Writers' Fighters
and Other Sweet Scientists

The Poynter Institute
For Media Studies

Writers' Fighters
and Other Sweet Scientists

John Schulian

Foreword by Studs Terkel

Poynter Institute for Media Studies
Library

ANDREWS AND MCMEEL
A Universal Press Syndicate Company
Kansas City • New York

Writers' Fighters and Other Sweet Scientists copyright © 1983 by John Schulian. All rights reserved. Printed in the United States of America. No part of this book may be used or reproduced in any manner whatsoever except in the case of reprints in the context of reviews. For information write Andrews and McMeel, Inc., a Universal Press Syndicate Company, 4400 Johnson Drive, Fairway, Kansas 66205.

Library of Congress Cataloging in Publication Data

Schulian, John, 1945-
    Writers' fighters and other sweet scientists.

    1. Boxing—United States—Addresses, essays, lectures.   I. Title.
GV1125.S38   1983   796.8'3   83-6002
ISBN 0-8362-6704-4
ISBN 0-8362-6703-6 (pbk.)

To my parents, who were there at the beginning, and to Paula, who wonders if the craziness will ever end.

Contents

Foreword by Studs Terkel	ix
Acknowledgments	xi
Introduction	1
1. A Mountain Named Muhammad	7
2. Sugar	39
3. Da Brains of da Operation	69
4. The Crooked-Nose Crowd	97
5. Heavy Artillery	127
6. Little Big Men	181
7. Beautiful Losers	205
8. Champions Forever	231

Foreword

Prizefighters are a singular tribe. Above—or below—all other athletes, they are a driven lot. When did you last hear of a football, baseball, or basketball player called "hungry?" Could you imagine Nelson Algren, the nonpareil of boxing fiction, choosing Joe DiMaggio or Jim Brown or Bill Russell as his battered hero? Or even the lesser ones? Only the ring, roped off, has that kind of loser, who almost made it, whose fate is punchy resignation. Even the champ, whose glory moment has passed before he knows what hit him. Ever on his own.

So, too, those writers, who are possessed by the "Sweet Science"—they are a unique breed. Need we mention the fat man, A.J. Liebling? Or Jimmy Cannon of the Depression and war years? Read their chronicles even now, of the gallant palooka or the dancing master; you see in your mind's eye today's ghetto alumnus—the black, the Hispanic, the poor white. "What rich man's son did you ever see with a broken nose?" asks John Schulian.

Schulian, who, it appears, can write salubriously of any sport, has *the* feeling tone for the prizefighter. In this collection of portraits, he offers us minidramas. Consider the middleweight who did time and was rehabilitated by Pappy Jack, a gentle mercenary. The hopeful fighter often "went in the tank but all he got was wet. There were no big fights, no big paydays, and pretty soon his Cadillac was gone, the collars of his ruffled shirts indicated they weren't making it to the laundry very often, and the cops were visiting Pappy Jack."

In reading John Schulian, you experience the shock of recognition as you do with a good short story. You remember your own encounter with a young black preacher, an ex-club fighter, who, before he was saved, threw a fight to Chuck Davey, the handsome college boy, at the urgent request of his own Pappy Jack. Davey, you may recall, was on his way up, with help from a small circle of friends, until he was boloed out of business by, if I remember right, Kid

Foreword

Gavilan. You remember Popeye, an ex-con, who confided that the coming heavyweight champ would be none other than the killer he was training—the one and only Jumbo Cummings.

Or a Schulian remembrance of Joe Louis: "He probably never realized how dank and dimly lit the basement hallway was. On his way to the ring, everything in Chicago Stadium must have been a furious blur—his handlers surrounding him protectively while he stared at the floor and contemplated the violence that was about to come pouring out of him. And as he returned to the dressing room, tasting the fruits of victory again, he made people wonder if he even noticed that his magic filled the hallway with the candlepower it lacked."

Or his portrait of Johnny Bratton, who had everything inside the ring and out until, whammo, he lost it. Everything. You'd see Johnny hanging around the lobby of a seedy South Side Chicago hotel, just keeping out of the rain. Oh, it once was a fancy place as the man himself was once a Fancy Dan. Oh, yeah, Johnny will tell you all. And there is no better listener than Schulian to really memorialize him. That's why he so moves you as a fighter's writer.

I imagine John Schulian a generation older than he is. I imagine his encounter with Oscar Nelson, the Battler. Onetime lightweight champion of the world. Was it 1908 or 1912 that he had those two classic encounters with Joe Gans? I ran into him some forty years after his glory days. It was a seedy old hotel once patronized by theatrical people. A dank room barely lit by one forty-watt bulb. He had his four huge scrap books laid out on the cot. There were photos of him and President Theodore Roosevelt. Another with the king of Sweden. Another in San Francisco as he was being honored for his multi-thousand dollar contributions to the victims of the 1908 quake. Another . . . oh, well, I imagine John Schulian hearing the man out and writing it down as only a fighter's writer can.

Though the Durable Dane is not remembered in this book—nor, for that matter, Bob Fitzsimmons and Stanley Ketchel—those of our time are indeed remembered. Indelibly. Glowingly.

Studs Terkel

Acknowledgments

The author and publisher wish to offer their gratitude to the following for permission to reprint previously published material:

Sports Illustrated, "On the Block: Way of All Flesh," March 4, 1974;

Baltimore Evening Sun, "The Lady in Red," January 7, 1975;

Washington Post, "Club Fighters' Savior," December 21, 1975.

The rest of the articles in this book originally appeared in the *Chicago Daily News* (R.I.P.) and the *Chicago Sun-Times,* so to them go the greatest thanks of all.

Introduction

Pierce Egan, the A.J. Liebling of nineteenth-century England, called boxing the "Sweet Science," and who am I to disagree at this late date? I have been enchanted by the musclemen, mystics, and mercenaries who gather under the umbrella of Egan's ironic description since I learned that Pappy Jack's prize middleweight had thrown a fight down in Texas. Though I wasn't more than fourteen or fifteen, I was privy to such hush-hush information because Pappy Jack's son was one of my best friends and keeping secrets was not the strongest part of his game. He loved to talk and the middleweight was his favorite subject, a heavy-lidded jawbreaker who favored ruffled shirts and pink Cadillacs and scared the bejabbers out of my friend's grandmother. I was a little unnerved myself the first time I shook hands with the middleweight and discovered that he was missing half his right thumb. An accident? I asked once he had disappeared in his latest Caddy. Oh no, my friend replied. A prison fight.

As a matter of fact, Pappy Jack had discovered the middleweight in prison. How he got him out was anybody's guess, but I suspect it had something to do with the rehabilitative effects of boxing. And maybe boxing really was good for him until some Mr. Big told him he had to throw that fight if he wanted to move within striking distance of Sugar Ray Robinson, Carmen Basilio, and Gene Fullmer. So the middleweight went in the tank but all he got was wet. There were no big fights, no big paydays, and pretty soon his Cadillac was gone, the collars of his ruffled shirts indicated they weren't making it to the laundry very often, and the cops were visiting Pappy Jack.

They knew that the middleweight had cleaned out a local appliance store; they even knew where he had the televisions and washing machines stashed; but all they wanted was to get the goods back where they belonged. Maybe the cops liked Pappy Jack and his middleweight or maybe they just understood how to produce results. Anyway, the middleweight quickly loaded Pappy Jack's garage with his swag, and in the dead of night, the cops hauled it all away. After that, the middleweight didn't come around much.

I suppose I was relieved, but now that I have spent more time around fighters, now that I have studied Muhammad Ali in full flower and ex-champions long after they have wilted, I wish I could have talked to the middleweight. My reasons are as basic as my need for pen and paper: Boxers not only lead more interesting lives than any other athletes, they are more willing to talk about them too.

Once you get past their boasts that they are the greatest thing since mouthpieces, the honesty comes bubbling out. I have listened to fighters recount shootouts and stickups, murder and mayhem, and never have I detected the self-consciousness that afflicts baseball players when it is suggested that they might be something less than angels. Not so many years ago, for example, Dave Parker of the Pittsburgh Pirates blew up at a St. Louis broadcaster who had described him as having spent a wayward youth that could have led only two places—the big leagues or jail. To a fighter, that would have been life in a shot glass, maybe even something to brag about, but then fighters are a different breed. Unlike the running backs of football and the sweet shooters of basketball, they don't grow up with people fawning over them. They spring from poverty—what rich man's son did you ever see with a broken nose?—and they make their way in a sport where there are no teammates to lean on. They are allowed no secrets in the ring and they keep few outside it. They are the subjects every writer dreams of.

With that in mind, I have lashed together this book. It is not a history, for I know as little about the Marquis of Queensberry as it is possible to know, and it is not the outgrowth of a calling I wish I had answered, for I always have been a devout coward. What you hold in your hands, rather, is a collection of newspaper columns and magazine pieces that I wrote in hopes of proving how sweet this strange science can be. Think of it, please, as a celebration of my favorite species.

I have written of fighters and writers, hustlers and hard guys, dozens of characters who subscribe to the theory that truth is richer than fiction, and try to prove it. I revel in their

Introduction

excesses and eccentricities, yet every time I come across Larry Holmes basking in the glow of his heavyweight championship, I am reminded of where these stories usually begin. When I first saw Holmes wander into the *Washington Post's* sports department, he had no luxury suite to live in, no Rolls-Royce to carry him around the countryside, no restaurant bearing his name. He was just a poor kid from an Easton, Pennsylvania, housing project, and all he owned was a cheap leather jacket and a dream of becoming a champ. To see him six years later is to realize that a harsh business can be conquered.

No matter how I inveigh against the fight racket's callousness and cruelty, though, I would be a liar if I didn't say that I am also fascinated by it. I may curse the blood specks on my shirt and I may nod fervently whenever I think of my friend Len Shapiro's observation that the only bad thing about boxing is what happens in the ring, but I return again and again. I guess it's because I want to know why a fighter won't surrender when he has no more hope or how a manager can keep sending a kid out there to be butchered. I have been this way since I heard about the antiquated trainer who used to shine a flashlight on wetbacks sneaking into the country from Mexico and ask the most essential of questions: "Ever fight?" Whether that makes me a humanist or a voyeur, I'm not sure.

For a three-month stretch in 1977, Don King, who still boasts the biggest pinky ring in the Sweet Science, thought of me in terms most kindly described as scatological. I was breaking in as a sports columnist at the old *Chicago Daily News* and King was bamboozling ABC-TV with something called the United States Boxing Championships. When I followed the lead of Flash Gordon, the fight racket's relentless underground pamphleteer, and pointed out the shamelessness with which the rules were being bent, King fumed. He could take being ripped in a newsletter whose readership amounted to no more than a cult, but not in a big-city daily read by other writers eager to take up the crusade. "John Schulian," he muttered when we met at a fight at his alma mater, the Marion (Ohio) Correctional Institution, "you're trying to cut my nuts off."

In truth, my aim was much higher. I was trying to write

Introduction

as well as the men who had come this way before me. You may not be aware of all of them, but to me, and to the apprentice wordsmiths like me, they were the truth and the light. They looked at boxing as something more than the school for scandal that the 1950s suggested it was. In newspaper columns as short as 800 words and magazine profiles as long as 8,000, they painted a blood sport in primitive colors and set it to bluesy music, and by doing so, made me want to do the same.

There was Mark Kram, who could make the pages of *Sports Illustrated* glow whether he was memorializing the wars between Ali and Joe Frazier or trying to describe the world that Gypsy Joe Harris saw through his one good eye. If Kram had a literary shortcoming, it was that he didn't write often enough. Then again, maybe that was a blessing, for I was forced to dig into out-of-town papers and yellowing anthologies to get my fix of boxing prose. So it was that I discovered Red Smith's poignant account of Joe Louis' last fight, Jimmy Cannon's salute to a gallant club fighter named Lou Graham, and Stan Hochman's bittersweet explanation of what makes writers' fighters, the piece that gave this book its title.

The bylines became like friends—Dave Anderson, Tom Cushman, Mike Katz, Jack Mann, Larry Merchant, Jack Murphy, Barney Nagler, Bob Waters, Vic Ziegel. And in time I learned that most of them were as eminently companionable over drinks as they were in print. They were not afraid to share their knowledge with a newcomer, nor were they embarrassed about displaying their healthy sense of the ridiculous. Their laughter always seemed to be nurtured by the Associated Press' Ed Schuyler, whose wild humor has appeared unattributed in hundreds of dispatches, mine included. My favorite Schuylerism sprang to life when he got his first look at Leon Spinks' bodyguard. "Don't cross Mr. T.," Eddie said, "or he'll dot your eyes." This may not be much of a repayment for having stolen it so blatantly, but I think it was the kind of line that would have had Joe Liebling jiggling merrily.

I say that without having met Liebling, for he died in 1963, the year I got out of high school. But I have read most of his books and feasted on *The Sweet Science,* and just as he tried to maintain the spirit Pierce Egan brought to covering British *boxiana* a century earlier, I have tried to maintain Liebling's. Granted, my efforts may not paint me as a boulevardier or be as concerned with using crowd scenes to capture the flavor of the times; and, surely, I dwell longer on the dark side of boxing than Liebling ever did, a habit that can be traced to my reading of Cannon and Kram. But when it comes to appreciating boxing's characters and understanding how well they transfer to the printed page, I have been under Liebling's influence since I called *Sports Illustrated* with the tale of a Baltimore boxing promoter who had a gym over a strip joint.

It was the best gamble I ever took. The freelance editor at *SI* in those days was Pat Ryan, a wonderful woman who had a genuine affection for crazy people whether she was reading about them or coaxing them to rewrite a few paragraphs. With Pat functioning as my fairy godmother, I got the story out of my typewriter and myself on the road to where I wanted to be.

Each year I make it to the World Series, the Super Bowl, the Kentucky Derby, and a lot of other splashy events as a columnist for the *Chicago Sun-Times*. Though I cherish each of them in a different way, I must admit that the moments I enjoy most involve boxing. Of course, there is something about watching Sugar Ray Leonard and Tommy Hearns redefine courage in their own images that will stir the juices of almost anyone, not just me. But more and more I find myself equally enthused by the stories that are waiting to be written about pugs who are forgotten but not gone.

The one who comes to mind immediately is Ron Stander, the battle-worn "Council Bluffs (Iowa) Butcher." We met in Washington years after Joe Frazier had redecorated his moon face and I wrote a feature about how Stander had become one more flank steak for boxing's grinder. Then I watched Ken Norton carve him up for five bloody rounds. When I stepped into his dressing room afterward, Stander was alternately sipping from a cup of beer and bellyaching that the referee didn't understand that it took him a while to get warmed up. Just as he was about to head to the hospital for another face full of stitches, he looked over at me and

Introduction

grinned lopsidedly. "Hey, John," he said, "thanks for the article." Ron Stander was a writer's fighter.

JOHN SCHULIAN ■

1.

A Mountain Named Muhammad

The great Ali, of course, and I use the adjective without tongue in cheek. When he said he was the best-known man on the planet, he wasn't dealing in hyperbole. He did more than give us golden moments in the ring; he took the heavyweight championship to Third World nations and created a following that would hover by the short-wave until the wee, small hours of the morning to hear the news of his latest fight.

Ali was a politician, a public relations genius, a master of the put-on. Part of his appeal was guessing which role he was playing. I remember when the Smithsonian Institution enshrined the gloves he had used to dethrone George Foreman. Ali must have said thank you sometime during the afternoon, but the words that stick with me came when he looked at the new wing he had been guided to and asked: "You guys gonna put a rug in here?"

Laughter was a constant when you were in Ali's presence and yet, as I think of the pieces I wrote during the last five years of his career, I cannot ignore the capacity he also had for turning a smile upside down. I'm not sure whether he did it on purpose or whether it was the inevitable result of being unable to cut himself free from boxing. All I can tell you is that he never gave anyone the same ride two days in a row.

"He's a Champ, He's a Clown"
New York
September 29, 1977

There were maybe a hundred gawkers and groupies in the gym listening to a sermon. The preacher was Muhammad Ali, his pulpit was a boxing ring, and his subject was an old favorite—himself.

With no regard for the scene's cosmic significance, Bundini Brown, Ali's alter ego and chief peddler of souvenir trinkets, suggested the great man move parts of his body other than his lip. It did not seem a bad idea, since Ali will risk life, limb, and heavyweight title against Earnie Shavers in Madison Square Garden Thursday night. But Ali responded less like a champ and more like Richard Pryor.

"Hush, nigger," he said. "It's my show."

"But we got to win," Bundini bawled in the buzz-saw voice that has cut through the roar of the crowd in so many arenas, in so many countries.

"Hush."

"We got to win."

"Hush."

"We got to win."

"OK, go ahead," Ali said. "Get yourself some publicity."

"I was big before I met you," Bundini sniffed.

"You was a Harlem pimp," said Ali.

Bundini doubled up with laughter.

It takes a while to get used to the hard edge of Ali's humor. Part of the process is making yourself realize that his sociological commentaries involve people you might expect to bring out the softy in him.

There was the gent in blue who showed up at the Garden's Felt Forum Tuesday for Ali's final sparring session. The one who said his name was Cassius Clay, Sr.

"You be the champ," he yelled at Ali. "You be the greatest."

"He's my daddy," said the former Cassius Clay, Jr. "Used to ride on the ice wagon and the coal wagon back in the prejudice days."

"Tell 'em, boy."

"Went to neighborhoods where he wasn't s'posed to go."

"Yeah, tell 'em."

"Jumped down off the wagon and beat up four white boys. Then he come home and whupped me. He's bad."

"Hee-hee. Tell 'em."

Muhammad Ali, at age thirty-five, exerts the kind of power perhaps no other black has ever had in this country. He tells the white majority things it doesn't like to hear, just as Martin Luther King did. But there is a difference in results. Martin Luther King, who preached peace, scared whitey. He scared whitey away. Muhammad Ali, who practices violence, scares whitey, too, but whitey always comes back because Ali is safe. Ali is an athlete, a champion.

As he gets older, the tendency is to think we have heard everything he has to say—once, twice, a thousand times. But on those rare occasions when his creative juices rouse themselves, the product is tougher, more biting than anything that has come before it.

It is as if he is trying to drive off the people who see him as an entertainer first and a boxer second. If that is so, Angelo Dundee, who trained him for all but the first of his fifty-six pro fights, can understand why.

"He's already done everything," Dundee says. "He has forced himself to the top of emotion—how many times? This will be his nineteenth defense. Maybe he's had it. Does anybody think he could go through what Ali has gone through? Ali is a champ, he's a clown, he is anything he has to be to make money. But after a while, it gets thin. Maybe he's trying to stop being anything but the champion."

The closest Ali will come to saying that is: "I know I'm the world's best boxer and I won't be for long. I gotta think about that."

Everything else he says is in code, a code virtually unbreakable for the layman. You listened as Ali described the psychological edge he has on Shavers, and you thought it was a joke. It wasn't.

"Acorn gonna be like a man jumpin' off a ten-story building," Ali said of the challenger whose shaved head inspired his nickname. "He never seen nothing' like the crowd gonna be there. When he walks in that ring and they start playing the National Anthem—ta-da-duh-duh-duh-duh-da—his heart gonna be beatin' faster and faster.

"Then I come in the ring and the fans are chanting: 'Ali! Ali! Ali!' He's gonna be sayin': 'How'd I ever get in here?' I'm gonna look over and say: 'I'm gonna crush you, Acorn.' And when the referee give us instructions, I'm gonna reach over and rub Acorn's head."

Shavers may be finished right there.

Cus D'Amato, perhaps the fight game's most mobile septuagenarian, has seen it happen to better men. "They turn around in the ring and face an Ali or a Joe Louis or a Ray Robinson," he says, "and all the power they thought they had goes out of them like air out of a balloon. I guess it's just a special force a few great fighters have."

The Force. It sounds like something out of *Star Wars*, or maybe it sprang from the playgrounds of Norman Mailer's mind. If Ali knows, however, he isn't telling. He is going to let Shavers find out about the Force firsthand. You know what a quaint sense of humor Ali has.

No Garden Party for Ali
New York
September 30, 1977

It had been a long time coming. Even Muhammad Ali, who is seemingly beyond blushing, must have been embarrassed by the delay. But at last there was a heavyweight championship fight that deserved the name.

The explanation for this startling development was so simple you would think someone would have thought of it before. What it boiled down to was that the other half of the human equation involving Ali was not Richard Dunn, a butterfly waiting for his wings to be picked off, nor was it Alfredo Evangelista, the walking Spanish omelet. It was Earnie Shavers, a brave man, a stubborn man, a tough man. And he was exactly what Ali needed to prove he can still deliver the quality on which he swears he has cornered the market—greatness.

True to form, Ali waited as long as he could before doing it Thursday night. For twelve rounds, he stuck just enough stiff left hands in Shavers' face to turn it an ugly purple and pile up the points to be sure he would walk out of the Madison Square Garden ring wearing his crown. Then he woke up as Shavers tried desperately to knock him out.

The thuggish-looking challenger, 211 pounds of muscle packed under a shining dome, stormed out for the thirteenth and clouted Ali upside the head. "Hell, yeah, he hurt me," Ali said later. "He hurt me four or five times."

At least one more of those jolts came seconds after Shavers' first bomb. The rest came in the hailstorm that was the fourteenth.

Ali started the round by trying to show Shavers he hadn't

been stunned. The ploy didn't work. Shavers went right back at him, tying him up against the ropes, banging away on Ali's kidneys and chucking him under the chin on the break. Then Shavers really got down to business.

He sent a looping right hand to Ali's head. And another. And another. Ali went stumbling backwards into Shavers' corner looking dazed, ready to be finished. But Shavers didn't move in. He moved ten feet away and stared at Ali as if it couldn't be true that Earnie Shavers, who just two years ago was fighting in dumpy gyms for a thousand grubby dollars, could have done such a thing.

"I thought he was faking," Shavers said afterward in the gentle, almost flutey voice that seems foreign to the rest of him. "He's a pretty good faker."

The problem was, Ali wasn't faking. "I was out on my feet," he said.

It didn't matter. In his corner, Angelo Dundee, the brains of the outfit, kept telling Ali it didn't matter. Dundee had a man in the dressing room watching the round-by-round scores as they were flashed on television, and he knew that Ali had the fight won if he could stay upright.

That was all Ali had to do. You had to wonder if he was up to it when Shavers raced out and popped him with the nastiest left he had the strength to throw.

Ali struck back with a left of his own. Shavers was more startled than hurt. Ali pumped two more lefts into his face. Now Shavers was hurt. Ali didn't need anyone to shout the news to him from his corner. He unlimbered the right hand he uses primarily for signing checks and rammed it upside Shavers' head. He was going for the kill. In a round that began with him in danger, in a round where he had to do nothing more than survive, he was putting on his greatest show since he and Joe Frazier gave us the Thrilla in Manila.

"He never hurt me bad," Shavers insisted. "I wasn't hurt."

If the round had lasted thirty seconds longer, Shavers would have known the truth. He would have been knocked out.

The brilliance of those final three minutes made a lot of things palatable afterward. You listened to Dundee say it was "the best fifteenth round I've seen in a long time," and you agreed with him.

"This is just Muhammad Ali," he said. "Muhammad always finds a way. He summons something up from out of nowhere and comes back. He's too much for all of us."

Even Ali, when he finally faced the press an hour and five minutes after he left the ring, had to be listened to seriously when he delivered his usual paean to himself. "I'm a courageous man," he said. "I have a whole lot of heart." Yes he does, and that is not all.

He has the ability to make us forget. Sad to say, there was much to be forgotten in this fight. There was the sleepwalking Ali did in the early rounds. There was the swing he took at Bundini Brown, his long-time good luck charm, after the fifth for telling him he should cut the comedy. There were the boos Ali heard when he tried to cover up some seventh-round soft-shoeing with a little showboating. And there were the boos Shavers' trainer, Frank Luca, is sure to hear for not being cagey enough to monitor the scoring on TV the way Dundee did.

It seems like an awful lot to be erased by just one round of boxing, just three minutes out of the lives of two men. But it happened, and when it was over, you realized something. Annoying as Muhammad Ali is, you are going to miss him when he's gone.

Straight from Champ's Mouth—Nothing
Las Vegas
February 14, 1978

Beads of sweat ran races down Muhammad Ali's fleshy torso. Ali, a heavyweight champion in training, paid them no mind. After ten straight minutes of bobbing and weaving and four more of boxing his shadow, he was thinking instead of how his thirst was running out of control. He grabbed a bottle swaddled in tape and tipped it to his lips. Then, like a miniature whale, he spurted water into the center of the ring. It was the only notable thing to come out of his mouth Monday.

The sound in Ali's camp for the time being is the sound of no lips flapping. The great man has taken what his obedient servants solemnly call "a vow of silence." Given all the ears he has bent in the past, this may prove the most beneficial aspect of his fifteen-round title defense against Leon Spinks Wednesday night. It already is the most novel aspect, no matter what some historians insist.

They are doubtless thinking back fifteen years to when Ali, cleverly disguised as Cassius Clay, had his mouth taped while training to fight Doug Jones. That maneuver differed from the current tapeless ploy because the idea for it came from his trainer, the esteemed Angelo Dundee.

"We just wanted to shut the kid up for a while," said Dundee. "But this business now, it's Muhammad's idea. I didn't have nothing to do with it. I was as surprised as anybody. Listen, if he didn't tell me he was gonna use the rope-a-dope against George Foreman, he's sure not gonna tell me about a little thing like stopping talking."

Speculating on the reason for Ali's silence has been so fascinating that only the wet blankets around the Hilton Pavilion are eager to learn the truth. In livelier circles, the guessing is that he has taken sides in an unpublicized split within the Black Muslims or that his pride has been hurt by vivid descriptions of his spreading middle. Or maybe he is simply tired of being an unwitting straight man, as he was when the Superman vs. Muhammad Ali comic book went public bearing a $2.50 price tag. "Champ," said an inquisitive fellow, "is the rematch going to cost $3.50?"

Nobody is enjoying the unsolved mystery more than Dundee. In his unfamiliar role as Ali's spokesman, he is getting more exposure than ever to the public as well as the press. "I'll bet some of these people didn't even know I could write," he said Monday after wading through a wave of autograph seekers. He talked with all of them along the way. "You know who else I'm talking to?" he asked at last. "Ali."

Their most fruitful conversations take place between four and six in the morning, after Ali has done his roadwork in solitude. If the hour is inconvenient, Dundee doesn't mention it, for he remembers too well that life with Muhammad used to be infinitely more difficult. "You'd go up in his hotel room and there'd be a hundred people there," says Dundee. "They'd be hustling this, hustling that, offering him every cockamamy deal you can think of. Muhammad was making movies, posing for pictures, doing everything but tending to the store the way he should have been." Now, where there once was chaos, there are only Ali's wife and two children and a handful of close friends. Tranquility has come to the Sweet Science.

It has done wonders for Ali's waistline as well as his work habits. When he checked in with Dundee ten days before Christmas, he was a bloated 241 pounds. Twenty of them have since disappeared. "He's in his best shape since he come back from the suspension seven years ago and beat Jerry Quarry," says Dundee, who refuses to notice the flesh that still jiggles everywhere on Ali.

Dundee prefers to see a champion to whom the $3.5 million he will earn Wednesday night is far down his list of reasons for fighting the wet-behind-the-ears Spinks. "Money isn't Ali's god," says Dundee. Similarly, Dundee refuses to consider the possibility that Ali really doesn't want to fight the ominous Ken Norton. "Muhammad would fight a cage full of lions," he says.

Obviously Dundee needs a while to get to the whole truth and nothing but the truth. At this point, however, it can't be avoided. "Muhammad Ali is thirty-six years old," he says. "He's at the end of the rainbow." With uncharacteristic subtlety, Ali is acting like it.

While Dundee has established a nostaligic mood by recounting the deeds of the champion as a young man, Ali has literally gone on a journey through his past. To begin preparations for Spinks, he used Dundee's charmingly dilapidated Fifth Street Gym on Miami Beach. When he walked up to the second-floor ring, he saw people who had been there when he was laying the foundation for his legend, people he hardly remembered. When he walked back outside, he was surrounded by the neighborhood's senior citizens. They call him "Mr. Ali," the way they always did. He had forgotten that.

What he did not forget was the most prized artifact of his career—the heavy punching bag he worked on before whipping Joe Frazier in the Thrilla in Manila. Ali deployed his forces to get it in Los Angeles, and they brought it back with its seams stitched and its canvas rotting from sweat. Ali has proceeded to knock the stuffing out of it regularly but not without a trace of fondness.

The champion was pounding out four-four time on the bag Monday when Dundee received his message. "Ali's gonna knock Spinks out," he said. "It will be in the eleventh or twelfth round." Ali only grunted when he heard Dundee. Sixteen hours before, he had been more emphatic. He was offering a mute hello to a few reporters in the lobby of the Las Vegas Hilton when an alcohol-soaked admirer came up to wish him luck against Spinks.

"Don't need no luck with the Duck," said Ali. He looked slyly at the reporters. "Whoops, I'm not supposed to be talking, am I?"

Not yet, anyway.

A Walk on the Quiet Side
Las Vegas
February 16, 1978

The fight was over. The press conference was over. Now Muhammad Ali, suddenly the former heavyweight champion of the world, had to walk through the crowd in the hotel lobby.

A platoon of security guards linked arms around him, but it wasn't necessary. The people milling about moved aside quietly, respectfully, the way they would if someone asked them to make way for pallbearers with a casket. "You're still the champ," a few of them murmured. Ali tried not to listen.

From the hotel's discotheque, a singer cut through the smoky air with off-key bleats. From the hotel's casino, there were the twenty-four-hour-a-day sounds of whirring roulette wheels and ice tinkling in empty glasses. Ali paid no attention to any of it.

He kept on walking, his head down so no one could get a good look at his battered, lumpy face. Sugar Ray Robinson, who knows from experience how it feels to be a handsome man made ugly by fists, offered his condolences. Ali said thank you with his eyes and moved on.

The elevator door was open when he got to it. He looked around at the security guards. "You guys don't have to protect me from nothing," he said. "Nobody want to touch me."

The guards dropped their arms to their sides. Ali stepped through them into the elevator. The door closed behind him and he rode to his twenty-ninth-floor suite alone with his thoughts about Leon Spinks and the championship that got away.

In the past year, there had been harbingers of just such a fall from glory. The awkward waltz with Alfredo Evangelista showed how much Ali was aging. The fifteenth-round escape from Earnie Shavers' steel fists marked him as a man who could be overwhelmed by the right combination of slugging and savvy. But Spinks, the Olympic gold medalist who had only seven professional fights before he clambered into the ring Wednesday night, was supposed to be all punch and no planning.

Bookies refused to take bets on his battle with Ali. Writers snickered about his often unintelligible ghetto dialect and the false teeth the Marine Corps issued him. Even after his split-decision victory over Ali had been announced and his porcine trainer, Sam Solomon, was squeezing him like a child, the 5,298 eyewitnesses in the Hilton Pavilion had to pinch themselves to believe it.

True, they cheered wildly at the savage beauty with which Spinks wrested the crown from Ali's head. But afterward there was a long, numb silence.

"I was really surprised," someone told Ali later.

"You're sitting down there at ringside drinking beer and you think you're surprised?" Ali said. "I was up in the ring getting my ass hit. You know I was surprised."

Angelo Dundee, Ali's guiding light for eighteen years, tried to warn him about Spinks. "This was no twenty-four-year-old kid," Dundee said. "This guy's mature. He's been in the Marines. He's been around the block. Nothing was gonna awe him."

But Ali, as audacious as ever, didn't believe Dundee until it was too late. Then he became charmingly humble. He had no other choice.

He wrinkled his brow at the idea that one judge, Art Lurie, a Las Vegas liquor store owner, could have thought he won the fight. And when his brother Rachman started screaming that he had been robbed, Ali angrily told him to shut up.

"You can't die because you lose," said Ali.

He has lost before, of course. A decade ago, the government won a unanimous decision against him after he obeyed the dictates of the Muslim religion and refused to go to war against "them Viet Congs." That cost him the three best years of his career. When he could fight again, Joe Frazier beat him for the championship. He regained it in 1974 by lassoing George Foreman with the rope-a-dope, and it looked as if he might never lose it again. Until Wednesday night.

"I'm thirty-six years old now," he said as he sucked on an ice cube. "Thirty-six is getting in the age. I want to take a couple months off. Let Spinks fight somebody else. I don't care who it is—Ken Norton, Earnie Shavers, Jimmy Young—they're in trouble. Let him do that and then he can give me a rematch.

"Yeah, I think that's what I want. There's something tells me to leave. Then there's something telling me to try one more time. I used to get hungry when I lost fights. I don't know if I can be that way anymore."

He bit down on the last of his ice cube and stared out at the people interrogating him. The left side of his face was red from where Spinks had been pounding all night. His eyes were swollen and on the verge of closing. He looked defeated, but there was more to it than that.

He looked like the oldest man on earth.

Last Night to Rewrite the Legend
New Orleans
September 15, 1978

It is as if Muhammad Ali has been planning for this night all his life, and how are we to know that he hasn't? He is boxing's consummate actor, the premier fistic sorcerer of the twentieth century, one of those rare athletes gifted with both greatness and the ability to understand his place in history. And now he has fifteen rounds—most likely the final fifteen of his career—in which to dictate how brightly his legend shall glow.

"You can't write a movie no better than this," Ali says. He will come to the Superdome as an aging king without his crown, and in one last bold attempt to get it back, he will fight Leon Spinks, the young varlet who plucked it from his head in February. If he succeeds, he will be the first man ever to be heavyweight champion of the world three times. The mere prospect is so improbable, so impossible, that maybe nobody would dare write a movie like this.

Curiously, as Ali strives to prove that real life always outclasses fiction, it is fiction that helps keep the fire within him burning. He ignores the odds that make him a twelve-to-five favorite over the fast-living Spinks and concentrates instead on the mutterings about his age, his loss of speed, his occasional clumsiness. Says Jose Torres, the fighter who became a writer: "Ali's profound paranoia is at work."

It has been with him from the beginning, taking root in his vanity. He didn't want to have his handsome face left scarred and lumpy, didn't want anyone to see him stretched unconscious on the canvas, so he danced and bobbed and weaved and roped one dope after another. He wanted enemies, adversaries, and foils. He needed a challenge like a flower needs water, and when he didn't think he had one seven months ago in Las Vegas, he let a kid eleven years his junior leave him in shambles. Now he wishes the bookies and the press would take up Spinks' cause, if only so he could do what he thinks he has always done best.

"When I beat Sonny Liston, I shocked the world," he says. "When I joined the Muslims, I shocked the world. When I beat George Foreman, I shocked the world. I am from the House of Shock."

You are sure Ali has used the line before, but you can't remember where or when. Meanwhile, he is up in the ring where he has been sparring, introducing his public to Gene Kilroy, the white interface of his entourage. "He's got the connection and the complexion to get the protection," Ali says. Someone behind you mutters, "Lewiston, Maine, 1963." You nod, bored, a trifle disappointed. Only later does it occur to you that, at thirty-six, Ali has no time to let his imagination float like a butterfly and sting like a bee. He has all he can do to prepare for his last stand against Spinks.

"Used to be," says Angelo Dundee, Ali's trainer since 1960, "Muhammad would spend four weeks in training camp and two weeks in the place where he was fighting and that would be it. Now he can't do that no more. He's gotta pay a heavy price every time he goes to the mat. That's why it don't matter how much he makes for a fight. The pain of getting ready is too much. It'll be the finish of him."

Long before dawn's early light, when even the best accountants care not about the $3.25 million he will earn or the $3.75 million Spinks will earn, Ali has slogged around Lake Ponchartrain. Then he has given himself over to Luis Sarria, who is not so much a masseur as he is a drill sergeant. Sarria speaks no English, understands no yelps of pain, and Ali is better for it after all those seventy-five-minute sessions in the ebony Cuban's torture chamber.

The belly is taut, the flab that once hid the top of his trunks is gone, the bounce is back in the legs. Everything is in order for getting revenge on Spinks, if only Ali won't give away the early rounds as he did in Las Vegas, if only he will poke his fists into the openings the champion leaves. "Spinks looks like a sucker for an uppercut," Dundee says, "but Muhammad didn't throw one last time." Ah, so much to be corrected and only fifteen rounds for the correcting.

"I'm gonna wipe out Stinks—I mean Spinks," says the unfazed Ali. But he has trouble working up the old braggadocio, the old outrageousness. Again and again he tries, excoriating Spinks for putting "bad juice" in his water bottle in Vegas, complaining that Spinks "hit me in my privates forty-two times." It is no good, though. His tongue won't flap the way it used to.

We are left to wonder if it matters, if the relative silence suggests a fading of the spirit and a sense of dread. In Spinks' camp, of course, there is not a man who doesn't want to believe that it does. "Ali might have needed a challenge before," says Georgie Benton, Spinks' chief strategist, "but now he can't stand a challenge." Benton says it over and over, trying to convince himself if no one else, but in the end, he can't even do that.

"You just can't guess on Ali," he says. "You tell yourself that he's had it and then he comes back, like there's some mystic force in his life."

How Ali would love to hear that. Someday someone will have to relay the message to him, for it conjures up so much of the magic he has achieved. But now is not the time. He has one more fight to be fought, one more conqueror to be conquered. Then his life as boxing's salvation will be over, and we will know how much Ali meant to us because there will be no one to take his place.

It's Ali!
New Orleans
September 16, 1978

Somehow, someway, Muhammad Ali rediscovered his old magic Friday night and wrote the most unlikely chapter in a story that seemingly has no end.

In the gaudy blue ring of the steaming Louisiana Superdome, Ali took Leon Spinks, the upstart who dethroned him seven months ago, and gave him a lesson in the virtues of combination punching and the evils of training in discotheques. And when Ali was finished pounding out his unanimous decision, he was heavyweight champion of the world for the third time. He was what no other man has ever been.

He has always said that there was never a fighter like him, of course, but he had to be worried about Spinks, eleven years his junior and light years ahead of him in pure savagery. You could see it on his face when his handlers guided him through the howling crowd of 70,000 and into the glare of the ring lights. But with each round, the furrow in his brow lessened and it became clearer and clearer that Spinks was not going to send him to retirement in the disgrace of defeat.

Retirement was supposed to be Ali's destiny, win or lose. But he is a man of surprises, a man who does not tolerate the expected. So it was only natural that he would say afterward: "I will wait eight months and decide. If I retire, I'll have a party. If I don't, I will take somebody else on." As always, his destiny was squarely in his hands.

It had been the same way in the fight just ended. After the twelfth round, all Ali had to do was stay upright until the final bell. All the referee and the two judges had to do was figure out whether they were going to give Ali the decision eleven rounds to four or ten to four and one even. It was that unanimous.

What it was not was the classic that Ali must have

prayed for, dreamed about. He had moments where he looked like a man trying to forget that he was thirty-six, and Spinks could never mount the brutal attack everyone kept expecting. But what should Ali care now that he has the victory he wanted so desperately?

It is Spinks who should go into retreat wondering why the fight was not even a shadow of the battle he and Ali waged in Las Vegas. Perhaps it was his corner, his controversial corner, that contributed to his overthrow. For one thing, all the men squeezed into it could think to tell him was, "Wiggle, wiggle, wiggle." For another, Sam Solomon, his trainer, and George Benton, the man he trusts the most, learned forevermore that there wasn't room for both of them.

"This is crazy," Benton said as he stalked away after the fifth round. "You can't have this many people here."

So Spinks was left looking helplessly at his corner, waiting for the words of wisdom that never came. The sense of abandonment was still with him afterwards. It was rapidly turning into surliness.

"I know I lost," he snapped. "You seen it. Don't ask a dumb question like that."

The real question, the question of how the twenty-five-year-old Spinks could lose so badly after devastating Ali in February, will have to be answered later. Was it because of the chaos in his corner? Was it because of all those hours living the good life when he should have been learning his trade? Was it because, as he insisted, "My mind wasn't into it. I just didn't feel right"? Or was it because Ali really did take him on a magical mystery tour?

Certainly the setting for such a tour was right. The fighters were being paid other-worldly sums. Every celebrity in captivity, from Miss Lillian Carter to John Travolta, found a way to ringside. The poor souls who bought the $200 seats pushed their chairs into the aisles and turned their high-society frolic into a cattle stampede. Best of all, Lucian Joubert, an electrician from New Orleans, didn't know he was refereeing the fight until an hour before Spinks and Ali climbed into the ring.

In the fifth round, Joubert tried to prove that he wasn't numb from shock. "Ali continues to hold Spinks behind the head," he shouted to the judges at ringside. "I warned him ten times." With that, Joubert gave the round to Spinks after Ali had won it with ease.

No matter. Ali was not going to be detoured. As if to prove it, he started the sixth by slamming a stiff left hand upside Spinks' head. No longer would he try to clinch with the 201-pound Spinks and use his twenty-pound advantage to wrestle the sinking champion along the ropes. Ali was ready to punch, and as the bell rang to end the seventh, he and Spinks were slugging away in the middle of the ring. Ali danced back to his corner. He knew what was happening.

The story was unfolding just as he had planned it. At the end of the eighth, he embraced Bundini Brown, the shaman of his entourage. In the tenth, he did the Ali Shuffle. In the twelfth, with Spinks searching desperately for a knockout, he startled the kid from the St. Louis ghetto with a right to the chest and followed it up with a pair of left-right combinations that came straight from a textbook.

Now the final seconds were ticking off on the clock and the crowd was chanting, "Ali, Ali, Ali." Spinks was still stalking him, but the life was out of his movements. He knew what had happened. So did the mob in his corner and the mob in Ali's corner and everybody with any sense at all.

Muhammad Ali had become the greatest again.

Ali Dusts Off His Old "Con"
New Orleans
September 17, 1978

The next eight months of Muhammad Ali commenced Saturday amid dire predictions that the saloons of the world will soon be swamped with requests for Cutty and watermelon. Ali didn't make the predictions, mind you, but he might just as well have. For he is chairman of the board of Champ Export, and Champ Export will distribute Champ Soda, and Champ Soda will come in seven natural flavors including you know what.

A toast, anyone?

Certainly a toast of some sort was in order. Leroy Johnson, a former Georgia state senator, wanted to raise a glass to his new Third World business venture with Ali, provided Ali didn't slip away from him while he was doing it. Jimmy Grippo, the nightclub magician who came to town specifically to coo Ali to sleep, was ready to salute the power of suggestion, which seemed to be putting his specialty on the line. And Ali, as usual, just wanted to say cheers to himself.

Not unexpectedly, Ali got his way, just as he had Friday night when he waltzed listless Leon Spinks around the Superdome's ring for fifteen rounds and became the world's first three-time heavyweight champion. The significance of that little piece of history was something he couldn't stress enough. "People knew I was good, so-called great," he said, "but they didn't know the extent of it until now."

In a way, the whole thing was a set-up for Ali. He harked back to February in Las Vegas and his first fight with Spinks, the fight he wasn't supposed to lose. He lost it, of course, and with it went his crown. That seemed a tragedy then; now it looks like a blessing. "If I beat Spinks the first time, I get no credit," he said. "When I beat him this time, everybody thinks it's something special." Which is just fine with Ali.

The prevailing sentiment puts him back on top in every phase of his beloved con game. "President Carter called to congratulate me an hour after the fight," he said. And that wasn't all. The president reported that he watched Ali on TV with Menachem Begin, who fights out of Israel, and Anwar Sadat, who fights out of Egypt. Try telling Ali he doesn't control all the pieces on the chessboard after that.

Some of them he has already moved. Others he is holding in abeyance, letting us guess what his next move will be, satisfying his taste for letting the public dangle.

If he weren't such a devotee of the mysterious, he wouldn't be saying "You just saw the last of the Greatest" in one breath and, "There isn't a heavyweight who can stay with me" in the next. It is as if he wants to be begged to return to the ring and begged to stay out of it. One can picture him sitting back contentedly and measuring how much he is loved, not just in the United States but "in South Africa, Manila, Morocco, Russia—all those places where they stayed up 'til two in the morning to find out if I won."

Like any savvy politician, Ali will try to visit as many of those faraway admirers as possible in the next eight months. After that, he will either have to retire or start training for the annual title defense the World Boxing Association demands of him.

"You want me to fight Larry Holmes?" he asked. "Holmes is twenty-eight. If you make him thirty-six like me, I wouldn't have no trouble staying with him. If you make me twenty-eight like him, no problem. If you make me twenty-eight, m-a-a-a-n . . ."

That is only a dream, though. Pugilistic reality is nowhere near as pleasant, so Ali is going to avoid it studiously. "I'm more than a fighter," he said. "I want to work for God and humanity." While he is at it, he will also make a television movie and worry about the way Champ Export is wheeling and dealing in oil, construction, heavy equipment, food products, concrete, and shipping. Earning $3.25 million that way will be slower than it was fighting Spinks, but it should be infinitely more pleasant.

And he will still be the champ, not the ex-champ. No one but Ali knows just how important that is to him, how much he relishes the power and the perks that the title brings. It is possible to guess, though, by examining the price he paid to prepare for Spinks.

"For six months, I killed myself in training," Ali said. "A lot of nights and days, I thought I was finished." But he made himself get ready for the eight good rounds he needed to be sure of victory, he made himself do away with the rope-a-dope defense that betrayed him in Vegas. And as the fight drew near, he fell asleep each night with Jimmy Grippo sitting at the foot of his bed telling him there was nobody better, for he was the Greatest.

"Jimmy Grippo is a great man, too," said Ali, summoning the sleight-of-hand artist from the Vegas strip into the midst of his meeting with the press. The first thing everybody noticed about Grippo was his curly brown toupee. The second was that he was infallible at what he did. The third was that once he got center stage, he wasn't going to surrender it without a struggle.

What seemed like hours later, after he had pulled cards and coins from every pocket and ear in sight, Grippo took Ali by the arm. "It's about time I taught you some magic," he said.

That really wasn't necessary, for Ali already knew all the

magic he needed to get through the day. He had made his press conference disappear.

A Painful Pilgrimage to Ali's Mountain
Chicago
March 2, 1979

There was an unscheduled ten-rounder last fall on a subway train speeding back to civilization from the South Bronx, a scabrous colony that even the World Series couldn't cheer up. The combatants were a little guy and a big guy, and the little guy was winning. He wanted revenge for the teeth no longer in his mouth and the knife scar across his belly. And the big guy, the victor in their previous fight, wanted out. "You the best," he wailed. "You the best." But his voice didn't portray his helplessness as vividly as his one open eye did. It was wide with pain and terror and disbelief, as if he couldn't comprehend how steep the price of his squalid existence had suddenly become.

Simmie Black had the same pathetic look about him the other night, when all he really wanted to do was see Muhammad Ali up close. That was the catch. To have his wish come true, he had to agree to take four rounds of punishment from a blossoming lightweight named Denny Daniels. "There's worse deals," Simmie Black insisted. "Shoot, I work at one every day."

So he bid adieu to the real estate man for whom he cleans apartments in Memphis and caught a plane to Chicago the morning of the fight. He came late to save the cost of a night's lodging, and he came alone because that is the way preliminary boys travel. No problems. There would be somebody to act as his manager and somebody else to act as his trainer. There always is.

The trouble began where it usually does for Simmie Black—in the ring. He entered with a towel over his head and no robe to hide his faded, frayed purple trunks. When he went out to receive his instructions from the referee before the first round, he surveyed the taller, better-constructed Daniels and decided it would be all he could do to give the customers a show. "I knew I weren't gonna beat the dude," he said. So he threw punches over and around the ref during clinches. He tried to draw Daniels off guard by playing possum. He staggered theatrically. And he responded to the one time he was knocked down by popping back on his feet like a Joe Palooka punching bag. But none of it was enough to spare Simmie Black from a unanimous-decision loss. The best he could do was make most witnesses forget about the terrible, hurt look in his eye when Daniels was pounding his head lopsided.

"I never saw some of that stuff you done out there," said the stranger helping him remove his gloves.

"I always try to give the peoples a good show," Simmie Black said.

"How much you getting paid?"

"Let's see, it was six rounds, wasn't it?"

"No, it was four."

"Yeah, four. That's right. Four rounds, I get $150. You got to excuse me, I'm kinda shook up. I'm a little punch drunk."

And Simmie Black, who says he is twenty-five and looks like he is forty-five, hit himself in the head to knock away some of the cobwebs.

He was still trying to make his eyes focus when the commotion started down the corridor. First, there was noise. Then there was a swirl of humanity through a rear entrance to De Paul University's Alumni Hall. Finally, there was a tall man in a tan suit striding through the chaos with blissful, almost regal ease.

"Who that?" Simmie Black asked.

"I think it's Ali," the man at his side replied.

Simmie Black was gone in an instant, lured by the siren song Ali was crooning as he poked his head into the packed gymnasium: "I'm gonna wipe this sucker out tonight. You can tell everybody. I'm gonna wipe this joint out." It is always the same with Ali, whether the occasion is a championship fight or a simple four-round exhibition, like this one with Luke Capuano. The hallway was crowded with old friends, gladhanders, and indescribably delicious women. Ali mugged with them and hugged with them, and then he disappeared through a door bearing a sign that said "Muhammed Ali only." He didn't stop to correct the spelling.

Having witnessed greatness, Simmie Black smiled.

"Foist time I ever seen Ali in person," he said, dabbing at the blood still trickling from his right nostril. "Makes me feel like a champion just bein' that close to him." Perhaps Simmie Black could have gotten closer if he had joined the line of people visiting Ali behind closed doors, but the suggestion evoked a shy, nervous giggle. "Nah," he said. "Why don't you tell me what's goin' on in there?"

In the dressing room, where the heat bordered on tropical, the predominant activity was sweating. Ali had the best deal of anybody because he could lounge around with his shirt off and not be accused of impropriety. While everybody gazed at his immense stomach, he toyed with the reporters, flirted with the women, and teased George Mostardini, the local heavyweight who calls himself the Italian Assassin. "Man, you don't wanna fight me," he said. "You'd be better off runnin' through hell with gasoline drawers."

The laughter resumed after Ali slapped Capuano around in the exhibition and was treated like delicate Dresden china in return. "Hello, foxes," Ali said to two sweet young things waiting for him in the dressing room. They occupied his attention while questions whizzed past his ears and photographers' flash bulbs snapped all around him. The room got hotter and hotter until a factotum pleaded for people without big business to leave. After they departed, the loudest voice remaining belonged to a dapper young man with a camera crew and a resolute sense of purpose.

"Now we're going to have a very sensitive moment here," he announced, "and we want you all to be quiet. Muhammad Ali is going to be filming a message to all of Montgomery Ward's store managers."

Ali did it, too, for five minutes without blowing a line. But, Simmie Black, you wouldn't have wanted to watch.

Ali Still Fast? Yes, Aging Fast
Chicago
September 12, 1980

An old man's dream ended. A young man's vision of the future opened wide. Young men have visions, old men have dreams. But the place for old men to dream is beside the fire. —Red

Smith, writing in 1951 after Rocky Marciano knocked out Joe Louis.

Someone should show Muhammad Ali the pictures from that October night. They came out of Madison Square Garden bearing the awful truth about what happens to former heavyweight champions who forget that their best is behind them. In one frame, Joe Louis was on his knees. In the next, he was outside the ropes propped on one elbow. Finally, he lay on his back, giving the world a lasting portrait of the bald, the paunchy, and the hopeless. He was thirty-seven, one year younger than Ali is now.

It would behoove Ali to think of that as he approaches October 2 and his first act of legal violence in two years. He should understand there is every chance that history will repeat itself in Las Vegas when he raises his fists against Larry Holmes, the king of the World Boxing Council. And maybe, God forbid, history will take a turn for the worse.

Remember, we are not going to see the Muhammad Ali who vanquished Leon Spinks in 1978 and walked away with an unprecedented third heavyweight title. The Ali now preparing to appear before us will be older and slower, and if he is not fat, he is odds-on to have stretch marks as a reminder of the blubber he has shed. But mere physical deterioration is not the greatest thing we have to fear. It would be wisest for us—and for Ali—to heed the warnings that his mind no longer sends messages to his muscles as fast as it used to, that the words that tumble out of his mouth ceaselessly are beginning to trip over one another.

Alas, we have no say in the matter and Ali has no apparent interest. He will not let himself be talked into retreat, even by those dearest to him. He has made a career of crusades, and now he gets a crusade that means far more than fighting tank-town exhibitions or even rewriting foreign diplomacy for the Carter administration. The only question that remains is whether his inspiration stems from simple vanity or the $8 million promoter Don King is paying him to fight Holmes in the parking lot at Caesars Palace.

"The parking lot," King proclaims, "is symbolic of the humble beginnings of these two gladiators."

What poppycock.

If there is anything symbolic about the arena that has been erected where Cadillacs and Continentals usually dwell, it is that such places are usually the sites of the meanest, grimmest brawls imaginable. Just think of how many middle-aged men have forgotten themselves, yelled at young thugs in flashy cars, and wound up getting stomped bloody for their lack of diplomacy.

The fear in these quarters is that the loquacious Ali has become irreparably middle-aged himself and that Holmes, eight years his junior, couldn't care less about it. "I ain't gonna let Porky beat me," the champion says. Porky? It is Ali who is supposed to bequeath the demeaning nicknames on his opponents, not vice versa. But there you have the unfortunate truth: Holmes has thrown down the gauntlet and Ali is a poor choice to do anything about it.

Perhaps his chances would be better if he had not shot for the moon in his first fight out of retirement. Indeed, when he announced his intention to return to the ring last March, the sentiment here was wholeheartedly positive because he was making noises about meeting Big John Tate before he tried Holmes on for size. Unfortunately, Tate lost his World Boxing Association championship to Mike Weaver and Ali lost his taste for adventure. If he fought Weaver and fared poorly, he might be denied his shot at Holmes. Ergo no $8 million. Ergo no test flights against lesser competition.

What awaits us then may be a mismatch on the order of cockroach versus heel. In one corner will be Holmes, undefeated after thirty-five fights and still close enough to the peak of his powers to be the most dangerous heavyweight in captivity. In the other corner will be Ali, two years away from throwing his last punch in anger and five years away from his last decent fight, the Manila Thrilla against Joe Frazier. The longer you look at the two of them, the better Marciano-Louis seems, and Marciano-Louis was hardly the Hundred Years War.

At bottom, the fight really had been a stepping stone toward a championship for the relentless young punching machine from Brockton, Massachusetts, the one everybody called the Rock. But surely Louis couldn't believe that. He had lost his title to Ezzard Charles just a year before, and in the months since, he had fought eight times, each time facing a little tougher foe, each time telling himself he was regaining the sharpness of his youth.

Marciano needed just eight rounds to convince Louis otherwise, to point the old man toward his dreaming place beside the fire. "I'm glad for myself," the Rock said when the deed was done, "but I'm real sorry for him." Louis had been knocked down by one left hook, knocked out by another, and knocked out of the ring by a right to the neck. For those long seconds that he lay on the ring apron, he was as sad and pitiful a sight as the fight racket has ever seen. But he did get up eventually and he did walk back to his dressing room, however slowly.

Pray that Muhammad Ali does so well.

Holmes TKOs Ali in the Eleventh
Las Vegas
October 3, 1980

The fire that made Muhammad Ali great was gone now. For the last three rounds, he had been wobbling from one corner of the ring to another, bouncing off the ropes and waiting helplessly for Larry Holmes to hit him with another punch. The thirty-eight-year-old Ali did not fight back, for he could barely lift his gloves. In a city that knows all about show business and broken dreams, he was just another star who had wound up as a pathetic lounge act.

When the bell rang to end the tenth round and Holmes was forced to end his brutal, pitiless assault Thursday night, Ali staggered back to his corner on legs made heavy by exhaustion. Through his glazed eyes, it must have been difficult to see the blue wooden stool that was waiting for him. But he made it, and when he did, Angelo Dundee, his trainer through twenty-one of the most memorable years boxing will ever see, told him not to get up again.

There was a sad, bewildered shriek from Bundini Brown, the obstreperous jester of the Ali camp. "But he's the champ!" Bundini squealed. "He's the champ!"

No, he wasn't.

Ali gave up the heavyweight title almost two years ago, opening the door to greatness for Larry Holmes and inaugurating a retirement he never should have surrendered. Holmes understood that; you could tell it by the savage, fearless way he fought in the parking lot arena behind Caesars Palace. And Dundee understood, too. That was why he fought off Brown, ignored the hands clutching at the sleeve of his jacket, and told referee Richard Green what had been apparent from the opening bell: Muhammad Ali, who called himself the Greatest and may well have been, was finished.

It will go in the record books as perhaps the best-paying eleventh-round technical knockout in the history of the Sweet Science. For what promoter Don King billed as "The Last Hurrah," Ali will receive $8 million. Yet no doubt he will feel short-changed. He didn't win his fourth championship; he didn't even come close. And his failure must hurt him even more than the boos that stung his ears from the sixth round on.

Nearly 25,000 gawkers and high-rollers sardined their way into the open-air stadium that Caesars Palace erected for just this night, and clearly they didn't think they got what a record $6 million live gate deserved. The reason for that, however, was not that Ali was involved in a daring robbery. It was that he had no business ever trying to trade punches with a man eight years his junior and light years his superior.

What Larry Holmes proved Thursday night was that he is the class of the World Boxing Council's heavyweights and every other organization's as well. He ran his professional record to 36-0 and won his eighth straight title defense the only way he ever has—by knockout.

For that and for refusing to let Ali win so much as a round, Holmes earned $3.5 million and the respect of the people who didn't know what to make of him when he first stepped under the canopied ring. Even with all his experience, he was still an unknown commodity—just the opposite of Ali, who entered the ring to an eerie, unfamiliar silence.

It was as if the crowd knew the sad fate awaiting Ali, as if the crowd could see that the skin around his middle still jiggled after the diet that sent his weight crashing down to $217\frac{1}{2}$ pounds. He smirked and winked; he tried to get the crowd to chant "Ali! Ali! Ali!"; he tried all the old tricks. But they did him no more good than his fists would in the ring.

Perhaps Ali realized what he was up against when he looked across the ring and saw Holmes' fierce countenance. All of the challenger's prefight barbs seemed to have had the wrong effect on Holmes. They were supposed to psyche him out, but instead they turned him into a study in ferocity that couldn't be cooled by even Gladys Knight and the Pips' mellow rendition of the national anthem.

So Ali reverted to low humor, biting his lower lip menacingly and faking sneak attacks on Holmes. All his hijinks got him was a slap from the 211-pound champion when their paths crossed. Holmes was not going to be intimidated. He wanted Ali's blood.

He would have it soon enough. From the opening round on, he beat down one of Ali's defenses after another. He squelched the peekaboo first, then the rope-a-dope, then all the useless variations Ali tried out of desperation. Time and again, Holmes' jab mashed the challenger's nose. Time and again, his right hand dug into the challenger's ribs. By the third round, Ali had a cruel red welt under his left eye and he must have been thinking he was crazy to ever get in the ring again.

Though mercy must have been on his mind, Holmes couldn't let it get the best of him. He had to stay on the attack, had to stay tough. Lord, how hard that must have been when the man who once was his idol, who once deigned to let him be his sparring partner, now was so helpless. When Ali tried dancing, Holmes danced with him. When Ali threw one of his rare punches—there couldn't have been more than ten of them all night—Holmes countered mercilessly, banging the challenger upside the head. The total effect was as ugly as the blood that began bubbling from Ali's nose in the fourth.

By then it was over. Ali lacked the energy to badger Holmes the way he had earlier. All he wanted, it seemed, was to stay upright through fifteen rounds no matter how much blood he lost or how many bruises he picked up. He has always been a fighter of heart, and now he seemed determined to prove it at any cost.

He endured through the tenth, endured until it was too painful to watch Holmes hit him anymore. And then Dundee, a kind soul in a brutal business, said Ali was finished, God willing forever. There was chaos in the ring—tears in the loser's corner, cheers in the winner's—but through it, you could see Ali slumped on the stool, silent and still except for his heaving chest. At last, after all these years, he knew the truth: He had run out of tomorrows.

A Has-Been Who Has Had Enough
Las Vegas
October 5, 1980

When he began his improbable journey, when the only thing faster than his fists was his mouth, Muhammad Ali possessed powers that seemingly could heal the sick, raise the dead, and make the little girls talk out of their heads. Now boxing's grand illusionist has but one trick left in his repertoire, and even it reveals him for what he really is. At the very sight of Ali—his steps slow and tentative, his eyes beaten into slits by Larry Holmes—you automatically long for the sweet used-to-be.

Your mind drifts back to 1964 and the February day when the doctors speculated that his thumping heart might jump out of his chest for fear of Sonny Liston, the mob skullcracker who had savaged his way to the world's heavyweight championship. It's strange because Angelo Dundee is thinking of the same thing—thinking of Miami Beach and the skittish, precocious kid he was training, the one who then called himself Cassius Clay when he wasn't trying to call a bully's bluff.

No one gave him a chance against Liston, and when he came howling back to his corner after the fifth round, Dundee wondered if the skeptics were right. "Muhammad was screaming, 'Cut the gloves off me! I can't see! I'm blind! There's dirty work going on! I want to show the world what a dirty fighter Liston is!'" To tell the truth, he had a point.

Liston had indeed been slathered with some sort of caustic goo. "I stuck my pinky in the corner of Muhammad's eye real gentle-like," Dundee recalls, "and then I put it in my eye and the stuff stung. I'm tellin' you, it stung." But the referee wasn't interested in that; he cared about nothing except the challenger's yelps of surrender. "I seen the guy comin'," Dundee says, "so real quick I grabbed Muhammad up off the stool—you know, to show the referee he was still going to fight." Never has the clean-and-jerk paid such dividends. One round later, Liston was all through, a disconcerted myth who refused to answer the bell and suffer the ignominy of a knockout.

"Hey," Dundee says to the reporters gathered around him, "look what all you guys would have missed if Muhammad lost that fight."

There would have been no phantom punch in Ali's rematch with Liston, for there probably would have been no rematch at all. And who knows what would have been denied the world after that?

The nutty poems and the nuttier datelines? The pride and power he infused into the burgeoning black movement? The unprecedented, probably never-to-be-paralleled third heavyweight championship? The great fights with Foreman, Frazier, and Norton and the even greater, surely more historically important fight with the draft board?

You can sift through all the programs and the newspaper clippings, the books and the TV news tapes and the movies, too, and the only sight you will want to be spared is the one that was thrust upon the world Thursday night. At thirty-eight, after two years of retirement, hypnotized by the prospect of a fourth title, Ali got the stuffing kicked out of him in the parking lot at Caesars Palace. He was just another old gaffer who had forgotten his age and tangled with a young squirt he should have given the right-of-way. When Larry Holmes was done defending his World Boxing Council championship, Ali slumped in his corner, judged incapable of answering the bell for the eleventh round and looking every bit like Sonny Liston sixteen years before. History had come full circle and trapped him.

Ali struggled to escape at first; some say he even threatened to punch Dundee in the nose when his trainer opted for surrender. Had Ali done that, it would have been the first blow he landed all night. He was a helpless, pitiable creature from the opening bell, and now he admits it. "I'm glad Angelo stopped the fight," he says. "I wouldn't want the newspapers to have those pictures of me on the floor, of the referee havin' to pull Holmes offa me."

Though the same pictures flashed through Dundee's

mind, he didn't want to prevent Ali from going fifteen rounds for the first time in his many-splendored career. "Sure, I stopped it," Dundee says, "but it was the hardest thing I ever had to do in my whole life." He tries to go on and fails. The words won't come out of a throat choked with emotion, and tears fill his eyes. Thirty-five years in the fight racket and Angelo Dundee is crying like a baby, crying for what he is afraid he might see in the future.

There is every possibility that Ali may refuse to return quietly to retirement. The speculation began when he said he wanted a piece of Mike Weaver, the World Boxing Association's heavyweight king, the morning after Holmes had humiliated him. Once that was out, it hardly mattered that the intelligentsia in the Weaver camp announced their disinterest in taking candy from Ali. Somebody else will like the idea, and Ali will be ready for them.

Already you can hear the gears meshing. He has convinced himself that he was dehydrated after losing thirty-six pounds in preparation for Holmes. His loyal followers nod their heads obediently and tell him that while he's rearranging his diet, he ought to get some better sparring partners, too. And beyond all that is the fact that he no longer splits the money he makes 50-50 with his manager, Herbert Muhammad; Ali gets more of the pie now, so why should he let the bakery close down?

It is frighteningly easy to imagine him as a latterday Jack Johnson, forlornly wandering around the country until he is in his fifties and putting on exhibitions wherever they will have him. Everybody will have him, of course, because he is Muhammad Ali, the man who calls himself the Greatest. But that is precisely the reason he should have nothing to do with them. To fight again anywhere, under any circumstances, would be to demean his legend and his name. If Ali doesn't realize that, Angelo Dundee does, and he cries along with the rest of us.

Ali Hated Being Lost In the Shuffle
Chicago
September 6, 1981

He loved the telephone. Everybody in the fight racket is supposed to. All they have to do is dial the right numbers and they can learn who got whacked out in Altoona last night, what kind of crystal such-and-such a heavyweight's jaw is made of, and where in Indianapolis to get a cup of coffee that doesn't taste like the inside of Rocky Marciano's shoes. Get enough good poop like that and you think the touchtone is your best friend, the way Angelo Dundee did.

He acted like he was just a busy signal away from asking Ma Bell to be his Valentine. And then he started getting messages from the area code that makes him wonder if the telephone isn't really a fool's horn of plenty.

The area code is 717, which will get you Deer Lake, Pennsylvania, and, provided your information is correct, the hideaway Muhammad Ali built on a mountain. The messages were from Drew "Bundini" Brown, and once the word on him was that when Ali got punched, Bundini felt it. The two of them were that close—a king and his jester, a soothsayer and his shaman, a preacher and his one-man congregation. It had been almost a year since Ali and Bundini shared the same corner of the ring, almost a year since Larry Holmes reduced the greatest champion of our time to helplessness, and yet some things never change. Angelo Dundee realized that as soon as he found out Bundini wanted him to call.

"I know the scene too well, you know?" Dundee says. "Drew Brown don't phone from Deer Lake unless he's got some news I don't want to hear."

Ali was back in training.

He was surrounded by Bundini and the rest of the obedient servants who didn't care that he turned thirty-nine in January or that the 240 pounds he was packing made him look like a dirigible. They were telling him that he was still invincible, still the champ, still the greatest, and the devil with those state boxing commissions that wouldn't license him to fight again.

For a while, it was a joke. Even Ali seemed to be winking

at his public as he bit his lower lip in mock anger and railed about winning the heavyweight title for the fourth time just to spite the Martians, the Ku Klux Klansmen, and all the other unnatural forces in his path. But the laughter turned to fears the other day when Ali announced that he will have his way after all. Come December in the Bahamas, he will return to the Sweet Science, and it won't be against Joe Frazier or Ken Norton or any of the other museum pieces who mistakenly think they won't break if they get hit. It will be against Trevor Berbick, the Canadian champ who last year delivered a message about the evils of violence that Ali would be wise to remember.

With a flurry of punches, Berbick sent a forlorn garbage collector named Big John Tate reeling pitifully across a Montreal ring. When Tate finally collapsed, his left leg twitched as if he were one breath from death.

While death likely is something Ali seldom bothers to worry about, there is no getting it off the minds of the people who care about him. It makes his increasingly slurred speech an afterthought and goes straight to the heart of Ali's problem—his ego. "You know the pride he has in his ability to take a punch," says Dr. Edwin Campbell, medical director of the New York State Athletic Commission. "He'll accept punches just to prove he still has that skill. That's what frightens me."

It frightens Campbell because too many punches lead to bleeding inside the skull, and bleeding inside the skull can lead to the unthinkable. "What could happen to Ali," he says, "is the same thing that happened to Willie Classen." Willie Classen, prizefighter, suffered fatal head injuries practicing his trade.

Still, Ali gives the impression that he never noticed. "He misses you guys, that's why," Angelo Dundee says. Gone is the faithful audience of reporters who served as his straight men, laughed at his "Me / Whee!" poetry, and found that he hit on more basic truths by mistake than most of us do on purpose. But the dearth of publicity accounts for only part of the hole in Ali's life. The rest of it must be attributed to the absence of something best understood by champions. "He misses the crowds, the roar," says Ferdie Pacheco, the physician who long ago was sent packing by Ali for suggesting retirement.

"The bell rings and it's just him. There can't be anything like it."

Ali always claimed that he would be different, that he could find life after boxing by making movies or hobnobbing with heads of state. He learned otherwise when he flopped both in Hollywood and as one of Jimmy Carter's puppets. Suddenly, there was nothing for him but his money and his Los Angeles mansion—nothing, in reality, but the emptiness that was compounded after Larry Holmes left him looking old and feeble.

Six months later, when Dundee checked into a Beverly Hills hotel and picked up one of those ever-loving telephones, he found Ali eager to see him, eager to relive old times, eager to be what he had been. While Dundee and his wife waited for him in the lobby, Ali signed autographs ravenously. Then he packed his visitors into one of his three Rolls-Royces and made a U-turn in the heaviest traffic he could find. No doubt it was what he thought a once and future champion should do, and yet he wanted to be sure.

"So what do you think about me fighting again, huh, Angelo?" he asked.

"You can't do it no more," Dundee replied evenly. "There isn't any water left in the well."

The hum of the engine filled the car and Muhammad Ali stepped on the gas a little harder.

Postscript

There never was an Ali fight I wanted to miss until the last one. It took place in an appropriately dreary old ballpark in the Bahamas. The promoter was a late entry who suffered the financial shorts almost until the bell rang and didn't have enough sense to realize that the combatants needed gloves. Trevor Berbick won a unanimous decision and Ali grabbed the stage afterward to boast that no other forty-year-old man could have survived ten rounds. But since when did Ali—the Greatest, if you will—become content with surviving? I'm glad I wasn't there to have my illusions destroyed.

2.
Sugar

Ray Robinson got to the nickname first, so I suppose there always will be a faction of purists who will hold that against Ray Leonard. What you have to realize, though, is that Sugar Ray II was as original as anyone who ever laced on boxing gloves. He didn't just make television commercials and play Ozzie to his wife's Harriet; after Ali passed from the scene, Leonard had to carry the entire fight racket by himself until his own retirement. I never would have thought it possible when I interviewed this gentle kid in his parents' tiny home as he prepared to march off to the 1976 Olympics. But looking back, I have to admit that it's nice to have been present at the creation of a personality who can make Johnny Carson stand at attention.

Sugar Ray Leonard Wants to Make Life Sweet for His Folks
Baltimore
May 14, 1977

Sugar Ray Leonard was signing autographs for urchins when the girl in the white turban caught his eye. "Sign my blouse," she said in the best come-hither voice a fifteen-year-old can muster. Sugar Ray, sweat-soaked from his labors as a prizefighter in training, stared at her. She stared back, as if to say he could do a lot worse than what she wanted.

"I be serious," she said in a corner of the Civic Center that had suddenly grown very quiet. "I be real serious. I been watching you and I like what I see. That's why I come here. I give you a kiss just to prove I be serious."

Sugar Ray leaned toward her and she brushed his cheek with her lips. Then she handed him a black felt-tipped pen and he autographed her gray blouse twice, across the back and over the heart.

"Lord have mercy," said Sugar Ray, and he smiled the

gap-toothed smile that makes him the most appealing figure in the sordid game of boxing.

They sing his praises in Montreal, where his charm might have won him an Olympic gold medal last summer if his left hook and dancing feet hadn't. They sing his praises at ABC-TV, where the hope is that showing his professional fights will make the public forget Don King. But nowhere do they sing his praises louder than in this gritty old city.

"I'm going to tell you the truth," says Eddie Hrica, a homegrown matchmaker with a reputation for doing just that. "If you put Sugar Ray Leonard on a street corner downtown and one of the Colts or Orioles on the opposite corner, Sugar Ray Leonard would draw a bigger crowd."

The city fathers hoped things would turn out this way. When Leonard decided to go pro last January, they decided to overlook the fact that he lives in Palmer Park, Maryland, a Washington suburb, and adopt him as their own. And, oh yes, promote his fights.

That meant he was expected not only to win, but to fill the Civic Center, which is a very large, very embarrassing municipal white elephant.

Leonard had no trouble with either task at his six-round debut in February. He knocked enough stuffing out of Luis "The Bull" Vega to win a unanimous decision and he drew a crowd of 10,200, breaking Muhammad Ali's house record by nearly 4,000 bodies. "A junior welterweight," says the 139-pound Leonard, "isn't supposed to do that to a heavyweight, especially when the heavyweight is my man Ali."

Now Leonard must see if he can produce a similar parlay Saturday afternoon on national TV. The trick will be tougher this time because he will be battling spring sunshine and a mean-spirited young factory worker named Willie "Fireball" Rodriguez, who has beaten Vega not once, but twice.

"Rodriguez has been doing a lot of talking about the kind of hurt he's going to put on me," says Leonard, "but talk doesn't bother me. Actually, I think it's kind of cute."

You would, too, at the wages Leonard is getting. Depending on what the gate is, he should receive in the neighborhood of $40,000 for six rounds of exercise. He knows that neighborhood well, for he also traveled its streets in his first fight. And although he insists he wouldn't step into a ring without a loving public behind him, there is little doubt about his primary motivation.

What separates him from the vast majority of American athletes is that he is chasing the almighty dollar for his parents as much as for himself. If Cicero Leonard didn't have to spend all night managing a twenty-four-hour ghetto grocery store, if Gheta Leonard, mother of seven, hadn't had a heart attack just before the Olympics, if it didn't seem that the two of them would never own their own home, then Sugar Ray Leonard would be a college student.

"Maybe college will come later," he says unconvincingly. "I'm concentrating on that home for Mom and Dad. No, I don't have one picked out yet. I'm just taking care of their bills first."

To truly enjoy himself, Sugar Ray must pull on boxing gloves. When he does, he has Angelo Dundee, Ali's trainer, to manage him and Dave Jacobs, the quiet humanitarian who has been with him since he was fifteen, to train him. Together, Dundee and Jacobs create a world where their protégé can concentrate solely on the business at hand.

They show him how to block punches and how to step and pivot. They tell him to put on poundage after the Rodriguez fight and become a true welterweight. One suspects they even told him to forget his twenty-first birthday in April and keep on saying he is twenty.

Only when Leonard steps out of this protective cocoon does he feel the true weight of fame.

"I'm William Hemphill from the East Baltimore Community Organization." In the Civic Center dressing room, an earnest young man was pumping Sugar Ray's hand soul-style. "We were wondering if you . . ."

One of Leonard's friends took the young man aside and explained that Sugar Ray has a business manager to deal with special requests. Sugar Ray showered and put his clothes on. When he turned to leave, the young man was there again. "If you could just remember my name," he said.

Sugar Ray nodded that he would.

The Power and the Glory
Las Vegas
September 30, 1979

Everything is perfect.

He stands at the main entrance of Caesars Palace, a tan suit setting off his handsome ebony face, and the dowagers crowd around, stroking him with hands they usually use only for slot machines. It is the same when he wanders into the casino; busboys and blackjack dealers alike yell that they are praying for him, and betting on him, too. Surely there can't be a safer gamble in the fight racket—not for the wagering set, not for the television networks. He is undefeated, untied, unblemished. And there is a very good reason why.

Everything is perfect because Sugar Ray Leonard works at it.

He has fought almost once a month for two years now, trying this, perfecting that, studying the curious marketplace in which he does business. "I hope you won't misunderstand me," he says, "but I understand what it takes to scale the majestic heights of stardom."

A stiff punch is mandatory, of course, and nobody should doubt that Leonard possesses one after the ease with which he demolished proud Andy Price in one round Friday night. "Who says I can't dominate now?" asks the North American welterweight champion, his ears still burning from past criticism. "I have combined the talents of Muhammad Ali, Sugar Ray Robinson, and Joe Louis. I have combined the talents of all the great fighters and made myself."

TV did the rest.

"Well, I'd say it helped, anyway," Leonard says. "I always try to smile at the right time."

Boxing needed someone who would do that, particularly with Ali strutting off into history. For a while, though, after he rode back from the 1976 Olympics on a wave of public adoration, Leonard wasn't sure he wanted to run the gauntlet of dirty dealers. "But after they started talking about a million dollars," he says, "I decided they had to be cleaning things up."

He has made his million and more, although he shies away from breaking it down to dollars and cents in public.

"Those figures are obnoxious," he says. "The higher they get, the worse they get." When the arithmetic gets too complicated, he can always seek counsel from his advisers back home in Maryland. No vultures, they. If they were, they wouldn't have arranged the future so he could become the president of Sugar Ray Leonard, Inc., a budding titan of commerce at twenty-three.

Even as he trained for his twenty-fifth straight victory, Leonard couldn't keep his mind completely off his new calling. This time, however, it was neither the state of his apartment buildings nor the size of his investment portfolio that had him worried. It was how he was going to decorate the den where he conducts so much of his business.

"The kid told me he wanted to use autographed pictures of the other fighters on the card," says his manager, the venerable Angelo Dundee, "so I went after them." When the mission was completed, Larry Holmes, Earnie Shavers, Roberto Duran, and the rest of an all-star cast had signed up, much to Leonard's obvious delight. "Hey, he don't say, 'Screw you, I'm mucky-muck,'" Dundee says. "He's for real."

The observation should come as no surprise, for though life is rosy now, Leonard has shed his share of blood and tears in the past. He learned the price of celebrity, for example, when the *Washington Star* splashed his paternity suit across its front page. As a result, he gives only so much of himself in interviews and absolutely refuses to let the press see his fiancée, Juanita Wilkinson, and their five-year-old son, Ray Charles Leonard, Jr. He can take a punch, you see, but not what he considers a low blow.

Marcus Geraldo didn't hit him with either when they fought last May. Instead, Geraldo led with his head and split Leonard's eyebrow.

"I'm seeing three guys out there," Sugar Ray groaned as he wobbled back to his corner.

"Go for the one in the middle," Dundee told him.

The strategy worked, but then Dundee's strategy usually does. The little paisano from the Fifth Street Gym in Miami has been the brains behind nine world champions, most notably Ali, and now he is working on number ten as unobtrusively as possible. After all, there is no sense in offending Dave Jacobs and Janks Morton, the trainers who have been with Leonard since the amateurs and who still put him through his paces at the Oakcrest (Maryland) Recreation Center. "I just come in and tie up the loose ends," Dundee says. It is a perfect job for a man with his connections.

He has arranged every one of Leonard's fights. "I give him tall guys, short guys, whackers, hookers, right-hand bangers," he says. What he has never done, though, is give Leonard someone who could beat him.

That will change December 1.

Wilfred Benitez, the World Boxing Council's welterweight champion, will be waiting in Caesars Palace with his undefeated record, his brilliant counter-punching, and his ominous arrogance. The Leonard people, however, are not impressed. "Don't use good when you describe my guy—use great," Dundee says. "He knows what being the best means. He can smell it. I'm telling you, there ain't been anybody like this since Muhammad."

Dundee rests his case on the evidence that is mounting daily. For one thing, Leonard will get $1.5 million for fighting Benitez while Benitez will have to settle for $500,000 less. And then there is the way heavyweight champion Larry Holmes reacted upon learning that Sugar Ray was on the same card with him Friday night: He hit the roof. In the long run, though, maybe nobody understands Leonard's clout better than Leonard himself.

Consider the way he handles the cries for him to do battle with the brutal Duran. He listened to them once again the other day from Don King, the promoter with the electric hair.

"I told him the minimum is $5 million," says Leonard. "He said, 'For both of you?' I said, 'No, for me.' He didn't smile too much after that."

Ah, but Sugar Ray Leonard did.

A King Acquires a Court
Montreal
June 18, 1980

Like ants in a bag of candy, they scurry to protect their vested interests. The one called Juice busies himself with tape and liniment while half a dozen somber young men in red-and-white baseball caps decide who gets inside the yellow rope and who doesn't. The fact that business is slow right now hardly diminishes their fervor.

There are two of them for every poor soul trying to get next to sweaty, workout-weary Sugar Ray Leonard, and still they are not satisfied. They insist that the rear be defended by Tiny, a reformed football player who has "6 ft. 6" stenciled on the back of his T-shirt and a frown indelibly imprinted on his face. Tiny is the ultimate incongruity for a boxing champion—a bodyguard.

The best argument that can be made for his presence revolves around Leonard's distaste for violence. "Outside the ring, I wouldn't hit anybody with my hands," Sugar Ray says. "I'd use a chair." Since breaking furniture over people's heads flies in the face of both good manners and the law, he includes Tiny on his payroll and thereby opens himself up for another line of questioning, the one about that dirty word "entourage."

He always has said he didn't need an entourage, didn't want to be surrounded by a small army of sycophants and bloodsuckers. That was for Muhammad Ali, who thrived on such attention, and Leon Spinks, who overdosed on it.

Yet now Leonard comes to Montreal with twenty-eight traveling companions, and everyone who has bought his party line in the past wants an explanation. So Angelo Dundee, the welterweight king's sagacious manager, tries this: "Ain't nothing wrong. These guys are from the community center, just like Ray." Ah, but throw in Mike Trainer, the lawyer with dollar signs in his eyes, and Charlie Brotman, the public relations man who is allergic to interviews, and the secret is out: Leonard is having a dalliance with the unspeakable.

To be sure, the foot soldiers in his army couldn't have picked a better time to follow their leader. On Friday night, in Olympic Stadium, he will put the World Boxing Council crown on his head and give the brilliantly malevolent Roberto Duran a fifteen-round chance to knock off one, or both. Already the savants of the Sweet Science are speaking of the fight in the reverent terms normally reserved for Ali-Frazier and Robinson-LaMotta. But what the beautiful dreamers shouldn't forget—and what Leonard's entourage should take pains to understand—is that Sugar Ray is returning to the city where he had a moment that may never be surpassed.

Four years ago next month, Leonard shucked the idea that he was just a glib kid with a stolen nickname and his infant son's picture taped to his socks. He came to the Montreal Olympics as the biggest thing in Palmer Park, Maryland, and left with a gold medal in hand and the love of the United States washing over him. It was a dizzying experience, literally.

"I nearly fell off the award stand I was so tired from the competition," he says. "Think of it: You have all those years of dedication and sacrifice, and in twenty or twenty-five minutes, everything is over. I'm telling you, it was almost too much for me."

Leonard needed a recovery period, not a victory party, so he ran for the camper that his parents had waiting for him. "It was supposed to accommodate nine," he says, "but there were twenty-one in all." Even today he isn't sure who everyone was. There were friends and relatives, of course, but the others—the ones who turned the camper into a sardine can on wheels—remain blurs in his memory. "I used to go out walking in the Olympic Village a lot," he says. "Maybe that's where I met them."

In retrospect, they are another of life's little jokes on Leonard. In person, they were the reasons he couldn't take one last look at Montreal and the part of himself he thought he was leaving behind. The Olympics were supposed to be the end of boxing for him and the beginning of a new existence as a student, a businessman, an ordinary citizen. "I thought I could be a success at anything I tried," he says. "I still do." What he has going for him now, though, is the clout he has acquired since his parents took sick and he discovered how his circuits are wired.

"I'm a fighter," he says. "It's what I love, it's what I'm best at. Can't you tell? Can't you tell?"

Leonard's smile is meant to be self-mocking. Instead, it succeeds only in underscoring the immensity of what he has accomplished at age twenty-four, after twenty-seven straight professional victories. To discuss his physical achievements is just part of it, of course, but discuss them we must, for here is a stylist who has dispatched all comers with relative ease and taken the play away from Duran with pure, undiluted effrontery.

They came face to face in New York two months ago before the press conference announcing their fight, and Duran's first move was to thrust his chin against Leonard's and grab a handful of the champion's coat. "It was kind of cute," Leonard says. "The only thing I didn't like was the way he wrinkled my suit." Sugar Ray retaliated when he got in front of a microphone and predicted he would "kill" Duran, a debatable choice of words at best. "It's really not my intention to kill anybody," he says now. "I was just trying to keep people from being bored."

If Leonard had any ulterior motive, it was to spare himself the discomfort that comes with signing up for a payday that will bring him between $7 million and $10 million. Even now, with the figures being splashed everywhere, he prefers to play the role of the financial innocent. "After you reach my position, you figure out you should have been happier with what you had before," he says. "Really, I could retire with $1,000 in my pocket and be comfortable." The next sound he hears is disbelief, and it doesn't stop until he resumes talking about Duran.

Left hooks more easily are grasped than the tax benefits of fighting in Montreal. The same goes for staying power and the ability to shake off a stiff punch. "On June 20," says Leonard, "reality takes place." It is a curious phrase when you consider that his lawyer is off trying to make him some more money, his public relations man is saying that's it for today, and Tiny is organizing a flying wedge to convoy him back to his hotel. But after all that, maybe Sugar Ray Leonard needs reality as desperately as anyone.

Leonard No Patsy, He'll Fight Duran Nasty
New Orleans
November 23, 1980

Under normal circumstances, Sugar Ray Leonard would not want to be Dale Staley for the simple reason that Dale Staley is a lout, and an unhygienic one at that. In the most memorable of his nineteen professional fights, Staley found himself facing a pacifist who, after being knocked down three times, discovered just how fast he could retreat. This vexed our hero, of course, and after failing to rekindle the action with taunts and glares, he did the only thing he could think of: He chased down the yellow dog and bit him on the cheek.

Staley's immediate reaction was that he should have doused his impromptu meal with ketchup. The referee thought otherwise; he disqualified the budding cannibal and, to hear Staley tell it, robbed him of a chance to do battle with the great Leonard. No doubt the moralists in the audience will find it meet and right to hear that Staley now serves as one of Sugar Ray's sparring partners. But they should be advised that even though he is older and presumably wiser, Staley remains a rotten guy.

"I do every wrong thing I can in the ring," he says, and for those nursing doubts, he spent the other afternoon proving it against Leonard. Staley fouled his boss with head, forearms, and elbows, and when he had Sugar Ray pinned in a corner, Staley defied the Marquis of Queensberry's etiquette book by grabbing the rope with one hand and thumping Leonard's noggin with the other.

Sugar Ray loved it.

"That," he announced, "is just what Roberto Duran deserves."

Maybe so, but it is Sugar Ray who is going to have to give it to the Panamanian rule-bender. The burden is right there in the contract that says the two of them will battle Tuesday night in the Louisiana Superdome for Duran's World Boxing Council welterweight championship, the very same championship he bullied away from Leonard only five months ago. With the memory of that mauling haunting him, with the need for the strongest possible revenge, Leonard wishes for the unlikely. He wishes that for just a few well-chosen seconds he could be the thuggish Dale Staley. Failing that, he works on his own brand of mayhem.

You could see it for yourself when he finally wrestled free of Staley's death grip. He clutched the villain's face with his left hand and set to rearranging it with his right.

"Dirty, wasn't I?" Sugar Ray cooed afterward.

His smile has never been broader.

It was the same smile that warmed America's heart at the 1976 Olympics and has sold Seven-Up, raised money for the Cerebral Palsy Foundation, convinced people to fill out their census forms, and turned ladies' heads around from Vegas to Vladivostok. When the sawed-off scholars from St. Paul the Apostle Elementary School bathed in his toothsome glow after the mean-spirited sparring session, they squealed as if Leonard were a silver-screen hero, not a solid-gold fighter. They wouldn't quiet down even when he was preaching the virtue of straight A's. That's how beloved he is. And that, ultimately, is what's so disconcerting about his campaign to add some venom to his arsenal.

A sneer hardly becomes Sugar Ray, but as far as his manager, Angelo Dundee, can see, the kid doesn't have any choice. "Last time, Duran thought Ray's decency and niceness and genuineness was weakness," Dundee says. The result was that Duran climbed all over Leonard on a drizzly Montreal night and piled up the early points that paid off in a championship.

Obviously, it was not the grandest moment in Sugar Ray's life, but he could live with it. What he cannot tolerate is the way Duran has carried on ever since. "For one thing," Leonard says, "he calls me the Devil." Yes, and Duran acknowledges Leonard by flipping him the time-honored middle-finger salute.

Roger Leonard, Sugar Ray's boxing brother, gets the same treatment. "Sign language," Dundee calls it. But Sugar Ray isn't laughing. He stopped the other day after his sister Sharon glanced at a car passing her on the street and saw Duran, who speaks little English, flashing a message that did not require an interpreter.

"He doesn't even act like he's human," Leonard says. "The way he carries himself, it's like he owns the world. He wants to intimidate not just fighters, but the people who are out in the crowd watching him. He wants you to bow to him, and then he doesn't understand why he's not loved, why he doesn't get endorsements. I guess that's why he hates me— because of my rise to stardom. But I try to accommodate people and he . . . Listen, even if we were old men in wheelchairs, we'd probably be going at it. He just brings the arrogance and hostility out of me."

On its face, such talk smacks of good old-fashioned wrestling hype and the feuds that always end with two fat slobs being disqualified because they are outside the ring throwing chairs at each other. The difference in the Leonard-Duran contretemps is that the stars of the show may be the two best boxers in captivity and that if they got down to throwing chairs, neither would be the least bit interested in missing.

Sugar Ray may not have believed he could be party to such animosity last June, but now he asks no questions. "I will do whatever is done to me," he says. He remembers Duran's first punch in Montreal, the one that clanged into his protective cup. He remembers the holding and the head butts and the forearm shivers. He remembers and he promises himself that Duran has a surprise coming.

The thought elicits a smile that on any other face would be deemed sinister. But this is Sugar Ray Leonard we are looking at and no one is more aware of his image than he is. Quickly now, he must assure his adoring legions that the snarl and the rabbit punch are simply tools to get him through a crisis, devices to allow him to stay as sweet as he's always been.

"I have to be mean and arrogant when I'm fighting Duran," he says. "Fortunately, I can erase that when I step out of the ring."

And you know who can't.

Leonard Takes Fight Out of Duran
New Orleans
November 26, 1980

For once, the warrior didn't get carried out on his shield. He simply waved his gloved right fist in the air to signal surrender, and when Sugar Ray Leonard dug a right hand into his belly before the referee could stop him, the warrior had no anger left to fight back. It was the end for him, the end for the reign of terror that Roberto Duran has inflicted on all the little men who have dared stand in his way. And none but the biggest dreamer could have guessed that he would go out so meekly.

Two minutes and forty-four seconds into the eighth round Tuesday night, Duran gave the World Boxing Council's welterweight title back to the sweet-faced manchild he took it from five months and five days before. He turned over the Brobdingnagian championship belt to Leonard, then clutched at the cramps he said were wracking his body and marched back to his dressing room through a Louisiana Superdome mob that called him "Quitter! Quitter!" If Duran heard them, he never showed it. He never showed it because, at age twenty-nine, after losing just the second of his seventy-four professional fights, he had something else on his mind.

"I'm not fighting again," the black-bearded Panamanian said through an interpreter.

"You mean you're retiring?" someone asked.

"Definitely," Duran said.

With that, he added one more surprise, one more mystery to a night that should have belonged to the brilliant Leonard alone. From the opening bell, the recrowned champion had fought with the composure and precision that eluded him throughout his dreary loss in Montreal. By the seventh round, Sugar Ray was working Duran over at will—whacking him with left hands, then dancing away and taunting his flustered target. "I've never seen Roberto so frustrated," said Ray Arcel, the loser's eighty-two-year-old trainer. But Duran refused to give Leonard the pleasure of knowing he had been humbled.

"Leonard was very weak," Duran insisted, "but my body did not allow me to pressure him. I had cramps in my stomach and in my arms. I just kept getting weaker and weaker."

But it wasn't until the end of the fifth round—when Leonard had already established his supremacy—that Duran started complaining that there was no tiger in his tank. Alas, he did it in Spanish and his gringo cornermen, Arcel and Freddie Brown, could only nod as if they understood. "I could hear Roberto," said his interpreter, Luis Henriquez, "but by the time I got to his corner, the round had already started."

So Henriquez had to wait until the sixth round was over

to hear the bad news that would become public knowledge barely six minutes later. And now Duran, who is supposed to make $8 million for this fiasco, must wait before he can collect his share of the Superdome swag.

The Louisiana State Athletic Commission handed down the edict only an hour after the technical knockout had been inked into the record book. Apparently there was just too much stench over the fight for the commissioners to do anything but order the loser in front of a doctor—too much stench and too many memories of Duran as anything but a candidate to go in the tank. "In all the years I've been with this kid," Arcel said, "I've never seen him throw up his hands and quit." But then maybe the sawed-off assassin called Hands of Stone—a champion first as a lightweight, then as a welter—had never faced an opponent as clever and savage as the twenty-four-year-old Leonard.

"If you got hit in the body with the punches I hit Duran with," he said, "you'd have cramps, too."

Leonard obviously was in no mood for listening to any talk about Duran's ill health or his own good fortune. For $7 million, he had given the most impressive performance of his twenty-nine-fight professional career. When the fight was stopped, the three judges had him ahead 68-66, 68-66, and 67-66, and it would have been easy to make a persuasive argument for a far more lopsided lead. Anyone who doubted that only had to talk to Leonard.

"Everyone said Sugar Ray was going to get knocked out," he half-shouted. "My friends back home in Maryland were betting against me. And now that I'm the champion, everybody wants an excuse. There is no excuse. I'm the champion."

Leonard looked the part from the moment he stepped in front of a crowd that was estimated at 40,000 and probably didn't add up to be half that much. Duran had entered the ring first, accompanied by a Salsa band and a cadre of uniformed Panamanian high-steppers who had the floor-boards shaking. It should have been a frightening sight for a kid who had looked petrified the first time he tangled with Duran, but Sugar Ray didn't flinch. And by the time Ray Charles arrived to sing "America the Beautiful," Leonard was flashing the smile that won America's heart at the 1976 Olympics.

"Oh, beautiful, for spacious skies," the great rhythm-and-blues shouter wailed, and the fighter started nodding his head in time with the music. A state boxing official leaned over and said something in his ear, and lip-readers at ringside could see his reply. "My mother named me after him," said Ray Charles Leonard.

He wasn't the least bit worried about Duran. It seemed folly then, but afterward Leonard's guiding light, the redoubtable Angelo Dundee, made it sound like being cool was all part of the plan. "My guy knew what he was going to do," Dundee said. "Those fifteen rounds in Montreal—that's when he went to school."

What Sugar Ray learned was that he couldn't fight inside with Duran, couldn't slug with him, couldn't play any of the rugged little wharf rat's games. So Leonard came out dancing and jabbing, never giving Duran a chance to draw a bead on him always moving until he saw the chance to deliver his own brand of punishment. "The name of the game this time was boxing," Leonard said. "Just boxing. Scientific technique." And it was too much for Duran, who had made a fortune fighting just the way he had on the streets of Panama City.

Oh, Duran had his moments, but they were the result of him lowering a shoulder and driving Leonard into the ropes, and there weren't enough of them to do him any good anyway. By the seventh round, he must have known that. Leonard surely did. "I was in control," he said. He could do anything he wanted. He could stick his jaw out and Duran couldn't hit it. He could fake a bolo punch, and while Duran let himself be mesmerized by it, the new champion would sting his nose with another jab.

Never in his life had Duran been treated this way. You could see it in his face. The hate that once burned in his coal-black eyes was gone, and there wasn't enough strength in his body to let him curl his upper lip in that familiar sneer. Sugar Ray Leonard had whipped him, and whipped him like a pup. Cramps or no, Duran was not a champion anymore. He was just a loser. So much for macho.

The Last Words in Boxing
Las Vegas
September 15, 1981

There must be an echo out here. No matter where Thomas Hearns travels, he hears the same preface for every question that is put to him. Sugar Ray Leonard says this or Sugar Ray Leonard says that, and by now Hearns must be wondering if the fight racket has turned into a debating society. He and Leonard are supposed to decide who the world's reigning welterweight is Wednesday night, but all anybody seems to care about is digging up old ground with a well-worn plow: Sugar Ray says . . .

To Hearns' dismay, witty answers usually escape him. He stands there with a blank look on his gaunt face, and the words that come to him are notable for nothing except their unadorned honesty. "Basically," Hearns says, "I don't have much to say." He is a puncher, not an orator who can contribute to the hype for the approaching spectacle at Caesars Palace. The best he can do is to show up and be bored out of his mind while staring at strangers who have given every round in the fight before the fight to the elegant, swellegant Leonard.

Take Sugar Ray to breakfast with the press, ask him why Hearns isn't there, too, and he says: "Hearns wasn't invited."

Let Aaron Pryor, an undefeated belter with designs on Leonard's stature, pop off from the audience and Sugar Ray sputters with mock anger: "Where is that fool? Send him up here. He needs the exposure."

Put a microphone in Leonard's hands and an adoring workout crowd in front of him and he'll explain what he perceives as the essential difference between the nation's reigning gladiators: "Tommy Hearns approaches boxing from a purely physical standpoint. I use my mind. Maybe Tommy would use his, too, if he had one."

The jibes are always there, partly the outgrowth of Hearns' demonstrated timidity outside the ring but also the result of Leonard's highly polished sense of who and what he is. Surely there has never been an athlete so perfectly molded for celebrity. What began with his gold medal at the 1976 Olympics and faltered ever so slightly with his indecision about turning professional has blossomed into a textbook study of success. So what if Hearns will make $7 million Wednesday? Leonard will walk away with $9 million, put it in the bank, and go right back to his special world of commercials, TV guest appearances, and a wife and son so perfect they must have been kidnapped from central casting. The life he leads makes "the Sweet Science" sound like a fitting description of boxing instead of flinty irony, and don't think Leonard doesn't realize that now more than ever before.

"Tommy Hearns is always going to want to be me," he says. "He's competing with both me the fighter and me the personality. If I showboat, he showboats. If I say something clever, he tries to say something clever. He just doesn't want to be upstaged by me."

There is more to it than that, of course. If there weren't, Hearns wouldn't have his 32-0 record, or his thirty knockouts, or the pleasure of proving that Emanuel Steward, his manager and trainer, was wrong for telling him long ago that he would never be a fighter, much less a World Boxing Association champion. He rode the bus when he decided to determine his own destiny, rode it from his home on Detroit's hardscrabble east side to the then anonymous Kronk Gymnasium on the west, rode it with a purpose we have since seen borne out magnificently. "If I told Thomas we weren't going to box one day, if I told him to go hit the big bag," Steward recalls, "why, he'd get on that bus again and go back home."

To look at Hearns' resolve in retrospect is to see a kid who somehow realized that being built like a No. 2 pencil wasn't going to prevent him from flirting with greatness in the ring. He had the kind of fortitude that allowed him to step aside last year and let lightweight Hilmer Kenty become the first champion off the Kronk's assembly line. And yet the twenty-two-year-old Hearns was so withdrawn as he began preparing his assault on Leonard's World Boxing Council title that he wouldn't leave the safety of his room to give anyone an idea of what makes him tick.

Only lately has he begun to realize that, in his position, he can't always refuse to answer the door when somebody knocks. What he can do, whether Leonard cares to believe it or not, is refuse to be somebody he isn't.

"If you go out and take care of your business and do it

right, the people will have confidence in you," Hearns says. "Then you don't have to be a big mouth."

It seems an eternity since one of boxing's solid gold main-eventers has acknowledged the dangers of too much talk and not enough action. The rowdy charm of Muhammad Ali hangs everywhere in the sport, like party crepe that refuses to be torn down. It has become a safety jacket for a thousand fighters you've never heard of and for Sugar Ray Leonard, too. But Thomas Hearns refuses to join the parade. He has his mother cooking his Las Vegas meals, the calculating Steward mapping his strategy, the guys from the Kronk keeping him company, and a growing sense of what it takes to keep the wolves at bay.

"Why are you late?" someone asks when Hearns finally shows up to meet the press.

"Because I want to be late," Hearns replies.

Obviously, you can't believe everything Sugar Ray says about his opponent's mental capacity. Nor should you put much stock in the mind games Leonard insists on playing with Hearns.

"But don't you think he's psyching you out?" a truth-seeker wants to know.

"If he is," Hearns says, "he's not doing a very good job."

The answer draws laughter and grudging respect, but it doesn't get him off the frying pan. He will stay there until the fight, and if he loses, even longer. Everywhere he turns, there will be someone who wants to know if his head is as hard as his fists, if he stays up nights practicing to be another Leonard, if he wishes he weren't going up against the country's most marketable athlete. Those are subjects Hearns shouldn't have to bother with as he loads up for the biggest fight of his life. But they exist, and you know why.

Because Sugar Ray says so.

Life Is No Longer a Piece of Cake for Jacobs
Las Vegas
September 17, 1981

He never wanted Wednesday night to get here. He wanted to close his eyes and hold his breath and make everything stop

Life Is No Longer a Piece of Cake for Jacobs

before Sugar Ray Leonard could risk his classic talent against Thomas Hearns' concrete fists. It was a surprisingly gentle stance for someone in the middle of a flesh peddler's sport, but in those long-gone days when Dave Jacobs watched over Leonard, they had a relationship that went far beyond trainer and fighter. They were so close that if Sugar Ray wanted his favorite German chocolate cake for dessert, he just called Jacobs' wife and asked for it.

Jacobs is forty-eight, too old to cry, but he couldn't escape teary sentiment as his personal hell week ground toward the welterweight championship fight he didn't want to see. He was bewitched by the fact that he was not with the fresh-faced Olympic hero he molded with his own hands, bothered by the ease with which he had imported two sparring partners for Hearns, and bewildered by the crazy emotions tearing at his insides.

"If they called this fight off," Jacobs said, "I'd be the happiest man in the world."

Few would ever understand exactly what was going on in his heart and mind. There was confusion and fear and, most of all, unshakable insecurity. A victory by Leonard would mean that he wasn't needed in the only place he ever really cared about. A victory by Hearns would leave him looking like a traitor. Jacobs didn't want to think about either possibility, but the questions about what he thought would happen kept filling his ears. And though he never came out and admitted it, he could only think of the worst for Sugar Ray. "If he gets knocked down," Jacobs said, "I'll be the first to pick him up."

After all, he was the first to put Leonard in a position to get knocked down. It happened in the Palmer Park Recreation Center, where Jacobs, an overgrown featherweight, used to train amateurs at night after delivering pharmaceuticals all day. He saw scrawny, timid Ray Charles Leonard walk into the gym eleven years ago and accepted him as nothing more than another kid who would learn how to wrap his hands and keep his dukes up. "Ray was just another guy from the neighborhood, you know," Jacobs said, "and then, after about six or seven months, I could see he was going to be more than that." He could see that Leonard was going to be a fighter so sweet they would call him Sugar.

The nickname rang from Washington, D.C.'s dreariest arenas to the golden splendor of the Montreal Olympics, and Jacobs was there to hear it every step of the way. "Wasn't nobody else," he said. You can forget about Michael Trainer and Janks Morton and Angelo Dundee, who guide Leonard's fortunes now. "The only person anybody ever seen with Ray Leonard back then," Dave Jacobs said, "was Dave Jacobs."

He wanted it to end in Montreal, wanted Sugar Ray to leave the ring and get his schooling and make a living with his brains and charm. But Ray's parents were sick and boxing was the fastest way to the kind of money that could help them, so Jacobs turned professional with the kid in 1977. It was a matter of loyalty. And for a while, his loyalty was rewarded.

He trained Leonard full-time and the venerable Dundee came in a week or so before every fight to apply a coat of polish. Jacobs didn't mind; he understood who the star was. All he wanted to do was look after the prize of his life in boxing. But the prize started slipping away from him, slowly at first, and then so fast that he had no idea where he would be going next. "I knew we were coming apart when I read in the paper that Ray was going to fight Wilfred Benitez," he said. It was Leonard's first million-dollar purse, an event that should have been made for celebrating, and Jacobs used the occasion to prepare himself for the worst.

Leonard's loss to Roberto Duran, the first loss of his career, was it. Sugar Ray kept saying he wanted to get back at Duran as soon as he could, and Jacobs kept arguing that he needed a couple of tune-up fights first. "Other people didn't feel that way," he said. The other people were Trainer, Morton, and Dundee, who had taken over the controls. There was only one thing Jacobs could think to do.

"I stepped down," he said. "I didn't get fired like some people say. I stepped down. Ray tried to talk me out of it. He came to my house and tried to convince me that fighting Duran again was in his heart. I told him he didn't need it—even when he beat Duran, I said that—but he couldn't understand. When he left that day, something stepped out of my life. I never wanted to be apart from Ray when he was in the ring."

Yet that was where Jacobs would be when Leonard

battled Hearns outdoors, behind Caesars Palace. In what shaped up as the toughest fight of Sugar Ray's life, the man who laid the foundation for him would be nothing more than a face in the crowd. He would be expected to cheer for Hearns because of the sparring partners he provided, yet he would also be ravaged by old memories. He would think of the good times with Sugar Ray, and then he would glance at his watch and realize once again that they were no more, that there was just one consolation about Wednesday night. Hell week would soon be over.

Leonard Saves Face with TKO
Las Vegas
September 17, 1981

After all those miles and all those smiles, Sugar Ray Leonard wasn't pretty anymore. He was a one-eyed man in an ugly fight that had nothing to do with the glitz and glamour that have become his calling card. There had been a time when he could have avoided this grim marathon, a time in the sixth and seventh rounds when he could have added Thomas Hearns to his list of victims. But the moment had passed and Hearns had escaped, and now Sugar Ray Leonard, his handsome face a scowling bruise, was struggling for survival.

It was the thirteenth round Wednesday night, and the catcalls had begun to fill the outdoor stadium behind Caesars Palace. There were 25,000 people baking in the remnants of another 100-degree afternoon, each of them seemingly intent on proclaiming Hearns a winner and Leonard a loser. In those opening seconds, you could see why as Hearns kept jabbing and moving and Leonard kept looking for a place to throw his right hand and never finding it. The frustration smouldered in his one good eye, smouldered almost hypnotically.

Then it was gone.

And so was Hearns.

The bomb that caught him was a right to the head that he never saw. Suddenly, the hit man from Detroit was on Queer Street, weaving under a flurry of lefts and rights, bouncing from one side of the ring to the other until Leonard bulled him through the ropes and onto his back. Hearns escaped without getting charged with a knockdown thanks to the largesse of referee Dave Pearl, only to find himself back on the second strand thirty seconds later.

"Off the rope," Pearl shouted.

The weary, wobbly Hearns refused the order with a shake of his head. He would not move until Pearl started counting, and he would never be the same.

Maybe the fight should have ended there, maybe Hearns should have been spared more punishment and Leonard the cause to deliver it. But that is not the way the Sweet Science operates, not when the guy getting his brains scrambled is ahead on the judges' scorecards by two, three, and four points. So on the beating went into the fourteenth round, on until Leonard had Hearns helpless against the ropes once again, on until a minute and forty-five seconds were gone and Pearl had no choice but to say that Hearns was undefeated no more.

Sugar Ray, the sweet slugger from Palmer Park, Maryland, was the winner by dint of a technical knockout and a quality he had never before had to use so heavily.

"I had to dig down in my guts," he said when $9 million, a 31-1 record, and both of the world's welterweight titles were his. "I knew I was behind, I knew I had to keep the pressure on. There wasn't anything I could do but find out what was inside of me."

Leonard was looking at the world through dark glasses. Under normal circumstances, you would have called them the normal trappings of America's busiest athletic celebrity. But on a night that found Muhammad Ali, Burt Reynolds, and Charo shoulder to shoulder at ringside, Leonard had bigger things to worry about than his image. "I suffered a slight injury to my left eye during workouts," he said, "and Hearns kept jabbing it." By the fifth round, Sugar Ray had a mouse the size of a small bagel. By the twelfth, it was a question of whether he could see at all. And even when Hearns had been dragged back to his dressing room, Leonard still squinted painfully at the glory surrounding him.

There never had been a fight like this, financially if not artistically. With 300 million people around the world watching on closed-circuit television and pay TV and who knows how many more waiting for the delayed videotape, the Leonard-Hearns showdown could gross as much as $40 million by the time the last penny is counted. Add to that the $6 million that the Caesars crowd paid for tickets ranging from $50 to $500 and you have the makings of a grand welterweight coronation.

The bookmakers had predicted the occasion would belong to Hearns. After being on the short end of the gamblers' good faith until two days before the fight, the snake-quick 145-pounder became a 6-5 favorite to add Leonard's World Boxing Council title to the one he already owned from the World Boxing Association. It made you wonder if the wise guys knew something the rest of the world didn't, and when you saw Leonard enter the ring timidly Wednesday night, your doubts turned to outright fears.

For the first five rounds, the 6'1" Hearns was in command, stinging Leonard with his jab and keeping his shorter opponent at bay with his vaunted seventy-eight-inch reach. Unable to get inside where he wanted to operate, Leonard had to fight outside, and he paid in pain. Not until the sixth could he solve Hearns' surprisingly good defense, and then he did it with a vengeance. A left hook to the head inaugurated the assault, and after that, there was no telling exactly what Leonard was throwing, just that he was throwing everything.

"He did something nobody ever did before," trainer Angelo Dundee said. "He was a better puncher than Tommy Hearns."

The record book shows that Hearns had thirty knockouts in his thirty-two victories, and thirty knockouts is a whopping figure until you realize that he had never fought anyone like Sugar Ray Leonard. Nor had he ever fought so long in such withering heat. No wonder he was in trouble again in the seventh, no wonder his long legs looked like rubber. But the greatest wonder of all was that Leonard, master strategist though he is, let Hearns get off the hook.

It could have been fatal when you think back to how Hearns rallied in the next three rounds, keeping Leonard off balance with his jab and becoming the stalker once again. In the far reaches of the stadium, the faithful from Detroit started chanting "Tommy, Tommy!" before the twelfth, and Hearns leaped off his stool to wave them on. Little did he know what Leonard had in store for him one round later.

Afterward, the fight judges would marvel at the savage beauty of Sugar Ray's surprise attack. They would talk about the lifeless glaze that came over Hearns' face when Leonard finally found the room to throw the combinations he had been saving all night. He used them until they were wretched excess and then he just banged away with his right hand. Twenty-three unanswered punches, one judge said. Twenty-eight, said another. The debate would range long into the night, and when it was over, there would be only one point everyone could agree on. Sugar Ray Leonard, the one-eyed man, never missed his target.

Leonard: Goaded by Ghosts?
Las Vegas
September 18, 1981

Maybe there is no other way to tap the greatness inside Sugar Ray Leonard. Maybe manufactured paranoia is the only viable fuel for the meanness he must have to survive in the ring.

What else can you think when you hear his brain trust whisper that the world is against him and see him dismiss the motherly smiles he gets from old ladies at the slot machines and the bons mots he has traded with Johnny Carson? Leonard convinces himself that everybody resents his success, that the ketchup he found splattered on his Mercedes back home in Maryland represented the knife the public would like to stick in his back. The hobgoblins of injustice are presumed to be everywhere and, to hear him tell it, they wouldn't let up even after he had proven that his heart pumps nothing but high-octane courage.

The occasion, of course, was Leonard's fourteen-round dismantling of Thomas Hearns and his quicksilver knockout punch at Caesars Palace. The sources of dismay were the judges' cards that said if the bruised and bedraggled Sugar Ray had not lowered the boom when he did, if he had allowed the fight to drag on to a decision, he would not have awakened Thursday morning as the world's undisputed welterweight champion.

In the land of the ten-point-must scoring system, one judge had him trailing Hearns by two points, another by three, and the third, most mysteriously, by four. To hear the weeping and wailing in Leonard's quarters when the great thinkers there got a load of that, you would have thought somebody had spiked his UnCola with Coca-Cola.

"I'm not saying Ray should be treated like Muhammad Ali," said attorney Mike Trainer, the power behind Leonard's throne. "I'm not saying he should win everything that's close. But, Jesus, give him a fair shake. If you look at those scorecards, it'll turn your stomach. They really make me think the powers that be in boxing are threatened by Ray. He's setting a tone, he's swinging the momentum away from the promoters and toward the boxers. And the only way he can be stopped is by the scoring. We just can't win any close fights, that's all."

Trainer's choice of words couldn't have been more inappropriate, for in thirty-two professional outings, Leonard has lost just once. His lone conqueror was Roberto Duran and the decision was split, but what does that matter now? Leonard came back to beat the scowling roughneck and put himself in a position to dig more gold than ever came out of the richest mine. He made $9 million turning Hearns' undefeated record to dust Wednesday night, and he did it the best way of all—by rendering the judges' cards useless. Alas, Trainer sees no point in paying attention to that and, not unexpectedly, neither does Leonard.

"People root against me," the champion said from behind dark glasses. "I'm like a diamond in the mud."

If Sugar Ray can shut out the love he basks in so readily, there isn't a chance he will hear the hosannas thrown his way by Chuck Minker, the judge who had him four points to the bad against Hearns. It was as blind a job of scoring as the tawdry old fight racket has been saddled with in a championship go— "At least the other judges saw the same fight I did," Minker countered lamely—but the potentially controversial points were washed away like sand castles at high tide. Leonard, after having Hearns on rubber legs in the sixth and letting him escape, dug down into a heretofore unknown streak of savagery and saved the night. Even Minker could see that.

"After twelve rounds, you looked at Leonard, you saw

his left eye closing, and you said, 'This guy's in trouble,'" the judge said. "Then, all of a sudden, he was swarming all over Hearns. That was what was so amazing about Leonard; the guy got in one good punch and he followed it with three or four. Beat up like he was and doing that? Coming out of nowhere like he did? You had to love Leonard's guts."

In truth, you had to love everything about Leonard and Hearns, from the record $36 million their battle grossed to the new light it cast on boxing's showdowns. Usually, they are bittersweet affairs, with age giving way to youth, Ali to Holmes, Louis to Marciano, that sort of thing. But this was a fight that matched two stars still on the ascent—Leonard, twenty-five, a strategist of the first order, versus Hearns, twenty-two, a devastating puncher whose seventy-eight-inch wingspan makes him seem like an octopus. "I never thought the sucker was that big until I got in there against him," Sugar Ray said.

Size, however, wasn't the half of it. There was also the matter of Leonard's left eye, injured two weeks ago by a sparring partner's misguided elbow and puffed up ferociously Wednesday night by Hearns' brutal right hand.

"But I wasn't able to hit Leonard with my best shot," Hearns insisted Thursday.

"Sheesh," said Sugar Ray.

Yet his surprise may have been more theatrical than anything else, for he had been the better puncher in that open-air ring, he had been the one who relied on the bomb to save his hide. Conversely, Hearns showed himself to be a far more accomplished boxer than anyone ever gave him credit for being; he jabbed and moved with Rockette precision and put up a defense that left Leonard looking like a man who couldn't find his keys. Back and forth the two of them went for thirteen rounds, one minute and forty-five seconds— switching styles, changing tactics, riding a psychological roller coaster. It was something to behold.

"I saw Thomas Hearns hurt and I never saw that before," said his manager and trainer, Emanuel Steward. "I saw Ray Leonard outboxed and I never saw that before, either."

Even though their man had won, even though nothing beyond that really mattered anymore, Sugar Ray's guardian angels wanted to debate the latter point. That's the way they go about their business, and their influence shows on Leonard like a cigarette burn on a custom-made suit. He couldn't make it through Thursday morning without getting stuck in the muck of his persecution complex. He had to moan about chuckle-headed judges, college graduates who don't want to see a fighter become a millionaire, and, as always, the omnipresent "they."

Who are they? Leonard couldn't say exactly. "Boxing critics," he guessed. And while you tried to figure out if that means fans, promoters, writers, or other fighters, he headed for home and the flooded basement he said awaited him. There was no chance to find out who or what caused the flood, no chance to hear if he was going to blame it on the forces he knows are out to get him. But you couldn't help thinking that if it will help him win another fight, Sugar Ray Leonard probably will point the finger at an enemy no one else can see.

The Choice Is Sight to Behold
Baltimore
May 12, 1982

Look at the pictures sometime. Then you'll know how much a part of Sugar Ray Leonard's presence his eyes are. They do more than accentuate a handsome face; they flicker with the electricity that allows no emotion to remain a secret for long. Of course, even a blindfold couldn't have hidden Leonard's excitement when the red, white, and blue flew high above him on the Olympic winner's stand, but it was different when a ring-smart thug butted his brow open. Bewilderment clouded his eyes and you wondered whether he had made a wrong turn.

The signs were there, for Ray Charles Leonard didn't want to waste his body this way. But his mother was sickly and his father was work weary, so he took the leap for the fight racket's gold. The next thing he knew, his head was ringing and he was staring through his own blood at a Marcus Geraldo who suddenly had become much trickier than advertised.

"I keep seeing three of him," Leonard moaned to trainer Angelo Dundee back in the corner. "What'll I do? What'll I do?"

"Hit the guy in the middle," the sage Dundee replied.

Leonard did, and he won, and you wonder if he remembers how it felt to be the master of his eyes now that he lives in a world that is 50 percent darkness. The doctors at Johns Hopkins Hospital tell him it is only temporary, and his wife, who sleeps on a cot beside his bed, pats his hand reassuringly, but the bandage on his left eye remains. It won't be removed as hastily as the intravenous needle that was taken out of his arm Tuesday, won't be removed by the telephone calls from Ronald Reagan and Ray Robinson, boxing's original Sugar Man, and the thousands of well-wishers who get no farther than the switchboard. Sugar Ray Leonard feeds on the bright lights, but now they are being denied him to save his sight.

The wunderkind who succeeded Muhammad Ali as the Sweet Science's savior spent two hours on an operating table Sunday having the partially detached retina in his left eye repaired. It was nothing that hasn't already happened to heavyweight Earnie Shavers and erstwhile welterweight challenger Harold Weston, Jr., and a multitude of fighters before them, yet the thought of it left your stomach uneasy and painted your imagination in torture-chamber colors. You weren't prepared to hear Mike Trainer, the guiding light of Leonard's career, suggest that his tiger may fight again, nor did you want to listen to Roger Stafford bellyache about how heartless fate robbed him of his Friday night shot at Sugar Ray's undisputed welterweight championship. Good sense and common decency never got a moment's play, but maybe we shouldn't expect them to in man's cruelest sport.

To enter the ring is to risk your life; to leave it with nothing worse than a cantilevered nose or an abundance of scar tissue or even a slightly scrambled brain is a blessing. The cost of an eye, however, is too much. You need only study the sightless pugs who populate the country's stinking gyms to understand that. They have been robbed of something the fortunate among us take for granted, and cursed to live in perpetual night. Unfortunately, Sugar Ray Leonard may not want to realize it unless he receives the proper counsel.

"Me and Ray, we're so stubborn," says Harold Weston,

Jr., whose beleaguered eyes turned him into a Madison Square Garden matchmaker. "Our souls can take it and our pride can take it, but our detached retinas can't. When Ray lays on his side for ten days with his eyes taped and he can't see nothing, he's going to say it's not worth it. He's just going to quit. If he don't quit, I'll go up and beat him with a stick."

At least Weston's message would be easier to comprehend than the source of Leonard's woe. Sugar Ray may have been done in by the sparring partner who accidentally elbowed him before he flogged Thomas Hearns into submission in September, or maybe Hearns did the damage himself. Then again, the culprit may have been the presumably harmless Bruce Finch, though he was gone by the third round of their February sleepwalk. The speculation will continue as long as there are men who remember Leonard, and judging by the display of heart he put on while weathering Hearns' bombs, he will be remembered long after he is gone.

Before he was rushed to Baltimore from his Buffalo, New York, training camp, Leonard was saying as much himself. "I'm content," he told *Playboy* magazine. "I have my place in boxing history." He has that and fame and $40 million and his standing as America's sweetheart—too much to risk by coming back and perhaps undoing the operation he just underwent, perhaps even ruining his good eye in the process. But how do you tell Sugar Ray Leonard that he has nothing more to prove in the racket he always has been too good for?

He is a creature of ego. Were he anything else, he wouldn't have beaten Roberto Duran in their rematch, wouldn't have bragged that he is Maryland's biggest taxpayer, wouldn't have taken so readily to yukking it up with Johnny Carson and Howard Cosell. But what Leonard should understand is that while he is trapped in this hospital room, none of that matters. Suddenly, his solid-gold life has been reduced to the bare essentials, and he would be wise to appreciate them for what they are.

He has a wife who holds his hand and a seven-year-old son who wonders when his father will be able to play with him again. So what if Hearns is out there waiting to be beaten once more and Marvin Hagler deserves to be taught a million-dollar lesson? Neither one of them is worth an eye; neither one of them is more important than the chance to see a sunset or a rabbit's tracks in new-fallen snow or a kid's face on Christmas morning. If Sugar Ray Leonard doesn't realize that, he should close his good eye and try to imagine what it would be like if boxing left him blind. In the darkness, maybe he would see the light.

Postscript

There was a lot to dislike about Sugar Ray Leonard's retirement party, starting with the fact that he felt compelled to have it in the Baltimore Civic Center and charge admission. Though the money was earmarked for charity, it was a harbinger of tackiness to come. Or do you really like using a ring for a stage, propping up Howard Cosell as master of ceremonies, and asking Las Vegas' own Wayne Newton to unload a little of his plastic sincerity on boxing's departing king?

I don't, and I'm not very crazy about being duped, either. But duped is what I thought I was after listening to Sugar Ray insist he didn't reach his decision until that night and then opening Sports Illustrated *the next day to read a story about his retirement written weeks before.*

And yet none of that matters very much.

What matters is that Sugar Ray Leonard was right in choosing health over more wealth, and if I am to say anything further about him, it won't involve grousing. I will, rather, simply hope that he never changes his mind.

3.
Da Brains of da Operation

Honesty is not a criterion for membership in the boxing promoters' lodge. It may even be grounds for expulsion. But that doesn't mean I don't have a special fondness for Don King, who is both the reigning wheeler-dealer and my favorite punching bag. Though I wouldn't trust him to bring back my change if I sent him to the store for a loaf of bread, there always will be a place for him in my prose because he makes me laugh.

Somewhere in the odyessy that has taken him from the numbers racket to prison to the fight racket, King learned the virtue of being outrageous. If it hasn't made him beloved, it has at least gotten him more ink than his arch enemy, attorney Bob Arum, who doesn't dress like a pimp or speechify like a storefront preacher. To hear Arum tell it, he is the class act in promoting, but his lack of soul means he doesn't get in my book any way except through the back door. I like my fight geniuses from the streets, not Harvard Law.

On the Block: Way of All Flesh
Baltimore
March 4, 1974

Baltimore is a gritty old strumpet of a city where unwritten sociological imperatives require a boxing arena to have Polish bakeries on one side, steel mills on another, and red-neck bars all around. Steelworkers Hall meets those criteria with the ease that home boy Joe Gans dropped pretenders to his turn-of-the-century lightweight championship.

Gans would have fit in nicely at Steelworkers because, if students of pugilism verité will excuse its newly painted exterior, everything about this unimposing brick pile seems the product of an imagination longing for another chance at yesterday. "Steelworkers," says a fighter who gets work there regularly, "is a little bucket of blood, just like you'd see in the movies."

I.W. Abel, the union boss, peers down from a photograph on the dingy wall, but he can't see the ring for the smoke. There are 1,225 tan metal folding chairs in the arena, and the critics who fill them cease puffing on cigars only to offer such advice as, "Hit him with a coconut, dummy." Everyone is hustling bets, even the housewife at ringside who puts a couple dollars on the red corner for one fight and a couple on the blue for the next. The action is heavier under the balcony, where a betting man can stop a boxer headed for the ring and tell him how many hundred are riding on him. Local fighters get most of the play—a commentary on their opponents as much as it is on their ability—and on those rare occasions when a decision goes against one of them, it rains beer.

"People gonna get excited," sputters resident promoter Eli Hanover, who is always excited himself. "This is a jumping-up-and-down sport. Who jumps up and down when someone carries a football four yards? Who jumps up and down when someone hits a single? Here people jump up and down just watching two guys trying to knock each other on their butt. Y'understand what I mean about a jumping-up-and-down sport?"

If you don't, check out Eli on a fight night. Up to greet an old pug with a roundhouse slap to the shoulder. And down. Up to find out if a preliminary boy has gotten the message that he is fighting. And down. Up to take another shot at convincing the sporting press that several boxers on the card don't belong in a rest home. And down.

Hanover enjoys the luxury of wearing himself out this way because he knows that all the hands in the till are an extension of his. Daughters Jackie and Gail sell tickets, brother-in-law Bernie runs the hot-dog stand, and wife Frances counts the money. The family approach helps keep the overhead low, which helps keep Eli in business, something he is very insistent about.

On occasion Hanover seems to have help from elsewhere. Take the time half of a midsummer's night main event decided he would rather stay in Puerto Rico and celebrate his last victory than fly to Baltimore and get beat on. Eli didn't learn of the change of heart until the afternoon of the fight. He sprayed $150 worth of telephone calls around the East, complaining that his stomach was killing him and assuming that everyone knew his wallet was, too. Four hours of trying produced a thirty-three-year-old Hartford, Connecticut, toolmaker named Jesus Alicia who hadn't been in a ring for a month and whose record was 10-20-4—but who was available. When Alicia showed up thirty minutes before the fight, the man filling out a medical examination card said, "What's your address, Jesus?" "Heaven, where else?" replied one of Hanover's cronies.

There is nothing heavenly about the location of the gym where Hanover makes his headquarters. It is perched over a strip joint on the Block, that swatch of East Baltimore Street famed for showing sailors and salesmen a good time and now as wrinkled, fat, and toothless as any atherosclerotic burlesque queen. The strip joint is the Jewel Box, and until last January Eli owned it. He sold out to Lou Barber, who managed several fighters Eli uses on his cards and who was recently convicted as part of a gambling ring that included local cops. So it goes on the Block.

The red door to Sports Activities, Inc. is next to the entrance to the Jewel Box. Anyone who picks the gym over the watered-down drinks and mush-bellied strippers gets a pained look from the Jewel Box doorman. Yet the gym's occupants aren't removed completely from the house of few lights below. The music from the jukebox pulses through the floor of the gym, massaging the ears and feet of everyone topside.

The Isley Brothers blend a burning question, "Who's that lady, beautiful lady?" into the normal gymnasium cacophony—the beeps and bongs of the automatic timer, the snorts of the sparring boxers, the splat of their gloves, the machine-gun bursts on the speed bag, the frantic lashes of a rope-skipping fighter struggling to keep pace with his trainer, who is singing "Tea for Two."

Up front Eli Hanover is talking. As usual. His audience is a man from the outfit that made the gym's ring. Like the one at Steelworkers, it is 18-by-18, smaller than the standard 20-by-20 because, Eli says, "I don't like to see nobody running away." The ring's size, however, doesn't keep Eli from telling the man, "All that canvas, sheesh, you guys must be making a fortune."

The man laughs. "You haven't paid for it yet," he says.

"It's better to give than receive," Eli replies.

Eli's Klaxon voice oogahs forward on the square wheels of a nasal Baltimore accent, grating to the uninitiated. The body is middle-aged Mickey Rooney. The head is Humphrey Bogart. But the dark brown eyes are strictly Eli. They dance like a nimble fighter stalking a night's prey. They take in all on the street below, from the wino slumped in front of a dirty-book store to the strippers high-heeling to work as night catches up with day. They water a bit when the fumes from Polock Johnny's sausage emporium drift through the open windows of the gym.

"This is the class street of the world," Eli says from deep in the recesses of his black executive's chair. "If you want to find it, come to this street. You got the greatest people that walk God's earth and you got some of the biggest stinkers." He notices a friend crossing the street. "Hey," Eli bellows. "Hey, hey!" The friend looks up at last to see Eli in the window, clasping his hands and shaking them over each shoulder, back and forth, back and forth.

It is the wave of the champion that fifty-two-year-old Eli Hanover, son of a Rumanian immigrant peddler, child of the tough East Baltimore streets, never was. He won fourteen of fifteen professional fights as a lightweight, but in the process he had the truth about his ability stitched onto his eyebrows. "I wasn't no great fighter," he says. "I was just a preliminary boy." A steadier future waited for him at sea, where he spent thirteen years sailing the world in the Merchant Marine. When he came ashore for good, waiting for him were his wife and the earliest of their nine children, an organizer's job with the seaman's union, and the chance to get back in boxing.

He paid his dues training and managing a series of nondescript fighters before he began promoting in the mid-sixties. There are pessimists in town who say it was more curse than chance. Before, Hanover could take whomever he was handling to Philadelphia or Washington or Richmond. Now he was stuck in Baltimore. Baltimore, where the only places he could put on a show were tiny Steelworkers Hall or the 12,000-seat Civic Center, which, a series of bad crowds has convinced Eli, is "a fat, greedy, white elephant." Rising land costs in the suburbs have kept him from building an arena with 3,000 seats that he insists he could fill anytime he stepped off the Block.

Such confidence has deserted Hanover just once in his decade of promoting. When an attractive Civic Center card flopped in 1970, he went incommunicado for eighteen months. He came back for another try, of course, declaring, "I feel like I just got outta jail."

Boxing was about to become a full-time job for him by then; he had retired from the seaman's union and he was getting ready to unload the Jewel Box. It wasn't money that brought him back; although Eli says, "I ain't going broke," friends indicate that he isn't getting rich, either. The lure, most likely, was that he was needed. Needed, that is, as much as any city whose populace remembers TV's Friday night fights needs a boxing promoter. Replacements had come from Philadelphia as well as Baltimore, and they had failed. That does much for Eli's already substantial ego, particularly now that his business is picking up. "Let's face it," he says. "I'm Mr. Boxing in Baltimore. This self-praise stinks, but we're talking about actuality."

Baltimore's last successful promoters, Lou Fisher and Georgie Goldberg, struck it rich in the forties. They put on two or three fight shows a week, and they always had one on Monday. "Except when it was Yom Kippur," says Hanover. But time caught up with them. The ice rinks and ball parks that housed their fights fell to ruin, and when the promoters grew old, there was no one to take their place.

There still isn't, as far as gimmickry is concerned. Fisher and Goldberg once had a heavyweight named Curtis Sheppard who was putting opponents' lights out upon request. That wasn't enough for them. They bought a hatchet, painted it gold, and gave it and the nickname Hatchetman to Sheppard. He carried the hatchet into the ring with him every fight after that. When he fought Jersey Joe Walcott, someone had to carry it out for him.

"The people that come to Steelworkers don't want no gimmicks," says Hanover. "They don't want no free T-shirts. They don't want no free boxing gloves. They want to see blood, that's what they want to see—blood. As long as it isn't theirs." The boxers who turn up regularly on Eli's cards seem eager to draw it or give it. "They are," he says, "ath-a-letes. You can't give the people what I call tomato cans. You know, no fluff-fluffs, no boo-boos, no ha-has. You do, you're out of business. You got to give the people ath-a-letes."

One of the fights Eli dreamed of would have matched Wes Unseld, the redwood-thighed center of the then Baltimore Bullets, with 6'5", 280-pound Bobo Renfrow. This is the same Bobo Renfrow who, when asked to sing his school song during a tryout with the old Boston Patriots, warbled the Schaefer beer commercial. Bobo turned to boxing when football rejected him, and when boxing became too hard, he went underground. "He's working on the subway in Washington," Eli says. "I think he's holding up the street."

So Hanover must settle for fighters of lesser physical stature but equally strange reputation. Light heavyweight Josh Hall's performances at Steelworkers have led to rumors of a jaw made by Libbey-Owens-Ford. But he is 4-0 in the parking lot of The Frigate lounge in suburban Glen Burnie. It is surprising that welterweight Buddy Boggs has time for boxing at all. He claims to have wrestled alligators, driven a motorcycle off a bridge for the Annette Funicello classic *How to Stuff a Wild Bikini*, and come up swinging after falling twenty floors in an elevator on a construction job. "Ronnie McGarvey, he's my Jesus freak," Hanover says. Once Eli paid McGarvey $650 for a main event at Steelworkers that the undefeated featherweight thought was worth more. "But I didn't argue the case with him," says McGarvey. "I just want to praise God."

Eli, meanwhile, is studiously watching the development of Leo Saenz, a nineteen-year-old middleweight whom Greyhound brought him last spring. Saenz is one of fourteen children born to an itinerant Mexican-American fruit-picker in Edinburg, Texas. When he was fourteen and his family had journeyed to Kalamazoo, Michigan, Leo set out on his own. He survived a brush with the law over some stolen pants and began learning his way around the ring. "I was just practicing with those other dudes," he says. "They was using me. They thought I wasn't going nowhere. And one day, this old guy—his name is Johnny Gale—he sees me practicing for the Golden Gloves and he said, 'You got it, man,' and he sent me to Baltimore."

Gale's judgment has held up through Saenz's first thirteen professional triumphs, eight by knockouts. Relentlessly aggressive, Leo is always hunting them. Trainer Terry Moore remembers Leo's reaction to one of the five decisions he has won: "Leo kept saying, 'I gotta knock him out, I gotta knock him out.' I said, 'Leo, you already done punched holes in the man.' He said, 'I know, but I gotta knock him out.'"

"This guy," Eli says of the kid, "is the best fighter I seen in the past thirty years potential-wise. If he don't become a champion, it's because he didn't try. He can be what you'd call your Rolls-Royce of boxing." Of course Eli says that, or something equally flattering, about every local product who appears on his shows and whose fists are worth taping. "If Buddy Boggs doesn't revive boxing in Baltimore," he once said, "then I'm getting out of the game." Bobo Renfrow was "the hottest, livest fighter in the country," and Ronnie McGarvey still "may be the best featherweight in the country." To every such pronouncement, regardless of its accuracy, Eli adds solemnly, "May this building fall on my head right now if that ain't the truth."

The carny barker's pitch is for the public, but the boxers aren't immune to Hanover's salesmanship, either. More than once one of Josh Hall's opponents has shown up over the weight limit. "My manager will be standing there," Josh says, "and I'll be trying to listen to him and Eli. Well, you know how Eli can talk. He'll look me right in the eye and say, 'You want to fight, don't you?', and the only thing I can say is, 'Yeah.'"

Hanover begins to wonder if his magic is evaporating when he has fight nights at Steelworkers like the one just past. The regular clientele showed up—Jack Pollack, Baltimore's fading political boss, and Simon Avara, Governor Marvin Mandel's barber, and a gang of old pugs remembered only by each other—but they wouldn't fill the place. The thought of it grated Eli so badly that he made friends of his nonpaying customers buy tickets. "I'm sorry," Eli said, "but even the pay phone ain't workin'."

Neither were the somnambulists in the first preliminary. "Hurry up and knock him out," a fan in the balcony yelled to lightweight Billy Bell, the local entry. "I got somewhere to go tonight." "Yeah, knock him out," cried a ringsider. "The man's got somewhere to go." Bell couldn't oblige them, but he remained upright and proved again that is the best way to ensure victory in Baltimore over an outsider.

The balcony dweller was helped toward the door by Donnie Branch, a paunchy heavyweight who delivered an unexpected first-round knockout, and Leo Saenz, who put away an alleged Nigerian prince in the second round of their fight. Each winner found himself with a shadow as happy as his victim was flat. Tagging along with Saenz was a rock 'n' roll guitarist who had strummed up $100 worth of action on his man. A cabbie named Doc had picked up Branch at Penn Station and decided to stick with him rather than head for Laurel Race Track and bet on Boone the Great, who wound up running last in the fifth race. "I'm driving my man home to Philadelphia," Doc announced after the fight from a perch on a well-padded wallet.

The happiness stopped outside the dressing room where Jesus "Pajarito" Nieves, Ronnie McGarvey's main-event opponent, was trying on gloves. "These are used," moaned Nieves' manager, Victor Cintron. "Anytime you fight main event, you supposed to get new gloves. A big city like this and you get these gloves my little boy wouldn't wear." Nieves, who speaks little English, shrugged and walked into the ring to take ten rounds of left-handed punishment from McGarvey. Knocked down once, staggered half a dozen times, Nieves endured with a stubborn nobility that earned him a standing ovation from the half-full house. It didn't change the unanimous decision against him, though. It didn't bring water from Steelworkers' dormant showers, either.

While Nieves toweled himself off for the drive back to New York City, where he would return to work in the garment district in the morning, Eli Hanover counted the night's receipts. Three thousand dollars. The break-even figure. Eli felt better than even the winners. He had proved again that he is where he is supposed to be. May the building fall on his head right now if that ain't the truth.

Club Fighters' Savior
Los Angeles
December 21, 1975

There was a time, believe it or not, when Muhammad Ali shied from shouting his own praises.

He was nineteen years old then, his name was still Cassius Clay, and tickets to his first main event in Los Angeles were selling like thermal underwear in July.

The promoter at Olympic Auditorium finally pointed Cassius downtown with orders to convince the masses that he was what he has said he is ever since—the Greatest.

Cassius returned momentarily. "I can't do that," he complained. "It's embarrassing."

Now there is being embarrassed and there is being broke, and the promoter explained the difference in a voice that could have raised a rash on a rock.

All Cassius said on his way back out the door was, "Yes, Ma'am."

Yes, Ma'am, because the promoter was a lady, and the lady was a champ.

She still is.

Aileen Eaton, sixty-six, who has outlived two husbands and seen three grandchildren and three great-grandchildren come into this world, is in her thirty-fourth year as the Grande Dame of the Olympic.

She is one of a kind, not because of her sex or her longevity but because of what she has accomplished while boxing is little more than a beat-up pug in rags.

With equal parts guile, chutzpah, and intelligence, Mrs. Eaton, as everyone from cabbie to congressman respectfully addresses her, has made L.A. the last great refuge for club fighters.

The only places that even come close are Miami, where Chris Dundee works harder to keep the sport alive than most boxers do in the ring, and Philadelphia, where the newest promoter is an imitation, however pale, of Eaton.

New York? It is no place for a club fighter to try to be somebody. Madison Square Garden wants only main-eventers. The kids on the way up and the dreamers whose day is done must fight when they can at Sunnyside Gardens, on

Long Island, under the el train tracks.

"What's wrong is there are very few class promoters around," says Eaton, who is not one bit fond of the occasional fights at the Forum in suburban Inglewood. "A lot of so-called promoters are in it for a fast buck on one or two shows. I've had a lot of them come in against me. They come in with a big flurry and they last one show.

"With them, boxing's a hobby—a lark or something. With me, it's a business. It was tough convincing people of that at first because there had never been a woman involved in boxing in any capacity, and I was dealing with the old-type managers who didn't do anything but handle fighters.

"But they got to know me. They found out I live up to what I say. I always have and I always will. I think almost anybody in the business will tell you that."

Except for smoking a daily chain of cigarettes, Eaton has none of a boxing promoter's outward characteristics. She won't allow swearing in her tiny office at the Olympic. She is clothes-consciously small (5'3", 120 pounds), and her hair is carefully tinted reddish blonde. When she slides behind the wheel of her majestic burgundy Cadillac, she looks to all the world like the doctor's wife she once was.

She came to L.A. from her native Vancouver, British Columbia, at fifteen. Already a high school graduate, she worked as a legal secretary until she met a bright-eyed young medical student named Maurice LeBell.

They married, he became a prominent L.A. osteopath, and she gave birth to two sons, Mike, now the Olympic's wrestling promoter, and Gene, who announces the wrestling matches on TV.

The family's happy days ended in 1941 when Dr. LeBell broke his neck in a freak accident at the beach and died after three months in a coma. His widow was left wishing she hadn't left Southwestern Law School after two years and wondering how she was going to support the boys.

"I went to work for an advertising agency," she says, "and one of the first things I did was arrange to trade the California Military Academy some publicity in return for schooling for Mike and Gene."

Her boxing-nut boss must have sensed something in that. One of her next assignments was to go down to the

Club Fighters' Savior

Olympic, which he operated, and find out why the resident promoter couldn't pay his bills.

"I had never seen a boxing or wrestling match," she says, "but after I looked around, I could see the place was in absolute chaos. I told my boss it ought to be closed down, and he said, 'What would I do Tuesday nights?'"

He never had to find out. He got rid of the old promoter and put two new people in the job—his attractive troubleshooter and Cal Eaton, a quiet, capable inspector for the California State Athletic Commission.

"Oh, we had a lot of fun," says Mrs. Eaton, the memory putting a glow on her face. "I was the serious one and Cal was so easy with people. When we got married in 1948, people asked him why and he just said, 'She's already handling all my money. I just want to make sure I can get half of it back.'"

But when the two of them set out at the Olympic, they had bridges of a decidedly unromantic nature to cross.

"We had a matchmaker, Babe McCoy, a great, great matchmaker," Mrs. Eaton recalls. "He walks in and sees me and says, 'What's the redhead doing here?'

"Cal says, 'I'm sorry, she came with the lease.' I made up my mind right there to learn everything I could about boxing."

On no fewer than fifty Thursday nights a year at the Olympic, Eaton proves she is a Phi Beta Kappa at promoting pugilism.

Tickets for her first show in January always go for a dollar. After that, anyone who buys his tickets ahead of time always gets a buck or two knocked off the regular $3.50-to-$7.50 price.

The program is a bargain, too, because it is free and contains a contest in which fans can win $50 by guessing the outcomes of three fights (winner, round, and how). "Every week somebody does it. Sometimes there are two or three of them," says Eaton. "I wish I knew how they do it."

What she has figured out is how to use the local TV station that shows the Olympic's bouts, both live and on tape. "The people can see who the up-and-coming youngsters are," she explains, "and when the kids are really hot, we switch their fights off TV. It hasn't failed us yet."

The source of almost all of the fresh talent is the Olympic's eight-year-old youth development program, which takes advantage of a quirky California law that allows amateurs to fight on the same cards as professionals.

Few other states allow this, which may well be why, in recent years, few other states have produced such fine fighters as Vicente Saldivar, Armando Muniz, Rudy Hernandez, and Danny "Little Red" Lopez.

They are carrying on the Olympic's tradition of gutty Mexican-American welters, feathers, and lightweights, which began in the forties and fifties with Enrique Bolonos, Lauro Salas, and Art "Golden Boy" Aragon.

Black fighters are a rarity at the Olympic because, says Eaton, "their people don't come out to support them." And Anglos and Orientals survive only if they are willing to stand at center ring and punch until somebody falls.

"We have a very demanding audience," Eaton says, smiling. The Chicanos who clamber into the 10,000-seat auditorium have been known to shower valiant preliminary boys with as much as $200 in coin.

When the mood turns hostile, however, there is nothing quite like it. A controversial decision in 1965 ignited a riot that forced the renovation of the Olympic, which was built in 1924 and had become as tawdry as the rest of central L.A. "Those wild men," Eaton recalls, "ripped seats out of the concrete that we thought could never be moved."

The excitement generated by the Olympic's face-lifting helped carry Eaton through some troubled times. In 1966, her husband, who had been the wrestling promoter, died. Little more than a year later, Eaton was flattened by a rare blood disease that blistered her skin and stole her strength.

"It didn't really clear up until 1971," she says. "But I was back in the office a long time before then. I figured that if I didn't come back to work, all the fighters and promoters in the country were going to start moving in on us.

"There wasn't any way I was going to let anybody take over boxing here. You know, I may not be a kid anymore, but I still feel the same way."

That's why the lady is a champ.

Boxing Better Dead than Led by Don King
Chicago
February 24, 1977

The shills tell you about the comeback boxing is making and you want to believe them. You want to believe that maybe now boxing will be all the good things it wasn't before it lapsed into unconsciousness two decades ago. But you know your wishes will never come true as long as Don King is helping pump the lifeblood back into the fight game.

King touts his United States Boxing Championships as the arrival of an era so clean it squeaks, but the tricks he and his henchmen are using are worn and dirty. Lusting after easy money, the King gang has resorted to phonying up fighters' records and stealing boxers from the people who really deserve to make a buck along with them.

If no one suspects King of masterminding such treachery, it is because he has received a better press than any ex-numbers boss who ever did time for manslaughter. To the public, he is a wizard who pointed Muhammad Ali toward an international fortune, an eccentric with glib charm and a head of hair that looks like a fistful of cotton candy carried by a chimney sweep.

A lot of people who should know better still see King that way. Take Roone Arledge, the major domo of ABC-TV sports. To televise key bouts in King's tournament, which began in January and won't end until June, Arledge has committed $1.5 million and twenty-three hours of air time, not to mention the network's prestige.

Perhaps he has been blinded by the glare of King's pinky ring. Or maybe he has just fallen for the line of self-serving jive King finds so easy to spiel. "My predecessors and my competitiors are only in boxing for what they can get out of it," King says. "I want to contribute something back into the sport."

Anyone who falls for that would do well to consider the conniving that grew out of a simple preliminary fight last June in Providence, Rhode Island.

It seems that light heavyweight Biff Cline, the son of one of King's men, came to town to pad his undefeated record against a tomato can named Johnny Blaine. Alas, Blaine did not cooperate. He pounded out a fourth-round TKO victory over young Mr. Cline.

But a little thing like that didn't keep King from advertising Cline as 16-0 before he fought on the tournament card at the Naval Academy this month and got his clock cleaned.

King's cronies contend that the Cline-Blaine fight was declared "no contest" by the Rhode Island Racing and Athletic Commission. What they can't agree on is why it was supposedly declared no contest; some say it was because Blaine hit Cline in the back of the head and others say it was because Blaine kicked Cline.

Helen Drummey, the clerk of the racing and athletic commission, thinks they are all taking liberties with the truth.

"We distinctly told those people that the decision in the fight was never changed," she says. "This fellow Blaine was winning all the way. And on the back of the scoring card I have in my files, it says 'Fair Fight.' I told that to a man from ABC."

The man from ABC may not have listened. More likely, he was overruled.

"We get our information on each fighter from *Ring* magazine," says Jeff Ruhe, an assistant to Arledge. "We have affidavits from *Ring* saying that whatever procedures they have used to rate fighters in the past, they will continue to use in this tournament."

Ring listed Cline as undefeated going into his Waterloo at Annapolis. Johnny Ort did the listing. According to the magazine's masthead, Ort is an associate editor. According to eyewitnesses, he is a lackey for King.

That does not exactly put him in a class by himself. The space at King's feet is crowded with Al Braverman, Paddy Flood, Henry Grooms, and Richie Giachetti. And isn't it interesting that they, along with King, control, book, or manage most every fighter who steps under ABC-TV's expensive lights?

Only welterweight Johnny Gant, managed by the esteemed Angelo Dundee, is a legitimate, no-strings-attached contender. That leaves the King gang with its mitts on Larry Holmes, Johnny Boudreaux, Richie Kates, Ray Elson, Edwin Viruet, Casey Gacic, Bobby Cassidy, Mike

Colbert, and Walter Seeley, not to mention a host of prelim boys with no business in the tournament.

So when Paddy Flood, speaking for King, says, "I really don't care who wins," you have to believe him. Because in most cases, no matter who wins, the King gang is going to come out money ahead.

This monopoly on talent should prevent fixes. But ABC can't be so grateful for that backwards blessing that it refuses to take a hard look at King's operation.

"If somebody would come to us with a complaint," says Arledge's spokesman, Ruhe, "we certainly would take steps to investigate it."

John McCafferty, for almost four decades a fixture in the Cleveland fight scene, would seem to have a gripe worthy of ABC's attention. He had booked Casey Gacic, a tough young middleweight, for two years, and this year he thought he and the kid were going to get somewhere.

"Al Braverman told me King wanted Gacic in the tournament," McCafferty says. "I've done business with Al for a long time, so I trusted him. Then this Rich Giachetti comes in and gets hold of Gacic. He tells Gacic he can't fight in the tournament unless Giachetti books him himself.

"What's Gacic going to do? He goes with Giachetti. Me, I'm sitting back in Cleveland thinking I was the victim of a con game."

McCafferty doesn't get much sympathy from Paddy Flood. "Let me tell you about boxing," Flood says. "It's the most treacherous, dirtiest, vicious, cheatingest game in the world. You never saw Cus D'Amato apologizing to that old man in Brooklyn for stealing Floyd Patterson from him, did you? That's the nature of the business. It's a terrible business."

Flood has his lines down pat. You ask him for a justification of why Gacic and Johnny Gant backed out on a Baltimore matchmaker when King offered them bigger, faster money, and Flood offers the same twisted explanation. "And don't think I'm losing any sleep at night," he says.

It's impossible to think that. In fact, Flood and the rest of the King gang have had such easy pickings this time around that they probably have been getting extra sleep.

If you dwell on that for a moment, no matter how much you love boxing, you wish it wasn't making a comeback.

Sure, King and his henchmen would have found another way to chisel people, but at least they would have had to spend some energy doing it.

Busted Flush: King Boxing in the Sewer
Chicago
April 22, 1977

The rain came down hard Thursday afternoon. It was a good time to think about the mess Don King and all the people under his voodoo spell have made of boxing. You knew that when you were finished, you would step out into the cleansing downpour, and in a few minutes, you would forget that you had been wading in a sewer.

It didn't have to be this way. Less than nine months ago, the public looked at the Olympic victory stand in Montreal, saw four bright-eyed young American boxers on it, and decided that maybe the fight game, the harlot of sports, deserved a chance to go straight. But Don King saw the same sight and decided there was easy money to be made.

King moved in on his prey swathed in the trappings of respectability. He had *The Ring* magazine, the Bible of boxing, at his right hand and James A. Farley, the urbane son of a former postmaster general, at his left. Better yet, he had $1.5 million from ABC-TV to finance his United States Boxing Championships. Suddenly, you weren't supposed to discuss the way he and his henchmen did business.

They were supposed to be absolved of stealing heavyweight Jimmy Young two years ago from Frank Gelb, the man who taught him to bob and weave. They were supposed to be above telling good-looking fighters like Edwin Viruet and Casey Gacic that the only way to get in King's tournament was to leave their managers and sign with the King gang. They were supposed to have too much integrity to stoop to paying kickbacks and falsifying boxers' records.

But the wise old heads on the inside of the Sweet Science knew things were going sour.

"This is worse than it ever was under Frankie Carbo and the hoodlums of the fifties," said one Miami fight man. "The racket guys would do business, but at least they tried to make it look real. These new guys just don't care. They're making wrestling look good."

King didn't like it when the press started digging up evidence to prove that, but he wouldn't say so. He was smart enough to know there was no sense in alienating the people who had painted him as the savior of boxing. He was also smart enough, however, to have flunkies who felt no such restraint.

"John," a voice rasped long-distance late last February, "this is Al Braverman."

Al Braverman is a porky fight manager and matchmaker who isn't always welcomed back in every arena he visits. At the time, he was one of King's lieutenants. Ergo the call.

"John," said Braverman, "you been writing some bad things about us. Now we never sued nobody, but we've got lawyers, you know."

The discussion got louder at both ends of the line after that. Finally, Braverman and another King lieutenant, Paddy Flood, were invited to hash things out face-to-face at King's next promotion, in the Marion (Ohio) Correctional Institution.

"I think we're going to be too busy to make it," Braverman said.

Now it is too late to talk to Braverman. When you phone Don King Productions in New York and ask for him, you are told: "Mr. Braverman no longer has his office here."

King made sure of that when he began to feel the heat from the federal grand jury in Baltimore that is investigating his wheeling and dealing. He suspended Braverman along with Flood and someone named Gordon Peterson. The implication was that they are bad guys and King is a good guy.

That is not the only time King has tried to shift the blame. When ABC announced it was canceling the semifinals of the tournament, King took pains to point out that *Ring* had supplied him with faulty rankings. Why that should be such a surprise is a mystery.

Ring's record keeping is a joke of long standing. The best recent proof of that comes from Barney Nagler, who serves *The Daily Racing Form* as the Henry Steele Commager of avaricious sports. Nagler says that on page 789 of the 1975 *Ring Boxing Encyclopedia and Record Book*, one Muhammed Wee Wee-Congo is listed as having fought eight times in 1974. His supposed opponents, says Nagler, included Tommy Farr, Pierre Charles, and Joey Beckett, who retired thirty, forty, and fifty years ago respectively.

"I was naive," King says. And ABC chooses to believe him, conveniently forgetting the street smarts he once needed to become the king of the numbers racket in Cleveland.

You can only wonder what will be discovered now that the network has appointed a savvy attorney to investigate the tournament's, ahem, "irregularities." His name is Michael Armstrong. Not so long ago, he was investigating corruption in the New York Police Department. Hopefully, he will tell us a lot about Don King. While he is at it, he might also try to find out how ABC wound up in this unsavory stew.

Can Roone Arledge, the network sports chief who is gunning to become boss of all that is news, really be so easily duped? And what of Howard Cosell? He roars that he is a fearless crusading reporter who tells it like it is, but he hasn't even come close to doing that this time, has he?

You remember that Sunday in March at the Marion Correctional Institution, where Don King did four years for manslaughter. He was coming back free and rich, and Cosell was along to throw verbal rose petals at him.

"How come you're shilling for King?" Mark Jacobson, a writer for the *Village Voice*, asked Cosell.

"Who are you, young man?" Cosell said.

Jacobson introduced himself.

"Well, I'm no newspaper reporter," Cosell said. "I'm a true journalist. I tell things as they are." And on and on he went until he reached his punch line: "How much money do you make a week?"

The unspoken answer was easy to figure. Jacobson doesn't make so much that he would be willing to swim in a sewer to get it.

Royalty of a Different Sort
Las Vegas
October 3, 1980

While a photographer's camera clicked lovingly in the background, Don King lit a cigar and sent up regal clouds of smoke. "Now look at the mirror," the photographer cooed, and when King did, he broke into a smile that rendered flashbulbs unnecessary. He was gazing at his favorite person.

It was only fitting that King should find so much joy in basking in his own reflection, for that is the essence of the ex-convict who has become the Barnum of boxing. He comes across as a cartoon character with his foot-long cigars, his shock-treatment hairdo, and his gold necklace on which "DON" is spelled out in diamonds. But not for a minute does he care if you consider him a tasteless joke. To do that is to drop your guard, and Don King makes his living off such carelessness.

You would think he would have run out of suckers after ten years in this dodge, but you couldn't be farther from the truth if you accused him of coming in through the back door. King always arrives at the main entrance and he never is at a loss for suckers, even if he must recycle them.

What other explanation could possibly hold water after the exhibition he put on at Caesars Palace the other day? He was hosting a press luncheon for the Larry Holmes-Muhammad Ali title fight— "the greatest promotion in the history of the world," naturally—and for the main course, he served ham-and-cheese sandwiches. It was a cheap meal, the kind King prefers when he is picking up the tab, but there were two problems with it: Muslims don't eat pork and Ali is a Muslim.

"Heh-heh-heh," said King, nervously flicking the ashes from his cigar.

Ali was glowering at him, and the Muslims who never leave Ali's side seemed to be considering how the well-fed King would look on a spit with an apple in his mouth.

"Ahem," said King. "Let me take this propitious opportunity to introduce you to the savior of boxing . . . the greatest . . . the biggest . . . the best . . . the only man capable

... please stand up and grace us with your wisdom, Muhammad Ali."

Ali rose to pontificate and, suddenly, the ham-and-cheese sandwiches were forgotten. "Heh-heh-heh," King said triumphantly.

Unmitigated gall has never failed him. Oh, there were years when he might have doubted its power. Four of them, in fact—the four he spent in the Marion Correctional Institution for manslaughter. But unmitigated gall had been King's trump card before then, when he ruled Cleveland's numbers racket, and since he got out of the jug a decade ago, he has refined his art until it shines like the gold he mines from the fight game.

King's secret is words. Some of them sound as though he grew up reading a dictionary that had no pronunciation marks— "misconscrew" and "afoxanado" —and others just leap off his tongue willy-nilly—a personal favorite is "trickeration." Silly as they sound, though, they have spared King from taking a fall for his phony United States Boxing Championships, charmed the bigwigs at Caesars Palace, and even hornswoggled Ali, a noted bulljiver himself.

"You see, as an afoxanado and a friend of Ali, I didn't want him to come out of retirement and fight Holmes," King said. "Ali couldn't believe that. He told me he was fighting for equality and justice, for the future of our children. When I heard that, I said, 'You're right, Ali.' And I promised him I would help make the fight, which is what my businessman's instincts had been telling me to do all along, heh-heh-heh."

To get the job done, King had to stave off no fewer than six rival promoters, including old foe Bob Arum and the entire country of Egypt. For Arum, his partner in promoting the Roberto Duran-Sugar Ray Leonard masterpiece, King had no regrets: "The man is a despicable and unconscionable cad, a low culprit." Egypt was another story entirely. "I saw myself standing on the bank of the Nile, overlooking the Pyramids," King said. "We was gonna fight for peace in the Middle East." Alas, the price of peace didn't meet his high standards.

So Vegas it was—a place where King could be in his element and nothing he said would be gaudier than the surroundings. He was back in his familiar fortress, and when threats of lawsuits came screaming across the Nevada desert, he didn't even flinch.

"It's mostly extortion and blackmail," he huffed. "All they want is money under the table plus two tickets to the fight."

King refused. He has his dignity, you know, and let us not hesitate to add that he also has his pride. There isn't a soul on earth who should believe his claim of being "a small businessman trying to make it in America." He talks in millions, kicks down boardroom doors, and considers himself the world's heaviest heavyweight.

Even Holmes and Ali must have gotten the message by now. It was waiting for them at the main entrance to Caesars Palace, where three gigantic cardboard cutouts stood to herald their fight. Two of the cutouts depicted Holmes and Ali, but the biggest, the boldest, the most ostentatious was of King. Just in case anybody forgot who the boss was, heh-heh-heh.

Barking Up the Wrong Tree
Las Cruces, New Mexico
November 3, 1979

There was no small amount of consternation the other day when Too Tall Jones stepped into the ring in which he will make his professional pugilistic debut and nearly fell through it. Thankfully, those scrawny underpinnings have been shored up and now, with the fight only twenty-four hours away, the ring appears to be in order. It measures sixteen feet by sixteen feet, as small as the law allows, to prevent the unfortunate Mr. Yaqui Meneses from running away from any rushes by the erstwhile Dallas Cowboy. Moreover, a fourth rope has been added lest the 6'9" Jones inadvertently topples into the ringside seats.

The only problem that remains sprang from a report that a gentleman was going to be blindfolded and handed a Samurai sword so he could chop watermelons in half as a preliminary to the fight and, presumably, Saturday Night Live.

"Uh, Frank," said David Wolf, Too Tall's manager.

Frank Mirabal, the finest promotional mind in all of Las Cruces, turned around slowly.

"It's about the ring," Wolf said. "It's not going to look good on national television if you have pieces of watermelon floating all over it."

"You know," said Mirabal, "I never thought of that."

Saturday is his first big one, his start toward what he hopes will be more money and more glamorous surroundings. "They tell me Sugar Ray Leonard's people will be watching," he whispers out of the corner of his mouth. He has to be careful, you know. There are a lot of jealous characters lurking about, and they might not appreciate a success story starring a forty-year-old upstart whose most lucrative business ventures in the past involved Christmas trees and firecrackers. Then again, maybe Mirabal wouldn't appreciate the story, because if there is anything he doesn't consider himself, it is an upstart.

"So I'm out in California," he says, "and it's 1965 and I'm involved in a promotion up in San Bernardino. It's a rock-and-roll thing and I've got this group coming in that's never played in the States. They had a little song out about then that you might have heard of. 'Satisfaction.' You know who I'm talking about now?"

Ah, the Rolling Stones.

"Right, right. I handled 'em all—the Stones, the Byrds, the Turtles. You remember the Turtles? You remember that hit they had, 'Happy Together'? Well, when that was goin' good, I got them to play a charity show for free. Signed 'em before anybody else knew who they were. Listen, I knew what I was doing."

Fourteen years later, with a three-week-old daughter at home and two grandchildren a long-distance call away and a ring physician who looks like Elton John at his elbow, Frank Mirabal is trying to prove that he possesses more than an overflowing imagination.

"Lemme tell you something," he says. "I can't always afford to live in the manner I like to, but I can damn well give it a try. I'll do whatever I have to, and I'm no flim-flam man, either. I think nothing of picking up the phone and calling Too Tall Jones, Lyle Alzado, Tom Landry, Muhammad Ali, Johnny Carson. Too Tall Jones is the only one of those guys I know, and the only reason I know him is because I actually called him. That's the business I'm in. If you want to call it promoting I'm a promoter. If you want to call it hustling, I'm a hustler. You decide."

At the very least, Mirabal is not a coward. As soon as he learned that Jones was abandoning the National Football League for the fight game last spring, Mirabal was on the phone offering his services as a manager. When that produced no results, the stubby, myopic former amateur lightweight bounded back with a scheme to produce Too Tall's fistic coming-out party.

Mirabal was knocking heads with the big boys in Dallas and Washington, D.C., as he tells it, and he didn't see how they stood a chance against him and Las Cruces. For one thing, he could get the Pan American Center at New Mexico State University for a $2,500 song. For another thing, Las Cruces is miles from urban angst but just a $52 airplane ride from Jones' old stomping grounds in Dallas. For yet another thing, Mirabal was sure he could unearth a Mexican opponent for Too Tall to tap the market of 600,000 potential customers in nearby Juarez. But best of all, Mirabal had the connections to put up the $45,000 guarantee Jones wanted.

"I've got a couple friends who are bankers," says Mirabal.

Now he knows what good friends they are.

Thanks to their soft hearts, he has been able to thrust himself into the spotlight, flitting here and there with his paeans to master promoter Bob Arum, and his ideas about putting kick-boxers on the card with Jones, and generally living it up. There is just one thing about the whole glorious process that gives him pause. "I think I've got about $3.10 to my name," he says. Judging from ticket sales so far, Mirabal may not even have that by nightfall Saturday. There are 14,000 seats in the Pan American Center and he has located just 8,600 people to put in them. "I don't worry about that," he says. Maybe his fearlessness can be attributed to a chronic difficulty with numbers. He has been predicting that between 400 to 600 media folks would turn out for Too Tall's debut, for example, but all he has to show for a press section are 20 reporters. "Don't talk that way," he says. "I like to think positive."

Nevertheless, Mirabal has been seen in public with his hands clasped, looking suspiciously like a lost soul praying for help. And just the other day, after dragging Too Tall in front of the local Rotary Club, Mirabal concluded his spiel by promising "better Christmas trees this year than I ever had before." If nothing else, the man knows how to hedge a bet.

In the Wrong Neck of the Woods
Chicago
June 11, 1980

It is hard to picture Michael from Great Neck as a boxing impresario because boxing impresarios aren't supposed to toil in vegetarian restaurants, consort with mystics, and wear their hair down to their shoulders. Michael from Great Neck does, and still the job description fits him like . . . well, one is tempted to say a new suit of clothes, but that would scarcely be accurate, for Michael from Great Neck hasn't had a new suit of clothes since his bar mitzvah.

This disdain for earthly goods can be traced to his days as a hippie, and while it may seem entirely laudable to refugees from the sixties, it makes no sense at all to the fight crowd. Even in Denver, where Michael currently plays it fast and loose, the fight crowd is fascinated by long, black limos, cigars the size of bratwurst, and pinky rings seeking second careers as spotlights. So when our hero does business, he does it as an outsider, a role that is anything but new to him.

"Jeez," he says, "when I was a hippie, people thought I was weird because I didn't smoke marijuana."

Now he finds himself confronted by a case of different surroundings, same image. The low-lifes who inhabit Denver's gyms and arenas have christened him Tiny Tim, after the fluttery geek who sang "Tiptoe through the Tulips." Michael, however, refuses to be dismayed. "Every once in a while," he says, "somebody will call me the white Don King." Perhaps the name has more to do with hair than anything else—King's sprouts upward, Michael's downward—but he likes to believe the nickname is also a salute to his burgeoning skills as a matchmaker, publicist, and wheeler of deals.

After all, he is the fast talker who got Eric Sedillo out of

Denver and into a main event in Chicago Thursday night, who knew exactly how much his man deserved for taking on undefeated heavyweight James "Quick" Tillis, and who didn't budge until he got it.

"For that," says Michael, "I think the least you can do is tell people my last name is Klahr. You never know who'll see your article."

Obviously, Michael Klahr, the pride of Great Neck, New York, has never gotten anywhere by being shy. It was brains and chutzpah that carried him to Columbus, Ohio, where he studied philosophy at Ohio State and human nature at a hillbilly bar called Dick's Den. It was nerve and wanderlust that led him to put upwards of 20,000 miles on his hitchhiking thumb. It was love of literature and the female form that made him only the second male student in the history of Baltimore's College of Notre Dame. And it was a sense of survival that spirited him out of Baltimore in the dead of night.

"I think the house we were living in was haunted," says Michael from Great Neck. He uses the pronoun "we" because, true to his hippie lifestyle, he was living in what passed for a commune in 1976. The door was never locked, the furniture was straight from a thrift store, the air was thick with incense, and the basement was inhabited by an ex-convict. "It was the ex-convict who was the problem," Michael says. "We should have expected it after all the other bad things that had happened to the people in the house. See, when the ex-convict married the little astrologer who lived downstairs, he got crazy. He wanted to kill all of us."

Exit Michael.

He hitchhiked to Denver intent on nothing more than meeting some old college friends for a river raft trip. But he wound up staying once his lady friend, the beauteous Melissa, pulled into town with all her worldly possessions piled into her car. They were married last summer the day before Michael turned thirty and long after he had begun establishing his legend in the West.

There are rumors that he announced his presence at the vegetarian restaurant where he still puts in two nights a week by asking for a few days off to go hunting. Instead of denying such scurrilous chatter, Michael merely points to his days as the Joltin' Jew, a two-fight career as an amateur featherweight in 1977 that left him with no wins and a scar over his left eye that can be seen only when his allergies act up.

"The most important thing I found out was that I couldn't take a body punch," Michael says. "My first fight, I got in there against some guy who had tatoos—he looked like a biker—and I thought, 'What's a small Jewish intellectual doing here?' I was so aware of the journalistic possibilities, and before I knew it, I was on the press table, gasping for breath. The guy had hit me in the stomach, and it felt like it was on the wrong side of my spine. Crazy, huh? You know, the real reason I was boxing was my asthma. I wanted to see how my breath held up in a stressful situation."

To no one's surprise, dealing with Eric Sedillo isn't nearly as taxing. Oh, Michael thought it might be after that night in '77 when he hopped an all-night bus to Las Vegas, touted all his gambling friends on Sedillo, and then watched the cement finisher get his lights put out at the Silver Slipper. But after that, Sedillo ran off twelve straight wins and made Michael proud to be part of his tiny entourage, so proud that he didn't mind loaning the big lug $500 even after S.T. Gordon TKO'd him his last time out. "Eric's got a mortgage and all these other middle-class responsibilities," Michael says. And Michael, he has Dee, the mystic.

"It's not like she predicts how the stock market will do tomorrow or anything," he says. "She just talks common sense to me. She gives me input to send white light on everything I'm dealing with."

Translated, that means Michael has decided that defeat was just what Sedillo needed to give him a new sense of purpose. Indeed, our hero fairly bubbles over with predictions of his man swarming Quick Tillis in the Conrad Hilton Hotel's ring and finishing him off early. To give Sedillo added incentive, Michael has offered to shave his head bald if Tillis falls in the first three rounds. "I haven't had a haircut in fifteen years," Michael says. It is his way of emphasizing the sacrifice he is ready to make. But then the sixties are over, aren't they?

Postscript

Eli Hanover died in the summer of 1975 and the word from L.A. is that Aileen Eaton has made a graceful, Ethel Barrymore exit from promoting. I haven't the slightest idea how Frank Mirabal did with his Christmas trees, but I do know that Michael from Great Neck has cut off his ponytail and is up in the Colorado mountains writing a novel. Don King, meanwhile, just keeps coining money.

Darwin would have loved the fight racket.

4.
The Crooked-Nose Crowd

It isn't just writers who become infatuated with fighters. Guys who are supposed to have brains do, too.

The most memorable one I've ever heard of found himself staring at a club fighter one night as if the kid had descended on a cloud. "I love that fighter," the guy kept saying in the reverent tone he usually reserved for stock deals, snazzy cars, and haute cuisine. He said it so loudly that a gentleman with a crooked nose couldn't help but hear him.

"Yeah?" the nosey one said. "Wanna buy the kid's contract?"

"You're putting me on," the guy said.

"No way. You want him, the kid's yours."

"How much?"

"A grand oughta do it."

"Hang on. I think I've got it with me."

Not until months later did the guy learn that the gentleman with the crooked nose had sold a fighter he didn't own.

The Lady in Red
Baltimore
January 7, 1975

You could see the Lady in Red right away, for a lot of reasons.

First, not many women had turned out on fight night at Steelworkers Hall. It was filled, as usual, with guys who were clouding the air with opinions and smoke from the cigars stuck in the corners of their mouths.

These guys are so steeped in stag bar machismo that they probably would have told you that this is the way it always should be.

It didn't help the feminine cause that nothing about the Lady in Red indicated that she knew a knockout punch from fruit punch.

She had a head of blond hair that looked as if it had

come out of a Reddi-Whip can. She was wearing a dress cut 1930s style, and her wedgies provided a pedestal on which to model it.

If the shoes were a pedestal, then the wall in the lobby beside the beer stand was a lamp post. She leaned against it and stared at the loud, gritty fight crowd bustling up the dirty arena steps. The fight crowd stared back.

The difference in stares was in the eyes. The fight crowd's eyes were ravenous, the Lady in Red's were wide with wonder.

That was one of the memorable things about her. Another was her mouth; it formed a perfect circle. "She looks like a cartoon character," said Michael from Great Neck, who is a regular at the fights. "You know, like Betty Boop."

But it wasn't the mouth or the eyes that you noticed first when you looked at the Lady in Red. It was her face. You could call it pretty, which it was unquestionably, but you could not let the description go at that. Her face was also shiny, as shiny as Elvis Presley's hair in *Fun in Acapulco*.

A woman who sat near her during the fights observed that most likely this was an example of the wet look that was fashionable a couple years back.

"Either that," the woman said, "or she forgot to wipe off her cold cream."

So it was hard to miss the Lady in Red as she sashayed to a seat in the second row. She got there because she was with a big spender who is very large in boxing circles.

The Big Spender fancies himself as quite the lady killer, but even he was a little surprised by all the attention his date was getting. "She's just a friend of a friend," he said with uncharacteristic modesty.

Then he strolled off to rub shoulders with his cronies, leaving the Lady in Red to make her own way in this scruffy hall filled with people yelling for blood and spilling beer on each other.

She stayed by herself for exactly one fight.

In the first row, almost directly in front of her, was this future middleweight champion of the world. Very charming, very dapper, and very handsome until the scar tissue started to redecorate his mug.

Somehow—you couldn't spend all your time watching

the Lady in Red—the next thing you knew, she was sitting next to him. He was pointing out little things in the ring to her. Her mouth was in a perfect circle, and so were her eyes.

She was so locked in on the Future Middleweight Champion that she didn't even notice the spray of boxer's blood and sweat to which most ringsiders knowingly subject themselves.

The Big Spender came back into her life when the fights were over. While the Future Middleweight Champion discussed the state of boxing with friends, the Big Spender hustled the Lady in Red out the door.

They wound up in a restaurant in Little Italy, at a table with promoters and matchmakers, writers and referees.

This was fine for the Big Spender until the Future Middleweight Champion walked in with his manager and trainer. The Future Middleweight Champion was one sentence into his pitch to get the Lady in Red to join him at another table when she picked up her things to go with him.

Now the scene started to get confusing. The Future Middleweight Champion asked the Big Spender to come to his table when dinner was over. The Big Spender grimaced. Someone a couple chairs away cracked up laughing. The Lady in Red returned to tell the Big Spender: "Excuse me, I didn't want to make a scene." Then she walked away again, leaving the Big Spender more baffled than ever.

He was just getting used to the prospect of a lonely night when the Future Middleweight Champion let him know he could have the Lady in Red back. The Future Middleweight Champion mumbled something about how his wife of three months would not have it any other way.

Everyone was feeling better, except the Lady in Red, who was starting to look like an overused ping-pong ball. Then the Big Spender and the Future Middleweight Champion stepped outside.

The first thought that came to mind was bare knuckles on the sidewalk. The second thought was: How good is the Big Spender at giving himself first-aid?

The only first-aid the Big Spender had to apply, it turned out, was to his wallet. He and the Future Middleweight Champion had stepped outside for a private debate about who was going to pay for the Lady in Red's dinner. As if there was ever any question.

Flash Gordon Zapped King the Merciless
Chicago
April 29, 1977

Don King must hate this. Here he is with his pinky rings and sleek limousines and velvet tuxedos, and he gets taken out by a guy who lives in a studio apartment, doesn't have a phone or a car, buys off the rack at Salvation Army, and looks like a cross between Woody Allen and Tiny Tim.

That's right. The muckraker who unearthed the villainy of King and his cronies was not a newspaper sportswriter or a TV critic or some talking head who showed up in living color on the twenty-one most wasted inches in your home. It was Malcolm Gordon, twenty-seven, of Queens, New York, founder, editor, publisher, and virtually the entire staff of *Tonight's Boxing Program*, a cantankerous weekly newsletter that makes up in passion and blunt honesty what it lacks in spelling and grammar.

Call him Flash.

He has labeled King a stinker, and worse, since the ex-convict-turned-fight-impresario choreographed Earnie Shavers' biggest payday and then made the woebegone heavyweight go to court to get his money. Last fall, when King talked ABC-TV out of $1.5 million and twenty-three hours of air time, Flash Gordon went bonkers.

He roared in print that King and company should call themselves "Extortion, Inc." He likened dealing with Al Braverman, one of King's chief flunkies, to "walking into a pool of sharks." He described Johnny Ort, King's connection at *The Ring* magazine, as "an office boy turned into (a) pumpkin-head at the clink of a few bucks." His kindest word about the leader of the pack was that the Justice Department should investigate King's caper, with its phony fighters' records and quaint financial practices.

This is very fashionable now, but Flash Gordon did it months before a beaten pug named Scott LeDoux opened the can of worms and knocked off Howard Cosell's toupee, all in one motion.

Flash's problem in spreading the word was two-fold. For one thing, no more than 250 fight fans pay $35 a year for a subscription to *Tonight's Boxing Program;* the rest of his readers stumble across him in front of Madison Square Garden or the Spectrum in Philadelphia as he hawks his sheet.

The other catch was his image. "People don't see what a beautiful guy Flash is and how he wants to do boxing a good turn," says his friend Abe Fox, a New York bus driver. "They look at him and say, 'Sheesh, what a freak.'" It is not an altogether surprising reaction. Flash stands 5'5", weighs 120 pounds with a good meal in him, perches his glasses on a titanic schnozz, has curly hair that reaches his shoulders, and sports a winter coat under which he could hide the cast from *Gone with the Wind*.

Now skeptics realize he is a walking, talking work of art, but Flash refuses to stand up and take a bow. It would be out of character.

Larry Schulz, a TV newsman when he isn't hunting the next great heavyweight, can vouch for that. He arrived in New York a couple of years ago and decided he wanted to debut with a feature on Flash. He wrote Flash a letter saying so and Flash sent it back to him—in a million pieces.

"Along with it was the most profane, hostile letter I've ever gotten," says Schulz. "A few months later, I saw Flash at a fight and I went up and introduced myself. I mentioned his letter and he said, 'Nothing personal, nothing personal. You're probably a very nice guy, but if you want to report on boxing, report on the fighters, not on me.'"

Flash obviously is cut from rare cloth. The first inkling of that was the way he celebrated his high school graduation; he moved out of his parents' home in the Bronx and into his present apartment, the one with the wonderful view of an alley. His reasoning was that he wanted to be near the fight shows at Sunnyside Gardens, two blocks away. But almost immediately he started traveling to Philadelphia to produce programs for promoter J. Russell Peltz. This inexplicable change of direction gave birth to the reigning conscience of boxing.

Working in his apartment with an offset printing

machine, Flash delivers the worldwide fight news that daily papers ignore. But his true calling is cheering the heroes and flailing the bums. "He's a little guy," says Michael Klahr, another of boxing's shoestring geniuses, "but he fights heavyweights."

Flash has no outside source of income to finance his crusade. If *Tonight's Boxing Program* doesn't sell, he sits on a flat wallet. Sometimes he sits on one even if it does sell. "Flash makes just enough to pay his rent," says Harold Lederman, a New York fight judge. "More than once I've lent him carfare to get to the fights. He always pays me right back. Flash is the most totally honest person I've ever met."

His honesty, couched in vintage Gordon vulgarities, had a tendency to make him unpopular with boxing's fat cats even before he started beating King over the head with his typewriter. The amazing thing is that he has never been sued. Or maybe it is not so amazing.

"Lawyers send him threatening letters," says Abe Fox, "but Flash just sends them nasty replies."

This is not a man to be trifled with. Ask Don King.

Dundee Made of Championship Caliber
Las Vegas
December 1, 1979

He remembers the days after the war, the big one, WWII. He was just out of the Army and his older brother, Chris, was on top of the world. Had a stable of twenty-five fighters and an office in the old Capitol Hotel in Manhattan. Room 711. Its sagging couch and cracked ceiling will stick with Angelo Dundee until he hears his last bell ring. Room 711 was where he slept.

"Couldn't afford nothin' else in them days," he says. "I was just a bucket guy."

When a fighter came into town on the train, it was Dundee who had to go to the station to fetch him. When there was a job nobody else wanted, Dundee did it. And yet the apprenticeship didn't rule him out of the perks of what he imagined to be royalty. It was home cooking for $1.25 at a little joint over on Forty-eighth Street, and the Lower East

Side to eat Chinese, and Toots Shor's on Fridays. Everywhere he went, Dundee kept his ears open, and sometimes he heard the sweet sounds that made up for a life of sour notes.

"So Charlie Goldman comes into the office one morning really hepped on this new fighter in a funny kinda way. He tells us the guy's short and balding with two left feet but, oh, can he punch."

Dundee shrugs helplessly.

"Rocky Marciano," he says.

He recalls only one other discovery from that era quite so well—his wife Helen. She was a model and a fighter's cousin, and the fighter just happened to be in Chris Dundee's employ. Angelo moved right in, and the next thing he knew, they were strolling off to a double feature. "She took me," he says. "I didn't have no money."

They have been married twenty-eight years now, the model and her sawed-off professor of pugilism. "She claims it's only been fourteen years," he says, "'cause I been gone so much."

There has always been a champion or a contender beckoning, and Angelo Dundee has always answered the call whether it took him to Manila or Michigan City. If it wasn't Ralph Dupas, it was Willie Pastrano. And if it wasn't Willie Pastrano, it was Muhammad Ali, the frenetic monologist who got in Dundee's door because Pastrano decided there wasn't anything worth watching on TV.

The fighters became part of their trainer's extended family and he part of theirs. Nothing very special about that. Not until the emergence of Ali, who made everything he touched special.

"'Entourage' became a dirty word when Muhammad was around," he says, "but all those guys was good for him. He lived offa that. He was like a master puppeteer. He would create situations; he'd get guys mad at each other and pretty soon they'd be squaring off. Who were they? Half the time I didn't know. Honest. Hey, I'm not curious."

Perhaps that is just as well. How was it that Dundee once described Ali? Opaque? Yes, that's it. "I can't see through this guy," he said. The view was murky and blurred, just the opposite of the one he has of his latest pupil. Small wonder, then, that he calls Sugar Ray Leonard "a lighter-upper."

Dundee felt Leonard's magic the moment he saw him in the Montreal Olympics. What went undetected, however, was the breadth of that magic. This is more than another meal ticket for Angelo. This is a kid who seems to have sprung from the drawing board of a boxing architect; there is some Dupas in his left hook, some Pastrano in his jab, some Carmen Basilio in his uppercut. Even when the ring is out of mind, when there is nothing to do but pass time with talk, Dundee can listen to Sugar Ray and sense another link with the past.

"It's a funny thing, we're both from hand-me-down families," Dundee says. "Hey, when I was growin' up in Philadelphia, I used to cop my brother Jimmy's coat so I could go dancin'. I was the youngest of five boys and it was the only coat we had. Jimmy caught me alla time because I'd wrinkle the sleeves. You know, they was too long for me and I had to hike 'em up."

The memory is as vivid as yesterday, and Angelo Dundee smiles. The fighters move on, but the old stories remain.

Boxing's Beautiful People Are Not a Pretty Sight
Las Vegas
December 2, 1979

He was gone with the wind. She was the last page of *The Great Gatsby*. Ridiculous and sublime, they meshed perfectly with the red-light district decor of Caesars Palace and the randy bleatings of the fight crowd. And never mind that the lady had been poured into a pair of silver lamé jeans that suggested another setting, another sport. The fight crowd can live with her kind of backfield in motion any day.

"Hey, hey," Don King, the crown prince of connivers, said when she strolled into the party.

"Awwww," he said when she strolled back out.

The scene was repeated half a dozen times as Friday night spun into Saturday morning and the lady's husband became more and more aware of the importance of a theatrical entrance. Stage left, stage right. What grand fun it was for this character in the black leather jacket and the blond vision on his arm. She got nuzzled by King, posed for a picture with heavyweight champion Larry Holmes, and strutted for everybody. Her husband just smiled.

"Do you know where she's from?" sputtered Scott LeDoux, the heavyweight trial horse. "Fargo, North Dakota. Fargo. Fargo. I didn't even know they had girls in Fargo. The only guy I ever heard of from there was Billy Petrolle, the Fargo Express. And now they're telling me she's Miss California. No kidding, man. Miss California. Well, she's not real big on small talk, but I told her husband, 'Man, take her home and lock her up. Lock the door, man, and if I ever come knockin', do not let me in.'"

Perhaps it is too soon to decide exactly what Miss California's role was in a week when fistiana was bound for glory and got sidetracked. Was she an antidote for disillusionment? Or was she just another decoy to keep us from looking at the unfortunate truth?

Boxing abounds with such web-weavers. They do their song-and-dance routines, beguile us, then move on. Moving, moving, always moving. And if you don't believe it, consider the case of Gil Clancy, the Madison Square Garden matchmaker, the erstwhile trainer who is admired by everybody except the fighters he discarded like used tissue.

Gil Clancy had a kid die on him last week. Willie Classen was a mill-run middleweight who was booked into the Garden to fight a young tiger named Wilford Scypion. With twelve seconds left in their ten-round bout, Classen got knocked out and began a trip that went from the ring to Bellevue Hospital to the grave. Gil Clancy didn't stick around to watch.

The day after Classen went on the critical list, Clancy was in Minneapolis doing color commentary for the TV fight between LeDoux and Mike Weaver. And Wednesday, with boxing staring at its eighth death this year, he was in Las Vegas trying to be funny.

"I got to talk a lot more now that Muhammad Ali's not around no more," Angelo Dundee, the brains behind Sugar Ray Leonard, was saying.

"Yeah, but I've got to help him," Clancy said over his shoulder. "Every day I've got to take him off to the side with me and go, 'How now, brown cow.' Isn't that right, Angelo? How now, brown cow."

It was not his wit that saved Clancy, obviously. It was the presence of Leonard, who has been hoisted onto the shoulders of boxing's hero worshippers and carried to the front of the national consciousness. With a hot property like that on the premises at Caesars Palace, there was neither the time nor the interest for a discussion about the possibility of boxing going back into the toilet. Instead, it was "Sugar Ray, tell us this" and "Sugar Ray, tell us that." And Leonard always came through.

When ABC wanted thirty seconds of his wit and wisdom, he delivered them. When ABC suddenly decided that forty seconds would be even better, he delivered them too. It was wonderful to see how easily Howard Cosell could be rendered obsolete.

Alas, the twenty-three-year-old Leonard talked better than he fought. Oh, he won the World Boxing Council's welterweight championship with a fifteenth-round technical knockout of Wilfred Benitez and called it "one of the greatest fights in history," but it was hardly that. It wasn't even one of the greatest fights in his three years as a professional. He was wary of facing his first truly dangerous opponent—painfully wary. The flash and dash that are his hallmark disappeared, replaced by cautious jabs and a right hand that went astray repeatedly. Poor Sugar didn't even win his prefight staring contest with Benitez.

"That wasn't anything," Leonard said. "It was just for TV."

Somehow, boxing always seems better when it is for real. As evidence, we have the fifteen-round draw that left Vito Antuofermo with his world middleweight championship and Marvelous Marvin Hagler in a funk. The ill feeling that developed between them when they were chopping up each other's profiles spilled over into the interview tent. None of that Leonard-Benitez kissy-huggy for these two.

"I had a cold all week," Antuofermo said, turning toward Hagler. "You heard me coughing in the ring. You can say that without lying."

"It coulda been the air," Hagler replied coldly.

They sat there with the blood still trickling from their

wounds and not an ounce of deceit between them. No one would be inviting them to appear on the "Tonight Show" or asking them to pose for a picture with some mysterious blond, and yet that was all right. They were fighters, not celebrities or song-and-dance men. They were fighters and they had the prettiest faces in the joint.

Lights Out—a Lesson Learned
Chicago
January 23, 1980

It was Omaha in '72. David Wolf was still a writer then, tagging along after Smokin' Joe Frazier and hanging on every word old Yank Durham uttered. Looking back now, Wolf understands that the heavyweight champion's manager was always more vivid, more interesting, more everything than the heavyweight champion himself. After all, Joe Frazier was just a fighter. Yank Durham was a dreamer and a con man, a failed preliminary boy who never let his past prevent him from coming on like the Einstein of fistiana. Obviously, he was someone to be admired.

So in Omaha, in '72, Wolf started filing away lessons for future use. Frazier was fighting roly-poly Ron Stander, known to the sporting press as the Council Bluffs Butcher and to local bartenders as one thirsty dude. The bookmakers were sending Stander off to the slaughterhouse as a 10-1 underdog, but even that didn't satisfy Durham. He sauntered into the Civic Auditorium, surveyed a bank of TV lights hanging from the rafters, and flew into a rage about a plot to blind Frazier.

"That's it," he screamed. "We ain't fightin'."

"Whaddaya mean?" Frazier said. "The lights don't mean nothin'."

"Shut up and start puttin' your street clothes back on," Durham hissed.

"But . . ."

"Do like I told ya."

Frazier did, and the TV lights went out. The poor devils in the closed-circuit theaters could squint if they really wanted to be sure Frazier was slicing up Stander. Durham was going to get every edge he could for his man, the rest of the world be damned.

There was a moral there, and it wasn't lost on David Wolf. Eight years later, the proof is in his press clippings. He is a writer no more; instead, he manages Too Tall Jones, the heavyweight escapee from the National Football League, with a savage zest that doesn't always translate well into print.

From Las Cruces, New Mexico, the site of Jones' pugilistic debut, comes word that Wolf hasn't paid all his bills there. In Washington, D.C., he got Too Tall his money while a world champion went begging. The pressbox literati in Dallas, meanwhile, are still cringing from his verbal assault on their "rampant ignorance" about boxing.

A hard case? You bet David Wolf is a hard case, in a way the late Yank Durham may never have imagined.

But then Yank Durham never had to make the quantum leap that David Wolf is attempting. Durham was a lifer in the fight racket, a hard-core insider, and Wolf is an outsider attempting to get in. It is a different gig than giving up day-to-day journalism and writing a book, the way he once did to produce *Foul!*, the bittersweet story of Connie Hawkins. And it is more extreme than the impish run at politics that George Kimball, the one-eyed underground sportswriter, made in the upside-down sixties. By the time Wolf is finished, his adventure may be considered nothing more than crazy. What better sport for it, though?

"It's so damned easy to get hooked on," Wolf says. "The more I covered it for *Life* and *True*, the more I realized it was one of the few sources of truly interesting characters—guys who'd done time and become champions, guys who wore pinky rings and talked out of the sides of their mouths, guys you just didn't find anywhere else."

Perhaps it was only natural that, in time, Wolf wanted to be one of them, even dared think that he could be better than they were. To be sure, he wasn't the first journalist to feel the urge. But in his case, he didn't have to park his dreams at the gymnasium door.

"Boxing has a—what should I call it?—a free-market environment," he says. "I mean, I could never come up with the money to buy a baseball team, and I'd have to put in twenty years in any organization to become a general manager. But with boxing, there's no structure at all. There's room for all kinds of variations. If you want in, you can get in. Simple, huh?"

At least it seemed that way in the beginning. Now, however, there are reasons to think otherwise. The first of them has to do with the old-timers' resistance to the training regimen Wolf prescribes. He is big on videotape, distance running, the Nautilus weight machine, and, contrary to the First Amendment he once leaned on, closed sparring sessions. The old-timers, on the other hand, are big on the medicine ball. "Hundred-year-old habits are hard to break," Wolf says. He might have better luck with them, though, if he managed fighters who threw the right kind of punches.

No such luck. "I wouldn't want to manage anybody I wouldn't want to write about," he says. Alas, the best story subjects seldom possess a sufficient propensity for violence. Witness Wolf's first fighter, Duane Bobick, the doe-eyed Olympic heavyweight; catastrophes against Ken Norton and Big John Tate left him with such emotional scars that he had to seek relief on an analyst's couch. Wolf insists there will be a happier end for Ray "Boom-Boom" Mancini, a head-hunting lightweight who is out to get the title fight his father never got. And yet the sawed-off Mancini is lost in the shadow of the 6'9" Jones.

Too bad for Boom-Boom.

Worse yet for Wolf.

He was overcome by the American love of size, and now he is paying for it. He thought Jones could play the big time, only to discover that he was barely ready for the cow towns. What do you say when the heavyweight champion of the future gets knocked down in his first fight, can't sell tickets to his second one, and beats up pugs in sneakers at every stop? You say what Wolf has: The press is stupid, the promoters are thieves, and the hotel in Las Cruces didn't deserve to be paid. Of course, the whole story won't come out until the book does. The odds, you see, are with writers, not fight managers.

Knockout *Fat City* Suffers a Club Fighter's Fate
Chicago
February 13, 1980

I still see his name once in a while, down in the small print at the bottom of fight stories from out of town. He had the stuff to make headlines and he blew it. I wish I could say I'm not surprised. But I was as big a patsy as everybody else who watched him climb off a bus at the Greyhound terminal in Baltimore and start coldcocking one pug after another. I thought he could be a champion, we all did, and he never had a chance. For deep inside him was a monster he couldn't control.

Wasted talent is the oldest story in boxing, yet one we seldom linger over for very long. Perhaps if those of us who inhabited Steelworkers Hall had done our homework better, we would have seen how it was going to be with this fruit picker's son who nearly got lost in jail and was supposed to find himself in the ring.

Everything was tilted his way; he had a promotor who worshipped him, opponents who were nothing more than learning devices, and a well-heeled manager who all but adopted him. And still he wasn't satisfied, still he needed a fix of the excitement his new surroundings couldn't provide. So he wallowed in booze and whores, pills and souped-up cars, and didn't stop until he heard the promoter's plaintive wail: "But you can be what you'd call your Rolls-Royce of boxing."

Flattery always could get the kid back to the straight life. What it couldn't do was keep him there. Sooner or later, as sure as the strip joints on Baltimore's scabrous Block open their doors every night, he would succumb again to the monster inside him, the monster that has made him a seemingly incurable loser.

I wonder if he realizes what has happened or if it is just one more blur that he shrugs off as the residue of stopping too many punches with his head. Long-shot player that I am, I wonder if he might somehow be jerked to his senses by seeing a wonderful, forgotten movie called *Fat City*. After all, it is his story—a lean, unsentimental accounting of a sport built on destruction and populated by a multitude of men on a fast train to nowhere.

Knockout *Fat City* Suffers a Club Fighter's Fate

To their everlasting discredit, American moviegoers put *Fat City* on the same train when it premiered seven and a half years ago. Never mind that, like the Leonard Gardner novel from which it sprang, it captured the fruitless existence of club fighters down to the last drop of sweat. Never mind that it should have put people in the mood to laugh off *Rocky* as nothing more than a Palookaville version of *Snow White and the Seven Dwarfs*. Failure was *Fat City's* lot.

Such a fate was hardly just, but maybe it was poetic, for now the movie is in the same situation as so many other creaky, cauliflowered warhorses. Now it must keep on trying comebacks like the one it will make Wednesday and Thursday nights at Chicago's Sandburg Theater.

I hope it can hang in there. I hope the revival-house addicts won't look down their noses at its fight scenes and sneer that there is more action just outside the Sandburg's doors, at the singles bars that clutter the landscape around Dearborn and Division. If anyone wants to see fights on film, he should get Jimmy Jacobs, the New York entrepreneur, to dig Sadler-Pep or Ali-Frazier out of his vast celluloid library. Yes, the same fight films on which Jacobs had to dub in the splats and thunks so they would sound as violent as they looked. In the end, you see, even the crème de la crème of fistiana isn't always enough. And when actors are involved, the best a movie can do is evoke a feeling about boxing, a tangible twang. *Fat City* does that better than anything that has ever been run through a projector.

It doesn't really matter that Stacy Keach, who plays Billy Tully, a forlorn never-was, can't remember to keep his chin tucked in and always lunges inelegantly. It is more important for him to look real as he scrounges for matches, shacks up with a floozie, staggers through a hangover while picking onions under a broiling California sun. He is a loser, and he can spot his spiritual kin in an instant. Enter Ernie Munger, portrayed by Jeff Bridges. Ernie Munger, a kid, a greenhorn, doesn't realize what is in store for him.

"I saw you fight once," he tells Tully when they meet in a gym.

"Yeah?" Tully replies. "Did I win?"

"No."

How many times have two lives been entwined so simply, yet so irreversibly? Surely director John Huston doesn't know. It is just something he got a sense of in his short undistinguished career as a pug, and *Fat City* gave him a way to express it. He could capture the insane dialogue: "Can you breathe through your nose?" "Not on a wet day." He could tell the world beyond boxing's sweat shops about the practicality of bragging big and dreaming big and never being surprised if none of it comes true. And he could show how a fighter can be a human punching bag—urinating blood, clutching aching ribs, wondering what next—and still hold onto his dignity.

But there is a fine line between honesty and sloppy sentiment, and Huston walked it painstakingly. To him, Muhammad Ali wasn't reality. Reality was fighting one night and going to work the next morning. It was trying to convince yourself you're headed for a million bucks when you're slurping coffee in an all-night diner. It was doing all that suffering and knowing there was no point to it. "Before you can get rolling," Billy Tully says, "your life makes a beeline for the drain." Those are words for a tombstone. A fighter's tombstone.

A Ticket to Immortality
Montreal
June 19, 1980

It was a glimpse of the future, and Ray Arcel refused to believe it. He had left the fight racket with his head caved in nearly two decades before, and now, on an autumn night in 1972, he was back in Madison Square Garden for the first time since then, just catering to a whim, nothing else.

He had come to see the main event—that much he remembers. But the pugs who were in it have long since been forgotten, both of them replaced in his memory by a scrawny Panamanian upstart who steamrollered his opponent with one punch and raced directly to the corner where Arcel's wife was sitting. They shook hands, the boxer and the lady he never had seen before, and off to the side, Ray Arcel did something he thought was beyond him in a fight palace of any description. He smiled.

"People don't realize how good Roberto Duran can make you feel," he says now. "But right away I told myself, 'This isn't some ordinary street urchin. This kid's decent. He's very decent.'"

The retired trainer's kind words, however, were supposed to be the signal of two ships passing in the night.

Hard experience had taught Arcel not to dream that eight years later he would have Duran knocking on glory's door for the second time in his career. That is precisely the case, though, for Friday night the erstwhile lightweight champion will strut into Montreal's Olympic Stadium and attempt to dethrone Sugar Ray Leonard, the king of the World Boxing Council's welterweights. It is a classic story of an aging fighter seeking the recognition that always has eluded him, and the tale is made all the more enchanting by the presence of Arcel, who is eighty-one years old and getting younger by the minute.

True to form, he refuses to acknowledge his status as a gerontological marvel. "Everybody keeps coming up and telling me how much they want to meet me," he says. "Who the hell am I? I'm a bum." The last person who believed that, it should be pointed out, was the strong-arm man who dented his skull with an iron pipe.

The year was 1953. Arcel was out of the training dodge then, busily putting together "The Saturday Night Fights" for television as an antidote to the wretched excesses of Frankie Carbo, Blinky Palermo, and the rest of boxing's riffraff. There were faster ways to make a buck, but Arcel was content to mine the talent he found in the outposts beyond New York City. So it was that he came to Boston on Yom Kippur, spent the Jewish holy day worshipping in a temple near the arena, and walked outside to meet the cruelest surprise of his life.

"I was just taking a little recess, you know," he says, "and I saw the manager of one of the guys fighting for me that night. So we're standing there on the corner talking, and all of a sudden, bang!"

When the pipe crashed down from behind and Arcel sagged to the sidewalk, a chill fell over boxing. This wasn't another fast talker from the east side of New York, you see; this was a gentleman who gave the sport grace, dignity, and, most of all, a sense of history.

To trace Ray Arcel's career, you must go back to 1917, when he was an undersized preliminary boy fighting for the most elemental of reasons: "I came from the only Jewish family on the block of Italians." Greatness eluded him, but he did get to know Benny Leonard's cousin. And not long after that, he got to know Leonard himself. And not long after that, he was training the mesmerizing lightweight in his comeback. Before Leonard was done, he had become the first of the eighteen champions Arcel has called his own.

The number is so astounding that it overwhelms the memories Arcel carries around in mint condition. Memories of a heavyweight who couldn't outrun him when he was fifty. Memories of a washed-up journeyman who upset a hotshot in Detroit and was embraced by the notorious Purple Gang. Memories of Angelo Dundee, Sugar Ray Leonard's manager, carrying towels in the forties. All kinds of memories, but the people want champions, so Arcel delivers.

Let's see, there were Tony Zale and Barney Ross, Jim Braddock and Billy Seuss, Frankie Genaro and Ezzard Charles. While the list goes on, Arcel stops at Charles. "He had Rocky Marciano beat, you know," he says. "Ripped Marciano's nose wide open. I thought they were gonna stop the fight. But Freddie Brown fixed the cut up and Marciano came out and put Charles on ice."

Arcel shakes his head, a half-smile playing on his lips.

"Funny, huh?"

Funny because now Freddie Brown, at seventy-one, works in Roberto Duran's corner, too, and he is there because Arcel couldn't stay retired. Lord knows Arcel tried, though. He was clean for eighteen years after his battered head mended, contenting himself with his job as a purchasing agent for an alloy company. But that didn't matter to Carlos Eleta, the Panamanian millionaire for whom he had trained fighters after World War II. "Carlos wanted me to come down and work with a couple kids he had," Arcel says. "You know how they are in Panama: When they see you on the street, they don't shake hands, they shadow box." That is a roundabout way of admitting he couldn't say no to Eleta.

It was Arcel's good fortune, although no one realized it at first. The second kid in Eleta's stable was the little jawbreaker from Madison Square Garden, the one named Duran. He did not hit it off immediately with Arcel. "I remember telling Eleta, 'You are going to make me hate you,'" the trainer says. "He had given me a colt to ride and I'd never even been on a horse." In time, Arcel learned.

Oh, Duran still calls him and Brown "the crazy Americans," but the respect is there. It grew out of the patience the ancient cornermen had with this child of the Panama City streets and the respect they have shown for his ability. "It wasn't anything we taught him," Arcel says. "He had it and it came out of him. The kid was another Jack Dempsey."

In a sport nourished by exaggeration, the temptation is to shrug off the comparison as just more bushwah. Yet something about Arcel moves his sincerity beyond reproach. Perhaps it is his refusal to be kept away from Montreal by age. "I'll be with Roberto until he packs it in," the old man says, and the pay will be the same as always. It will be nothing, because Ray Arcel figures the fighter has already rewarded him with greatness.

Death in the Ring Is a Fact of Life
Chicago
July 9, 1980

Fighting is not a coward's business, no matter how much the air is polluted by cries that this pug is gutless and that one has no heart. To lace on a pair of eight-ounce gloves and climb into the square circle, face to face with a man intent on relieving you of your senses, is to give the world irrefutable proof of your courage before a punch is thrown. The hope here is that somehow, some way, this provides at least an ounce of solace for the wife and child that Cleveland Denny left behind.

Surely he could not have bequeathed them much in the way of diamonds and gold, for he was of the genus club fighter. When his day at the factory was done, he had more long hours ahead of him at the gym, and if he didn't like the idea, he had an option that never varied: He could quit.

It is easy to say now that Denny should have done just that. But such a retreat would have been foreign to the instincts that made him what he was and to the impulses that sent him charging up to Gaetan Hart, the Canadian lightweight champion, screaming with the profane wrath born of their first two fights. "I'll kill you!" Hart shouted back. And how was anyone at an otherwise innocuous weigh-in to know that when the two of them battled under a weeping Montreal sky, Hart would lay the groundwork for his threat to come true?

Sixteen days later, Cleveland Denny was dead at the age of twenty-four. He had been in a coma from just before the Duran-Leonard fight until just before the Holmes-LeDoux fight, and then he became part of boxing's tragic history. The Associated Press sent word immediately that his was the fight game's fifth death in the last seven months, and in the instant it took to read that statistic, the word "game" became as bitter as a mouthful of bile.

Now we await the cries of rage and indignation that are sure to follow. They will show up on the editorial pages of our newspapers and on the commentary segments of the television news. They will bemoan the fate of our fighters and beleaguer the slice of society that lives off exhibitions of man's inhumanity to man. They will do everything except provide workable solutions for a breed of athletes beyond the comprehension of great thinkers who seldom descend into stinking arenas.

Too bad, for in those arenas dwell a precious few men made stronger by their surroundings, men with too much pride to peddle flesh guilelessly and too much savvy to assume that boxing can be policed like any other sport. The one who comes to mind immediately is Angelo Dundee, trainer of Sugar Ray Leonard and passing acquaintance of Cleveland Denny. "I said hello to the kid when we was getting our pictures taken for our credentials up in Montreal," Dundee was saying Tuesday. "When I heard he was dead, right away my mind flashed back to the way he looked that day—healthy, smiling, happy. And now he's gone, you know. It just leaves you empty."

On the heels of the emptiness is frustration. It has its basis in the extensive tests that every fighter underwent to become part of the evening that saw Roberto Duran win the World Boxing Council's welterweight championship. The malevolent Duran himself was called back to the hospital repeatedly to make sure an irregular heart beat was not hazardous to his health.

"They were giving these guys everything," Dundee said. "The electrocardiogram. The electroencephalogram, where they put the needles in your scalp. Everything. And then this poor kid dies. I'm tellin' you, it drives you outta your mind. What else can we do?"

Assuming that the medical profession has done its all, perhaps the answer is nothing. Protective head gear, so popular in the amateurs, has earned the professionals' disdain because it creates a blind spot and promotes a false sense of security. Gloves with thicker padding are dismissed with equal alacrity because they encourage fighters to stay on their feet longer, thereby inviting more sustained beatings. "Maybe bare knuckles is the answer," Dundee said. "A kid would get flattened out and that would be it." You can imagine how that would go over with faint hearts and pacifists. Most likely they would just start another futile campaign to legislate boxing out of existence.

Simply put, there isn't an emptier dream anywhere. Even if the law did dictate against fisticuffs, men would fight for prizes in cow pastures, on riverboats, and in the back rooms of saloons, the way they have done in the past. They would fight because it is their nature, because it is as much a part of them as painting was a part of Van Gogh and writing was a part of Hemingway. And they would pay no more heed to the possibility of being hurt, maimed, or even killed than any of the tough guys presently marching into combat.

"If something bad's gonna happen, it's gonna happen," Johnny Lira said Tuesday, and his shrug spoke as loudly as his fists have while making him *Ring* magazine's eighth-ranked lightweight. "Hey, people get hit by cars, you know. People fall down stairs, you know. I can't worry about dyin' when I'm trying to put some guy to sleep."

There will be those, of course, who will laugh off Lira's pronouncement as the posturing of a fighter who has known no pain worse than a split eyebrow. In that case, it would be wise for the doubters to remember Davey Moore, who lost his life in 1963 three days after losing his featherweight championship to Sugar Ramos.

After leading the fight for the first nine rounds, Moore walked into Ramos' right hand and toppled backwards, striking his head on the bottom ring rope. Though he climbed off the canvas, Moore was finished, destined to be knocked out seconds later and sent into a world where the pounding in his skull didn't stop until his heart ceased beating. But before he lost consciousness, before he so much as left the ring, he sought out Angelo Dundee, Ramos' trainer, and asked a question that should stand as a memorial to what boxers are made of: "Angie, you're gonna give me a rematch, ain'tcha?"

Liebling Means Love—of Boxing
Chicago
December 5, 1980

On its bruised and bloody face, the fight racket seems as repugnant as a sport could be. There is the violence, of course—the furious destruction of scar tissue, brain cells, even lives—and there are also the little murders committed with ballpoint pens in smoky back rooms. Promoters steal from managers, managers from fighters, fighters from the public. The evidence is in every gutbucket arena where a four-rounder was ever fought, yet the heart refuses to heed what the head tells it.

When A.J. Liebling wrote about boxing as the "Sweet Science," he struck a note that rang as true as the one Rocky Marciano discovered by putting Jersey Joe Walcott to sleep with a one-punch rhapsody. Alas, explaining this phenomenon, this perplexing love affair, is as difficult as convincing an antivivisectionist that sleeping canines never know the difference.

But the reasons for adoring fistiana can be found if one is willing to sift through the all-too-well-publicized carnage. Boxing's indestructible charm dwells in the dese-and-dose patois of a trainer with a face like a baked potato, and in the street-smart existentialism of a ghetto kid who had just two choices in life—the ring or the can. And if the sight of such rough-hewn noblemen doesn't move you, doesn't make you understand how something beautiful can flower in a sweat-sour gymnasium, then surely Joe Liebling's prose will.

"It is through Jack O'Brien, the Arbiter Elegantiarum Philadelphiae, that I trace my rapport with the historic past through the laying-on of hands," Liebling wrote. "He hit me, for pedagogical example, and he had been hit by the great Bob Fitzsimmons, from whom he won the light-heavyweight title in 1906. Jack had a scar to show for it. Fitzsimmons had been hit by Corbett, Corbett by John L. Sullivan, he by Paddy Ryan, with the bare knuckles, and Ryan by Joe Goss, his predecessor, who as a young man had felt the fist of the great Jem Mace. It is a great thrill to feel that all that separates you from the early Victorians is a series of punches on the nose. I wonder if Professor Toynbee is as intimately attuned to his sources. The Sweet Science is joined onto the past like a man's arm to his shoulder."

Only the daft or the sacrilegious would dare suggest that there has ever been a better paragraph written on boxing. It is funny, stylish, slyly irreverent, and, above all, affectionate. Those were the hallmarks of Liebling's work, the reasons he could entice the *Police Gazette* set to read his stuff in the usually forbidding pages of *The New Yorker*.

Seventeen years after his premature death at the age of fifty-nine, there are still those of us who won't be satisfied until we have devoured his every word not just on boxing, but on war and food, politics and newspapers, Chicago and other foreign ports. We prowl second-hand book stores hoping to discover a dusty copy of his beloved *Between Meals,* and we cherish the Lieblingesque nuggets we find squirreled away in the damnedest places. In New York, for example, there is a sportswriter named Stan Isaacs, an elfin scamp who in his formative years covered some of the same fights Liebling did. Their friendship remained a secret, however, until the teetotaling Isaacs invited Vic Ziegel, a scribe of the nonteetotaling persuasion, to meet him in a sleazy Eighth Avenue saloon.

"Stan," Ziegel said after he walked in and got a load of the dump. "Why here?"

"Joe liked it," Isaacs replied.

That was all he had to say. To Ziegel, to anyone with good taste in boxing chroniclers, Liebling will always be Joe. He will always be the bald fat man whose feet jiggled uncontrollably when he wrote a good line, the unpretentious adventurer who enjoyed an honest rainmaker as much as he

The Crooked-Nose Crowd

did a commodious greasy spoon.

But until recently we never thought we would know any more about him; he seemed doomed to remain America's unacknowledged literary genius, cursed because he was a journalist instead of a novelist. And then Raymond Sokolov, nominally a food writer (how the perpetually hungry Liebling would have loved that), rescued him with a biography called *Wayward Reporter*.

The critics have debated the book's virtues loudly and not entirely favorably, but true Liebling devotees refuse to be deterred. There was much to know about their hero and now they know it—the good as well as the bad, the funny as well as the sad. Abbott Joseph Liebling was kicked out of Dartmouth for missing chapel too often and fired by *The New York Times* for playing games in small print. He considered newspaper editors to be tools of the devil and nicknamed Chicago "The Second City" because he couldn't see any place finishing ahead of his native New York. He was a sucker for race horses and women, and neither treated him well, especially the women. They left him with little for company except the gluttonous meals that eventually killed him—a tragic end for an affectionate soul.

If *Wayward Reporter* does nothing else for Liebling's memory, perhaps it will encourage people to hunt up *The Sweet Science*, the collection of his nonpareil boxing tapestries. Therein lies the true measure of the man called Joe. He could make you smile by describing a pug "so hairy that when knocked down he looks like a rug." But when he studied the antique Archie Moore fruitlessly trying to knock out Rocky Marciano, he refused to scoff. "Would Ahab have been content merely to go the distance with the White Whale?" he asked.

It takes a special talent to put words—and feelings—like those on paper. And no matter how beset by personal despair he may have been, Joe Liebling must have known what he was to *The New Yorker* and its readers. Quite simply, he was irreplaceable, as the late Jack Murphy, a splendid wordsmith from San Diego, discovered when he went knocking on the magazine's door.

"So what is it you'd like to write for us?" asked William Shawn, the editor.

"Boxing," Murphy replied.

"I'm sorry," Shawn said, "but we stopped covering boxing when Joe died."

Futch Looks Back with Joy
Detroit
June 13, 1981

Places change, memories remain. Even in the part of town where the fires of despair have torn the hearts out of buildings, it is impossible to erase the sweet used-to-be for Eddie Futch, a fight man come home from the West Coast. He has returned to counsel Larry Holmes, the heavyweight champion, but out of the corner of his eye, bantam Eddie looks back at a time when Joe Louis played hooky from his violin lessons to learn how to box.

Both of them lived on Clinton Street and both of them trained at the old Brewster Recreation Center, a natural progression for the poorest of the Depression's poor. "The city didn't sponsor boxing anywhere else," Futch says. "In the more affluent areas, they had tennis and golf, but with us, I guess they figured fighting was natural." So down in Brewster's basement, they cleared out space, put up a ring, and began throwing leather. For Futch, who had hawked fight extras for the *Detroit News* and studied Jack Sharkey on the newsreels, it was the inauguration of a life's work.

Unofficial historians of the Sweet Science in Detroit remember Eddie Futch as a welterweight who didn't let his birdlike physique prevent him from winning the Golden Gloves or sparring with the heavy-fisted Louis. "Joe used to say, 'If I can hit you, I can hit anybody,'" Futch says. "Oh, his hands were fast. I had to devise ways and means to keep from getting killed." And yet there was reason to believe that Louis actually did have his sawed-off target's well-being in mind. Futch started believing that the night he got knocked down four times in a three-round fight of his own.

"What a war," he says. "I was up against this fellow named Frank Pomper at a Catholic parish over on the West Side, and my trainer wanted me to quit. He said Pomper was too strong for me. But I'd knocked him down twice, I knew I could beat him, so I told my trainer I'd never speak to him again if he threw in the towel. What could he do? Pomper came out for the last round all confident and everything, and as soon as he went to throw his right—bang!—I hit him with a left hook. Down he went.

"Afterwards, Joe Louis came up to me and asked if I knew why I'd been getting hit so much with right hands. I said if I knew I would have done something about it. Joe laughed and said I'd been giving the fellow a square target; I should have been on more of an angle, with my left shoulder and foot out in front of me and my chin tucked behind my shoulder.

"You know, I had twenty or twenty-five fights after that and I never got hit good with a right hand again."

The Brewster Recreation Center's honor students took care of one another that way, guarding a treasure that the rest of the world only gradually realized they possessed. Louis, of course, was the standard bearer—perhaps the greatest heavyweight ever. But even though he is dead and Brewster has been renamed the Wheeler Rec, the tradition that was born fifty years ago remains in full flower among the heavies. Futch trains Holmes, the king of the World Boxing Council. Del Williams trains Leon Spinks, the obstacle in Holmes' path Friday night. Ray Barnes trains Mike Weaver, the World Boxing Association's champion. Futch, Williams, and Barnes—all of them Brewster boys.

The odds against that happening were probably as great as those against Futch being so impeccably well-preserved. Two months shy of his seventieth birthday, with three children, seven grandchildren, and six great-grandchildren, he looks like a kid of fifty-five. Maybe that says something about the joy of having trained both Joe Frazier and Ken Norton in their primes. Maybe it's even a hint that boxing—the sport he couldn't turn pro in because of a heart condition—functions as a fountain of youth.

"Don't you ever slow down?" someone asks Futch.

"You must have been talking to my daughter," he says with an impish smile.

To slow down would mean to stop commuting between his La Puente, California, home and the stable of young fighters he schools in Phoenix. It would mean not answering

Holmes' distress signal after the champ fired Richie Giachetti, the trainer who had been with him throughout his career. There is even a possibility that Futch, moving at half-speed, wouldn't be able to find an audience for the stories he tosses around like Christmas candy.

He can tell you about Louis, obviously. But he also can tell you about the fighters you should have seen. Take Holman Williams, for example. "He couldn't punch and he wasn't strong," Futch says of the Brewster graduate he trained as both a welterweight and a middleweight, "but he was the greatest infighter anybody ever saw. Joe Louis always made Holman spar ahead of him just so he could watch and get ideas." Likewise, the scholarly Archie Moore had a brainstorm after losing a ten-round decision to Williams. "He saw Holman was getting tired the last two rounds," Futch says. "When they had their rematch, Archie made sure it was for twelve rounds. In the eleventh, he knocked Holman out."

To get over his disappointment, Futch leaned on the shoulder of his prize welterweight banger, Lester Feldon. The kid had just cleaned Carmen Basilio's clock, and now he was aiming for Sugar Ray Robinson. "Everything was fine," Futch says, "until he got married without my approval." Not that Eddie disapproved of the fairer sex—or sex itself, for that matter—but he figured Feldon didn't need any distractions at the moment, and his new wife most certainly was a distraction. "She spent all the money I'd been saving for Lester," Futch says, "and then she started telling him he was a set-up for Robinson. She made it sound like I was working against him." By the time she finished, Feldon was a zombie prime for a whipping and Futch knew it was time to get out of Detroit.

He was burned up, all right—as burned up as he has ever been. But that's the way life is: You think something is the end of the world, and thirty years later, it's a story to be told at homecoming.

The Fight Game: A Chemical Composition
Chicago
October 4, 1981

There are some gentle souls from the FBI who don't seem to understand how boxing can be called the Sweet Science. For the past year, they have been tracking down various scientists and inviting them in for tape-recorded chats, as if to suggest that the sport is populated primarily by gypsys, liars, tramps, and thieves.

While the intrepid G-men may have a point, they fail to realize that the presence of such characters is exactly why the fight racket earned its sugary pseudonym. Irony, you see, is very big in scientific circles. In fact, the only challenger it has is absurdity.

"This is the most ridiculous foggin' sport in the world," says Paddy Flood, the resident poet of New York's Grammercy Gym and the concerned citizen who tries to tell the investigators they are wasting the taxpayers' money. Flood's thesis is supported by historical passages from every level of the game. Among its high-rolling promoters, for instance, we have Bob Arum warding off a reporter who just caught him in his own tangled web by saying: "All right, already. Yesterday I was lying. But today I'm telling you the truth."

The truth, however, means different things to different people, which is why James J. Johnston, an old-time fight manager with the guile of a safecracker, could gaze with fatherly pride at a pug named Fainting Phil Scott. "My Philip," said Johnston, "earned more money than the president of the United States last year just by sitting on the floor and holding his groin."

Such theatrics were beneath Greasy Johnson, no pun intended. When he was not being sought by the police for his shopping habits—Greasy didn't believe in paying—he toiled as the kind of heavyweight every kid on the way up wanted to have on his dance card. It wasn't a ticket to gracious living, but it paid enough to keep the bill collectors at bay. So you can imagine his consternation when he got a job at a parking lot between fights, messed up his punching hand in a freak accident involving a woman driver, and much to his dismay, found that she didn't realize he was an artist of sorts. Greasy had no choice but to fight his next main event in court.

"Uh, Mr. Johnson," the woman's lawyer intoned, "you tell us that you have lost the ability to function as a pugilist because of this mishap. But I see by your record that you have hardly distinguised yourself in your field. You have, if I may quote from *The Ring Record Book*, lost, lost, lost, won, lost, won, lost, lost, lost ..."

Greasy was speechless, but his trainer, the redoubtable Angelo Dundee, wasn't. "Lemme tell you something about Greasy, I mean Mr. Johnson," Dundee said when he took the witness stand. "He's what you call a perfect opponent. And there's a market for perfect opponents. Common sense, right?" Not even the FBI could have argued with that. Greasy won his case.

The temptation is to wish everything would go that swimmingly in the Sweet Science. Alas, that would rob it of too much of its perverse charm. There would have been no Al Braverman denying he was using a foreign substance on a battered fighter by claiming that it was made in this country. Nor would the late Subway Sam Silverman, who ruled New England boxing from a throne made by Cadillac, ever have been able to employ the wiles of his wife, Helen the Pencil. "You didn't mind getting the shaft from her," Braverman says. "She always blushed a little."

If Bob Arum and Don King had the decency to do likewise, it might be easier to accept the way they have enlarged upon the shell game that Subway Sam and Helen the Pencil played. But vainglory is more their style, so verbal abuse is their inevitable reward. "You know what I tell Arum and King?" Paddy Flood says. "I tell them, 'You ought to be in the gas chamber, both of youse.'"

Flood laughs at the numb silence that greets his pronouncement. "What the fog, they know it," he says. "It's just a big foggin' joke, boxing, that's all."

Perhaps no fighter ever accepted the racket's inherent ridiculousness better than Chuck Wepner, the New Jersey heavyweight who sprung enough leaks in his career to be hailed affectionately as the Bayonne Bleeder. The cuts other pugs would have called gushers were little more than shaving nicks to Wepner. Indeed, there were times in the tanglefooted, granite-jawed liquor salesman's career that his best

The Crooked-Nose Crowd

chance for a win was making his opponent sick.

But it was not without masterful leadership and inspired oratory that Wepner rose to the heights he did while losing to Muhammad Ali. He was slumped on his stool between rounds, looking like a ketchup commercial that hadn't panned out, when Braverman whispered in Flood's ear and Flood delivered an impassioned speech that still echoes through boxing today:

"Listen, Chuck, I know you're a big man in Bayonne, and you don't need this fight, and you don't need the heavyweight championship. You got your whiskey route and your bar, and you're a big man with all the ladies. But, Chuck, me and Al, we been poor bums all our lives. We got nothin' but boxing. You understand? Nothin'. So will you do me and Al a favor, Chuck? Will you do it for us?"

Wepner lost anyway, but maybe that was only fitting. Boxing isn't for happy endings; it's for getting rid of the fancy-schmancy mystique that surrounds too many other sports. When you deal with a fight guy, you get everything from his warts to his crazy bone. You cry, you laugh, and sometimes you do both at the same time, the way Flood did after watching his light-heavyweight tiger, Ray Elson, lose a war with Victor Galindez.

Flood was out watching the main event that followed when Tony Canzi, the sawed-off cornerman, started tugging on his sleeve. "It's about the kid," Canzi said. "He's taking a shower and his girl friend is in with him."

Flood thought about it for a minute, then cracked a lopsided smile. "Hey, Tony, the kid just fought his heart out," he said. "Let him go."

What better way to prove it's the Sweet Science?

5.
Heavy Artillery

With all due respect to Muhammad Ali, who said he was the last one worth watching, and Sugar Ray Leonard, who said little men have replaced them, heavyweights remain a source of fistic sustenance. It is not just that their size and punching power strike a respondent chord in a country which, but for the price of gasoline, would gladly go back to driving blocklong sedans. It is also that heavies seem to know instinctively when writers need fighters.

As proof I offer Randall "Tex" Cobb, who was simply trying to stay in shape and out of trouble when a Philadelphia newspaper columnist knocked on his door. The columnist had been roughed up by some barroom types who took exception to his point of view, and now he was looking for an equalizer. Cobb might have been one, too, if the characters in the bar hadn't decided to ensure their might with tire irons and baseball bats. He wound up with a broken arm while the columnist got his head caved in, and I suppose the whole episode could be described as a disaster. But if you're a writer, the sentiment still outweighs the results.

Style Took a Beating from Spinks
Las Vegas
February 17, 1978

It was good-bye for Muhammad Ali. He headed out the door of the Hilton bound for Bangladesh. "Have a safe trip, champ," cried one of those people in his entourage who have a face but not a name. Ali turned around sharply. "You don't have to call me champ to be my friend," he said.

It was hello for Leon Spinks. With a flunky carrying the World Boxing Council's incredibly tacky heavyweight championship belt, with a headache he couldn't pass off, Spinks prepared to meet the press. "Everybody," he rasped, "no smoking, please." He waved his arms to clear the air. He should have done the same with the questions that came flying at him. Some he misunderstood. Others he understood, but the words that would have answered them collided in his mouth and never got out.

What we have here, quite obviously, is a difference in styles.

Ali could be maddening or flattering, puritanical or satanical, but he never failed to be entertaining. Even when he swore off talking as he prepared to tap out against Spinks Wednesday night, he was the best show on the Vegas strip, Charo and Jack Jones notwithstanding.

Spinks, at twenty-four, is something else again. "We're going to try to make him a class guy," his trainer, Sam Solomon, said Thursday. The implication was obvious. Even Spinks, who acquired a lifetime supply of rough edges from the ghetto where he grew up and the Marine Corps, seems to realize his limitations as a public figure. He talks about giving himself a new image. He says he wants to make up the intellectual ground he lost when he dropped out of school in the eleventh grade. He suggests that he wants to be cosmopolitan, perhaps even continental.

"I'd like to rest up by taking a boat to England," he said Thursday.

"You mean a cruise?" someone asked.

"A cruise?" said Spinks, as if he had never heard of such a word.

He will take some getting used to. He is not Ali, but then as the genial, insightful Solomon says, "There will never be another Ali. You might as well get used to the fact that Leon Spinks is Leon Spinks."

He has a wife named Nova, a nine-year-old stepson, and two sons of his own, ages seven and four. He lives with them in a pleasant spread near the Philadelphia city line that is a million light years away from the seamy, sleazy St. Louis streets he roamed as he grew up. "I was the nicest guy on my block," he says from behind the toothless smile that has become the quickest way to identify him. "It was a mean block, but I was still a nice guy."

It didn't seem that way after he joined the Marines at nineteen. At least twice he decked drill sergeants who came down on him too hard. He might have wound up in the brig.

Instead he wound up in the ring, and the ring saved him from going home to a life of loading barges down on the Mississippi River. The Montreal Olympics beckoned and he answered by winning a gold medal as a light-heavy. He would turn pro afterward. That was never a secret. What no one knew was whom he would entrust with his future.

The honor fell to Solomon, who ounce taught bobbing and weaving to both Sonny Liston and Ernie Terrell. He didn't even have to do any recruiting this time. He was working for Top Rank, Inc., the promotions outfit, on the Ali-Ken Norton fight in 1976 when Spinks came calling, escorted by a young slick named Butch Lewis.

"Butch asked did I want to train him," says Solomon. "Do a fish need water?"

Seventeen months later, Solomon has a heavyweight champion. At 197 pounds, Spinks is the smallest one since Joe Louis. With eight professional fights, including his fifteen-round split decision over Ali, he is the least experienced one ever. But he is still the champion, no matter how much that discombobulates the musty world of boxing.

The WBC, for example, made loud noises about forcing Ali to fight Ken Norton for the fourth time if he defended his title successfully. Now the upset victory raises the question of whether the commission will threaten to strip Spinks of his title if the first man he defends it against isn't Norton. Jose Sulaiman, the WBC's president, was supposed to talk about the confusion Thursday morning, but the Hilton, for some unknown reason, refused to let him have a room in which to do it.

Only one of the leading heavyweights in the country thinks Norton should have first crack at the new champ—Norton. In the crazy hours immediately after Ali was dethroned, someone asked Norton if he thought Spinks could beat him. "Is there a chance of God coming down right here and talking to me?" he shot back.

Larry Holmes already has publicly asked to take on Spinks. Surely Jimmy Young and Earnie Shavers will do likewise. One can imagine Joe Frazier coming out of retirement, particularly since he has never stopped training. George Foreman might even find a loophole in his unwritten contract with Christianity that will let him commit violence for money.

"I don't see why we can't have two heavyweight champions," said Don King, boxing's P.T. Barnum. Of course, there is no other way for King to think, for Bob Arum has the contract rights to Spinks' first six title defenses. Whom Spinks will fight for openers is apparently a long way from being decided. "Absolutely no commitment has been made," said his lawyer, Milton Chwasky, "and that's the honest truth."

Thursday, as Spinks emerged from a hotel room littered with everything from Hare Krishna propaganda to the Superman vs. Muhammad Ali comic book, fighting seemed the furthest thing from his mind. Twelve hours before, he had done all of it he could stand for the time being. He had pounded away at Ali's rope-a-dope defense until he became the first man ever to get inside it. "When I heard the decision," he recalled, "I kept saying to myself, 'I did it, I did it.'" Now he wanted to continue the celebration that started with the final bell, the celebration that would make up for the short shrift he got from the oddsmakers and the opinion makers, the celebration to end all celebrations.

Destiny's stepchild deserved it.

A One-Way Street Called Chaos
Chicago
March 22, 1978

When the cops pulled Leon Spinks over in St. Louis the other night, they asked him what he thought he was doing driving the wrong way on a one-way street. He said he didn't know. When the cops asked him for his driver's license, he said he didn't have one. There was no muttering about it being in his other pants, there was no sputtering about how real criminals were out committing real crimes. Leon Spinks just went along quietly, for at age twenty-four he is already a beaten man.

It was the fight game that got him. The World Boxing Council finished the job last weekend by yanking its tacky-looking heavyweight championship belt from around his waist. By then, this unsophisticated, unsuspecting ex-Marine was punchy from being picked to pieces.

The vultures were promoters and attorneys, managers and trainers, TV executives and most everybody else who claimed to have his best interests at heart. If it is any consolation to Spinks, it was nothing personal; they would have done the same to whoever dethroned Muhammad Ali.

There is a priceless bit of irony here. In knocking the good humor out of Ali, Spinks vaulted to the most visible position any athlete in the world can hold, and he did it after only seventeen months as a professional fighter. But at the same time, he was destroying the rock on which the resurgence of boxing is built. Given all of his balderdash, given all of his unpredictability, Ali was the stabilizing force in a sport that normally is ruled by whim and greed. With him out of the way, confusion was ready to make a comeback.

The chaos began minutes after Spinks filled the legendary Ali's mouth with the sour taste of mortality. Larry Holmes stood up to challenge him in a press conference and Bob Arum, Spinks' Svengali, replied that he appreciated Holmes' interest, but not his guiding light, Don King. "He's not Don King's fighter," a stubby gent named Richie Giachetti shouted from the rear of the room. "He's my fighter." For an instant, it looked as if Arum and Giachetti might be promoting a spur-of-the moment main event between themselves. What they were doing, though, was getting into the spirit of things to come.

The WBC certainly had no trouble doing likewise once Arum told Spinks to refuse its order to make his first championship defense against Ken Norton. Jose Sulaiman, the council's president, puffed up his chest and threw Spinks out on his derriere. Naturally, the World Boxing Association used the occasion to solemnly vow that Spinks will remain as its heavyweight champion until he is beaten in the ring.

Now that we have two champs, one wonders what the next step in this lunacy will be. Perhaps each major television network will decide that it wants a champion of its own. CBS would have to stick with Spinks, of course, since it played no small role in his decision to forget his contract to fight Norton and covet a more lucrative rematch with Ali. Over at ABC, Norton would get the call, provided nobody remembers how he did the last time he worked for the network as a sportscaster. The perpetual latecomers at NBC would have the rest of the field to themselves. They could have Jimmy Young or Joe Frazier or George Foreman or Earnie Shavers, or maybe they could just rotate the title and keep everybody happy. That makes as much sense as anything else TV is doing with boxing these days.

The heavy thinkers at the three networks seem to have forgotten that they almost killed boxing two decades ago by overexposing it. How else can you explain why fights were televised last Friday, Saturday, and Sunday? As if that isn't worrisome enough, there are new fears that Spinks' fellow Olympic golden boys, Howard Davis and Sugar Ray Leonard, may be forced into championship fights before they are ready. "Some wise guy is going to see what Spinks did against Ali and think that these kids can do the same thing," said an East Coast matchmaker. "I'm afraid of what Carlos Palomino (the welterweight champ) would do to Davis. I'm afraid of what Roberto Duran (the lightweight champ) would do to Leonard." The operative word is murder.

If any boxer is going to benefit from TV immediately, it should be Norton. The networks aren't going to care that he was given the WBC title and thus became what is known in the fight racket as "a cheese champion." One of them will be only too glad to show him taking on the winner of Saturday's Young-Shavers exercise. When that happens, when millions of people in millions of living rooms hear him described as a champ, he will have the sort of legitimacy that can be undone only by a knockout punch.

There are those who argue that Norton deserves it. They think he won his last fight with Ali. They think Ali shafted him by promising to fight again after he beat Young. They think he got stabbed in the back once more when he called Arum's bluff, signed to fight Spinks for 200,000 measly dollars, and still had to watch the new champion run off for the promise of a $3 million brawl with Ali.

By the standards of polite society, they are absolutely right. But nobody said boxing is polite, and the only standard it ever has had is that lying and succeeding often go hand in hand. Imagine the dull stares and falling jaws when, suddenly, after decades of frightful injustices, the WBC decided to put its foot down. To Leon Spinks' dismay, the foot landed on him.

He was hardly a deserving recipient of such bad luck. For one thing, he was already laboring under the handicap of a manager he couldn't get rid of. That manager still has the right of approval on all of Spinks' opponents, and he still gets 30 percent of Spinks' winnings.

The burden on Spinks got even heavier after he beat Ali. His two trainers had a falling out in public, and one of them stormed back into Joe Frazier's camp. Then Arum began wheeling and dealing in the fashion of the best riverboat gamblers. One minute Spinks was fighting Norton, the next he was saying he had a rib injury that wouldn't be well until it was time to face Ali in the fall. If he tried to say anything more, Arum had an attorney of his own choosing at Spinks' side telling him to keep quiet. The only problem was that Spinks wanted to pick his own attorney. He did and Arum roared in protest.

The noise was just dying down when the WBC made Spinks a former champion. He accepted his public disgrace without a word. His silence may have been a sign of strength, but more likely it was testimony to how deeply he had been hurt. He is young and he is being torn apart by half a dozen different interests, and all he had to show for it when he was arrested was the $19.70 in his pocket. It is a wonder he didn't do something worse than drive the wrong way on a one-way street.

Spinks Lost a Decision to Fate Long Ago
New Orleans
September 16, 1978

He is a man to be pitied. Never mind that he failed to defeat Muhammad Ali again. Never mind that he couldn't erase all doubts that he deserved to be heavyweight champion of the world. The star that shined on Leon Spinks was always a bad star.

His fists were supposed to make everything better. No one believed that more firmly than Leon Spinks himself. He thought of how he used his fists to knock the crown from Ali's head in February and it all seemed so simple to him. "Nah, Ali wasn't the toughest fight I ever had," he said before he entered the Superdome Friday night. "The toughest fight I ever had was in the street."

You watched him in the ring and you could picture him battling on the crumbling concrete in the St. Louis housing project where he became a man while he was still a child. The fury of the ghetto was upon him. He attacked and attacked and attacked. There were no steps backward. The object was to destroy the enemy in front of him.

Your reaction was to feel sorry for his opponents, and for a moment it was meet and right. But now it is easy to see that Leon Spinks may become just as much a victim of his savage style as his old victims were. "He'll never last ten years," predicted a man in his camp. "He'll self-destruct." Then where will Leon Spinks be? And what will become of the friends the championship brought him? They were everywhere before Friday night, joyously slapping hands if they were everyday people, gleefully counting their money if they were $125-an-hour attorneys. Leon Spinks was their man.

It was only a coincidence, of course, that he didn't recognize even one-fourth of them.

He was their man, and the people who had his ear told him this was good. They surrounded him with doctors and lawyers and judges, and they used his money to buy airplane tickets and hotel rooms and fight tickets for one and all.

There were fifty of these guests on Leon Spinks' list the first time it was submitted to the promoters. The gimmick almost didn't work, because the promoters balked and gave Leon Spinks the money it was going to cost him. They told him he should spend it the way he wanted to. So the people who have his ear talked some more, and when Leon Spinks went out to fight fifteen rounds Friday night, he had sixty-one guests cheering for him. At least he assumed they were cheering for him. After all, he was spending $7,000 a day on them.

That is as close to positive public relations as Leon Spinks ever gets. That and the display of affection he put on when the National Baptist Convention came to town last week. Hundreds of elderly black women surged toward the twenty-five-year-old champion, eager to mother him, to be called "baby," to get an autographed picture. Leon Spinks did not disappoint them.

The rest of the world should be so lucky. Throughout training for his second fight with Ali, he was grumpy and moody and undependable. He missed workouts to visit the dentist and to buy stereo speakers. He bridled when the promoters wanted him to do those small things that sell a fight. And in those rare moments when he wasn't being unreasonable, he expected a pinch of graciousness to earn him forgiveness.

"There are good points and bad points to being champion," he said. "The bad point is trying to be a human being, just an average human being like everybody else. I would like to be able to do a job and when it is over, enjoy my life."

Leon Spinks did not understand that it is never easy for those in the spotlight, and the people who had his ear were not going to explain it to him. "You're the champ," they said. "You can do what you want to." It was what everybody would like to hear. It was what Leon Spinks, of all people, needed to hear least.

He is hooked on trouble, both the headline-making kind that gets him arrested and the insignificant kind that eats away at his self-respect. But nobody has done anything about it, perhaps because the ride until Friday night was too pleasant. And now that it is over, the friends of Leon Spinks can move on.

Leon Spinks will not be so lucky. He will be by himself, and it will do no good to tell him this is the way he has always been. It will be the first time he has ever realized it.

Nothing Mickey Mouse about "Goofy" Leon
Detroit
June 11, 1981

It says something about the life and hard times of Leon Spinks that he should be trying to regain the world heavyweight championship in a city where he was once found naked and unconscious in a flophouse bed. His memories of that ignominious winter night involve drinking in a joint called The Last Chance Bar and being set upon by a pack of ghetto rogues. Eyewitnesses, however, suggest that the rogues never existed and that a scarlet woman did. Whoever it was had some pretty exotic tastes in thievery, for when Leon regained consciousness, he was missing not only the small fortune he had stuffed in his pockets, but his two front teeth.

No wonder that when King Larry Holmes granted him the chance to do battle Friday night, the brains behind Spinks spirited their man out of Detroit and into the northern Michigan woods. Up there, Leon could breathe deep, train hard, and think pure thoughts. Alas, pure thoughts get pretty boring when you can't do anything at night except listen to the crickets chirp. At least that was the explanation after the conversation in camp turned to wife-beating.

Everyone seemed to have a story about the glories of it except Leon. With him, the iron fist in the family belonged to Nova Spinks, the ebony Brunhilda who used to cradle him in her arms when they weren't at war. "I never beat up on Nova, she beat up on me," he said. "When we was datin', I'd come home with a bloody nose and my mother would ask me what happened. I'd say, 'The niggers got me.' But it was Nova. She didn't give me no bruises, but, man, she beat my ass. Tell you how tough she was: When I walked down the street with her, wasn't no niggers gonna bother me."

The hard-won security is gone now, the victim of Nova's discovery that a divorce suit packs more of a punch than she does. "Yeah, she's tryin' to beat my ass again," Leon grumbles. Not that he is surprised, you understand. Life's circumstancs haven't done right by Leon Spinks since he was born into St. Louis' infamous Pruitt-Igoe housing project twenty-seven years and eleven months ago.

He had a father who used him as a punching bag and a mother who told him he was going to grow up to be a bum. The olders kids in the project christened him "Goofy Leon" and beat him bloody with frightening regularity. Not until he had won an Olympic gold medal in 1976 and upset Muhammad Ali for the heavyweight title two years later did he have the slightest chance for respectability. And then he blew it.

There were the cars he wrecked and the driver's licenses he never had, the drugs he consumed and the clocks he ignored. His was a life out of control, and he proved it when he trained in New Orleans' all-night discos before Ali turned out the lights on his party. Ever since, Leon Spinks has been a joke, a reason to nudge the guy next to you and ask if he is interested in buying advertising space on Leon's mammoth false teeth.

"I hear what people be sayin'," Spinks says. "They forget I got experience now. They lookin' for me to play the fool. That's why when I want to freaky-deaky, I got to go behind closed doors."

He is like that these days—wry and able to laugh at himself—but no longer is he anyone's unsuspecting jester. With fifteen rounds to separate the undefeated Holmes from the World Boxing Council championship at Joe Louis Arena, Spinks has no doubts about who he is and, more importantly, where he is. "If I wasn't on the comeback trail," he says, "I wouldn't be here right now, would I?" Comeback seems a strange word to associate with a fighter facing only his fifteenth professional go, but not surprisingly, Leon is hardly a typical case. In his 10-2-2 record, you can find that he was knocked out by the undistinguished Gerrie Coetzee and held to draws by a pair of plumbers, Scott LeDoux and Eddie "Animal" Lopez. His worst moment, however, was one the history books don't show. Before he flattened Alfredo Evangelista, Leon paid for it when a right hand he never saw turned his knees to jelly. And you know what they call Evangelista, don't you? The Spanish Omelet.

Perhaps the indignity was what made Spinks such a willing worker in the crusade for his own redemption. He enlisted a new trainer—Del Williams, whose reputation in Detroit fight circles stretches all the way back to the Louis era—and gave himself over to a manager who doesn't believe in burying money in the backyard—Jerry Sawyer, a reformed banker. As soon as the team was complete, Spinks set out to achieve a lofty goal: "All's I could think of up there in the woods was fighting the way I did against Ali in Las Vegas."

Oh, there was a bit of a flap when the spartan decorum of training camp was disrupted by the arrival of a Cadillac Eldorado bearing vanity plates that said "MS GIN" and containing the twentieth-century fox who went with them. Other than that, though, Leon really was serious about being the only heavyweight in captivity with a thirty-two-inch waist. "I pushed myself harder than ever," he says. "I made myself hurt just to be sure I'm ready."

The idea behind the torture was that Holmes will hurt even more after dealing with the kind of swarming style that has troubled him so much in the past. Even now, with the reality of the fight upon him, Spinks refuses to be deterred by the champion's boasts of a five-inch reach advantage and promises of a knockout. "How do you expect to escape anybody that swings at you?" he says. "Move your head, right?"

He has become the essence of mother wit, this toothless child of the streets. Once he was a laughingstock, and now he understands that the joke doesn't always have to be on him. His pocket dictionary is everpresent, his guard forever up.

"I've been through some stuff, don't you think?" he says, not really expecting a reply.

"What was some of that stuff?" a reporter from a radio station asks with feigned innocence.

"Like you don't know," Leon Spinks says. "Don't be askin' me to embarrass myself."

At long last, he has too much dignity for that.

Larry Holmes a Born-Again Somebody
Las Vegas
November 10, 1978

He can sign for anything he wants. It is one of the perks that go with being Larry Holmes, heavyweight champion. In this shrill, gaudy oasis for tinhorns and tarts, his signature is golden. The people who accept it as currency don't care that he must share the peak of boxing's tallest mountain with Muhammad Ali. They just automatically assume that everything will be taken care of eventually, because Larry Holmes, a nobody for so long, has finally become somebody.

Somebody, do you understand? Larry Holmes has never heard a sweeter song.

His personal "Hallelujah Chorus" bounces off gymnasium walls and show-biz marquees, following him hither and thither like an obedient puppy. He called off training for his imminent title defense against Alfredo Evangelista a day earlier than pugilistic decorum dictates, and everybody said it was good. He had promised to referee a handful of kids' boxing matches for the North Las Vegas Optimists Club in the ring he helped buy. The only compensation he sought was some cheers, some love, some proof that the assembled multitude was aware of his rising star.

"Did you see the two little dudes out there at the beginning, man?" he asked later. "Yeah, the two in the first fight. They couldn't have been more than six or seven years old, but they was banging on each other. They was trying to impress me. They said, 'Man, this is Larry Holmes.'"

The high rollers escorting him said the same thing a different way. He had ridden to his refereeing gig in the back seat of a county sheriff's car, but that was deemed unfitting for a man of his status and stature. "We got you a Cadillac to go back to the hotel," said the chief high roller, surveying all of the 6'3", 210-pound Holmes. "There'll be more room for your legs." Left unsaid was that there would be more room for his ego, too.

It is seemingly insatiable, and yet there is a charm about it. The credit for that goes to Holmes' forthrightness. "I am arrogant," he says, "but I always thought I could get along with people by telling 'em where it's at from the beginning." So it doesn't seem so awful when he orders one of his brothers to snatch his pasteboard likeness from the lobby at Caesars Palace and stash it in their suite. It doesn't seem so awful when he strolls through the casino in a workout suit the color of a twenty-four-hour gambler's eyes and offers to draw a crowd at any crap table you pick.

"You could put me in a category with all the stars and celebrities. I'm one of them," he says. "People want to say they shot dice with me."

After waiting nearly twenty-nine years for this, Holmes cares not that the price of visibility in Vegas is high. He can afford to be $1,000 behind, as he was a week ago, and it is nothing but a joke if he gets $900 ahead, as he is now. To him, such money is "chump change."

And why not? He will receive $1.5 million for defending his World Boxing Council crown Friday night in the Caesars Palace Sports Pavilion. That is $1 million more than he received for knocking said crown off Ken Norton's swelled head in June. But, to Holmes' chagrin, it is also $1.2 million less than Norton made for their memorable brawl. Explanations, quite obviously, are in order.

The handiest one is that Alfredo Evangelista is a stiff even though he is ranked fourth among the world's heavyweights and is getting his second shot at the title. The hulking Uraguayan, who fights out of Spain, is slow, awkward, and bereft of a great punch. His biggest asset, proven when he battled Muhammad Ali, is that he can withstand fifteen rounds of punishment and still walk out of the ring. Unfortunately, that hasn't convinced any local bookmakers to take bets on his chances against Holmes. Applying their logic, maybe the champion doesn't deserve a bigger payday.

The other explanation—the juicier one—revolves around Holmes' relationship with Don King. In a word, it is tenuous.

"I told Don King I'm his last hope," says Holmes. "If he mistreats me, misuses me, he don't have a heavyweight champ anymore. And if he don't have a heavyweight champ, what kinda promoter is he? You hear what I'm saying?"

Behind Holmes' indignation is the unshakable belief that King has denied him his due ever since he was an apprentice left-jab artist. "Don didn't want to give me a chance," Holmes says. "He always believed in other guys." There were Johnny Boudreaux and Jody Ballard, Dino Denis and Stan Ward, all of whom have been relegated to agate type while Holmes gets the headlines. In the beginning, they were King's favorites. It is one of many slights Holmes hasn't forgotten.

Apparently fate decided that it wasn't enough for Larry Holmes to have an absentee father, to drop out of school in the seventh grade and go to work washing cars, and to fight in saloons for hamburgers and hot dogs. The kid they called the Easton (Pennsylvania) Assassin would have to struggle even after he had found his calling in life.

The word on him was all mouth, no heart. Trainers avoided him studiously. Gil Clancy, who molded the great Emile Griffith, announced that Holmes would never amount to anything. Angelo Dundee watched him spar with Ali for five years and let it go at that. And so it was left to Richie Giachetti, who used to run an auto repair shop in Cleveland, to guide Holmes' career out of nothingness.

"The other guys just thought, 'I'm older than you. I've been around longer and my way is the right way,'" says

Giachetti. "Me, I always been one to sit down and talk things over with Larry."

Talking and arguing are synonymous in their stormy relationship. For years, the rewards it brought them hardly seemed worth their trouble. The Norton fight changed that. It also changed Holmes' image as a worthy candidate for a heart transplant. In the thirteenth, fourteenth, and fifteenth rounds, he tapped a source of raw courage no one knew he had and won the championship he wasn't supposed to get a sniff of. It would have been perfect were it not for Ali and the schism between the WBC and the World Boxing Association.

The WBA title is Ali's and there seems no way he is going to let Holmes have a crack at it. "I know him, I know his style, I could beat him," Holmes says. "But if I did, people would only say it was because he was old and dried up. It would be one more time when I didn't get no credit."

For a moment, the thought casts a pall on Holmes' suite. It is as if he is more concerned with the apparition of Ali than with the reality of Evangelista. Only the sight of his brothers can bring Holmes out of his funk. They are in a corner wolfing down room-service delicacies. "Anything you want, just sign for it," says Holmes. The words make him feel better. They make him feel like what he has become—somebody special.

Holmes vs. Ali: Shadow Boxing
Las Vegas
October 1, 1980

Like everything else in the land of the big cuff link, Caesars Palace rose from the desert sands to offer the pleasures Mama never allowed. It lures high rollers and easy marks with the whirring of the roulette wheel, the stirring of ice in tall glasses, and the purring of painted ladies. But out in the stuffy gymnasium that sits behind the glamour and the glitz, Larry Holmes didn't expect to do anything but sweat. For three rounds of sparring, the proof of his labors had been cascading down his muscular torso, and now, suddenly, he felt a chill. Muhammad Ali was at ringside.

He was half-heartedly shushing the crowd Holmes had

drawn and throwing straight right hands that were clearly an answer to the jab the world's heavyweight champion was polishing. The act was vintage Ali, which is to say we have seen it a thousand times before, yet Holmes couldn't help but sneak glances out of the corner of his eye. And when he peeked, Ali caught him.

"I want you, Holmes!" he roared.

"Here I am!" Holmes shot back.

It wasn't exactly what Ali expected to hear; the defiant tone caught him off guard, and he shook his head, the head that was littered with gray hair until he started using a black rinse on it. "Holmes is my Frankenstein," he said, his voice softer now. "The monster's done broke loose and I gotta go get him." The fact that Ali actually thinks he can do it after two years of retirement underscores one of the main themes of Thursday night's championship fight: Larry Holmes has a past he doesn't want to remember and nobody else can forget.

His problems go back thirteen years, back to when he was seventeen, just an amateur trying to punch his way out of an Easton, Pennsylvania, housing project. When Ali drove into town, Holmes climbed aboard his bus and took the ride of his young life. Anytime Ali posed for a picture, there was Holmes trying to sneak into the background. "He was the heavyweight champion and I was a kid," he says. "Shoot, man, you couldn't tell me nothing. I was on cloud nine." It was a sight Ali would never forget.

Perhaps that explains why he later hired the kid as a sparring partner. He had this vision of him as cannon fodder, and even though he would shout about "the next heavyweight champion," his praise rang false. For one thing, Ali had no time for heartfelt sincerity; it was 1974 and he was on the road to the second of his three titles. Joe Frazier and George Foreman stood in his way, and Ali had to figure out a way to remove them.

The kid was part of the solution. He was big, fast, and rangy, and if flattery made him work harder, Ali was only too happy to dish it out, for he was the one who would profit from it in the end.

Profit he did, of course—to such an extent that he can't really believe that Holmes wears the World Boxing Council's crown now, that Holmes has won all seven of his title defenses by knockout, that Holmes remains undefeated after thirty-five fights. Ali looks at the odd shape of the champion's head and still sees a gawky dreamer, a walking joke who stands between him and his fourth reign as the king of the heavyweights. "I call Holmes the Peanut," he says. "I'm gonna shell him and send him to Plains, Georgia."

The crack is nothing Holmes can't laugh off. What bothers him is that he doesn't hear many other people doing likewise. When he is thirty and at what he considers the peak of his powers, he is demeaned by laughter. The sting of that sound has sharpened his sense of purpose.

"I'm not just fighting to defend my championship," he says. "I'm fighting for my identity."

There is, after all, so much we should know about Holmes, about his wife Diane and their six-month-old daughter Kandi, about his sense of humor and his disco back in Easton. He calls it Round One, a name that sounds perfect for spotlighting boxing's latest contribution to music, Joe Frazier and the Knockouts. "Oh, no," Holmes says. "I don't want to scare my customers away."

To think of him spending a lifetime catering to lounge lizards, however, is to get the wrong impression of him entirely. At base, he comes across as the most decent and modest of fellows. It is for Ali to rattle on about how 800 million Chinese are waiting for him, waiting to buy blue jeans and tennis shoes and anything else he can ship in from the States. For Holmes, it is enough to think of the home he is having built in Easton, the one that will replace his garage apartment and feature a swimming pool shaped like a boxing glove. There is even an architect's rendering of his personal Versailles gracing one of the walls in his Caesars Palace suite, but few visitors notice it. Their attention is grabbed by a four-color poster of Ali and the scars, bruises, and blood with which Holmes has decorated it.

"It just shows what happens when you thirty-eight and you try to fight," he says.

"You mean you won't be fighting when you're thirty-eight?" a man asks.

"You kidding?" Holmes replies. "I'm gonna be watching these guys on TV. I'm not gonna be in the ring taking punches. I ain't crazy about getting killed."

The good sense in Holmes' observation seems as obvious as the edge he holds over Ali in youth, strength, and savagery. But the obvious has been obscured since he came to Las Vegas to fight in a $1 million stadium that was built on the Caesars Palace parking lot for one night, and one night only. There have been rumors that Ali is getting to Holmes with his constant badgering and that the bloody nose Holmes got when he blew too hard while sparring was really a cut eye. The more the truth suffers, the faster the odds on Holmes drop. Once he was a 2-1 favorite; by Thursday night, he may be no better than even money. The only way he can prove the doubters and the prevaricators wrong is to bloody a legend.

"I loved the man, I really did," Holmes says. "Ali was everything to boxing, a real hero. But he got to learn . . ."

The words are coming slowly now. Holmes wants to get this right.

"Look, George Foreman told Joe Frazier to retire twice; he did it with a left hook and a right hand upside the head. Nobody ever told Ali to retire; he just got a warning from little midget Leon Spinks. Well, I'm going to tell Ali to retire. It ain't gonna be no fourth championship for him. I'm just hoping I don't hurt the man."

Maybe that is all anyone really needs to know about Larry Holmes.

Food for Thought
Detroit
June 12, 1981

The grind gets old. All of them find that out sooner or later. They begin with the stink of the housing projects on them, and when they are finally rid of it, when boxing has made them smell sweet at last, they realize the price they are paying. It is the 5:00 A.M. roadwork, and the endless rounds of sparring, too—the sparring and the butterflies on fight night and the old men who growl that women weaken legs. Even the champions can endure only so much of boxing's endless torture, and when they reach their limit, they start hating it as much as Larry Holmes does.

"I can't be lying to people," Holmes says. "I'm looking

forward to retiring."

He is undefeated in thirty-seven fights, the heavyweight champion of the World Boxing Council's half of the planet, and the 4-to-1 favorite to put Leon Spinks' head on a platter Friday night, but he doesn't really want to think about any of it. The joy he used to feel in the ring has been surpassed by the dreams that came true for him. "I wanted a little store on the corner and a little house and a little wife," he says. "I got it all—and more." The bonuses are a baby daughter and a summer camp for the kids back home in Pennsylvania, a bar called Round One and a restaurant where the walls gleam with the pictures of champions past and present.

"It's the Four Corners Lounge," Holmes says. "You ought to come and see it some time just to get you a menu. I named all the dishes we serve after fighters and guys that hang around us. Muhammad Ali is a plain hamburger and Howard Cosell is chicken fingers. Me, I'm the delmonte steak."

"What about Spinks?" someone says.

Holmes looks puzzled by the attempt to drag him back to the present. He had slipped away so nicely, done it while everybody around him assumed he was sitting in front of them on a dressing room table in Joe Louis Arena, and now he has been caught.

"Oh yeah, Leon," he says sleepily. "Maybe I can put him on the menu after Friday. He can be whipped potatoes."

In the room, there is both laughter and a sense of the way fighters change. Not so long ago, Larry Holmes could have worked up a good hate for the star-crossed Spinks. Remember, it was Leon who used his Olympic gold medal to get a shot at Muhammad Ali's title after just seven professional fights. "It made me bitter," Holmes says. "I'd had twenty-six hard fights by then." But added together, they still didn't amount to as much as Spinks' upset victory over Ali. Holmes could only fume as the winner and new champion boogied down a one-way street to self-destruction, mindlessly insulting Holmes' wife at a boxing diner along the way. "I owe him a whupping," Holmes snarled then. When he looks at his snaggle-toothed challenger now, though, he sounds as much like a parent as he does a potential executioner. "Leon's talking better than he used to, don't you think?" Holmes says. Malice seems the furthest thing from his mind.

Perhaps he is just weary from the battles he has fought already. In the beginning, there were sparring sessions against Joe Frazier. Later, there were main events against Muhammad Ali, Ken Norton, Mike Weaver, and Earnie Shavers. Surely, no heavyweight trading punches today has hoed a tougher row, yet the thirty-one-year old Holmes never has received the public acclaim he deserves. It is partly because he followed Ali to the throne, of course, and partly because the championship is split between the WBC and the World Boxing Association. You can even throw the proliferation of television boxing into the stew if you wish, for it no doubt has diminished Holmes' stature as well as his taste for wooing prospective fans. Simply put, giants don't like to be treated like midgets.

What may have driven that point home to Holmes was his relationship with his erstwhile manager and trainer, Richie Giachetti. "I have no hard feelings about Richie," he says. "He's just a no-good mother jumper." The champion reached that conclusion when he learned in a grand-jury hearing earlier this year that Giachetti had been taping their private conversations. Giachetti's plan, apparently, was to gather enough verbal TNT to blow promoter Don King off the top of the boxing world. Since King hasn't been judged guilty of anything except having a hairdo that defies gravity, you must read between the lines about his hold on Holmes. But rest assured Giachetti touched enough of a raw nerve to get himself exiled.

"I carried Richie for years, paid him over $1.5 million, and day by day I'm finding out more about the things he was doing all along," Holmes says. "He's a disgrace to the human race. He never taught me a thing. All Richie was good at was pouring water and getting my mouthpiece in place within ten seconds."

"Then why was he around for so long?" someone asks.

"I liked him," Holmes says.

But he likes his new trainer, Eddie Futch, more for three very good reasons: honesty, Frazier, and Norton. The first led to the vital role Futch played in the development of those two big names, and Holmes has been seeing its evidence since he was a babe in boxing trunks. "Even when Richie had me," he says, "I'd ask Eddie what I was doing wrong. I just had to be—how do you say it?—yeah, subtle, that's all." Now that they are publicly affiliated, Holmes finds himself trying to build up a head of steam as much for Futch's sake as for his own. He talks as hard as ever, but somehow his threats of violence are tinged with too much humanity. "I want to knock Leon out quick," he says. "If it goes past four rounds, he could get hurt, all the punches he takes."

Holmes tries to harden the edge on his great thoughts by claiming that he couldn't be seen in his new Rolls-Royce if Spinks beats him. And to be sure, there is some merit to his position. But it would be easier to believe he has a tiger in his soul if he had a different car in his garage. In boxing, you see, a Rolls is for retirement.

Who's Hue?
Detroit
June 14, 1981

There are varying reports on how much blood Howard Cosell lost, but the important thing is that Larry Holmes hit him. With one swipe of his arm, the undefeated champion of the World Boxing Council's heavyweights struck a blow for truth, justice, and the right of every free-thinking American to watch a prizefight without risking his hearing and sanity. Unfortunately, Holmes wasn't aiming at Cosell.

Maybe that in itself is commentary on the parlous state of boxing among the giants or, more specifically, the wafer-thin defense of Leon Spinks, whom Holmes dispatched so hastily Friday night. But ABC-TV paid its money and took its chances, and while Spinks was being reassembled in Joe Louis Arena, some network genius decided a bonus was in order. As Cosell interviewed the champion for the nation's edification, a great white hope named Gerry Cooney was rounded up and deposited in a location where he was guaranteed to catch Holmes' eye and ire.

The champ went bonkers and Cooney put up his dukes, but the only casualty was Cosell. He was left holding a split lip, which was just what he deserved for trying to inject show business into a sport that already makes *Rocky* and all those other fight movies look like so many board of directors meetings. Just eleven hours later, in fact, Holmes stared balefully at the Saturday morning rain and rumbled, "The mother lover ain't never gonna beat me." He was not talking about Howard Cosell.

The lantern-jawed Cooney has gotten so much attention so effortlessly—a No. 1 ranking and a *Sports Illustrated* cover without beating a top ten fighter—that Holmes can't help thinking it's a matter of pigmentation, plain and simple. "If Cooney wasn't white," he said, "he wouldn't be nothing." Alas, the undefeated Irishman from Long Island, New York, stands as the only interesting competition available for Holmes. Sad commentary perhaps, but no other conclusion can be drawn after the bill of goods Detroit wouldn't buy from Don King.

When it was over, puddles of red ink were everywhere in Louis Arena. Barely half of the joint's 21,000 seats had been filled, no matter how hard King's drumbeaters tried to see double.

"My guess is 16,000," propagandist Murray Goodman said.

"Shame on you, Murray," an old acquaintance replied.

"Hey," Goodman said, his feelings obviously hurt, "this ain't Chicago."

To recount that exchange, however, is not to suggest that Motown deserved the three-penny opera that paid Holmes $2 million and Spinks $500,000. It was a sad thing to watch, no matter how brilliant the champion was, and the tone was set in the preliminaries by the young studs who are supposed to be the hope of the heavyweight division. Greg Page put everybody's favorite punching bag, Alfredo Evangelista, on ice forty seconds into the second round of their little waltz, but in the process Page looked like a diamond who may be turning into a broken bottle. He was too flabby and he did too much jiving with his jab, and in comparison, Michael "Dynamite" Dokes should have been just what his nickname suggests. As it turned out, though, Dokes had to beat Great Britain's hapless John L. Gardner with a left hook because his right hand, the hand that should be his best weapon, is just a firecracker.

It was enough to make one think that Leon Spinks really was, as Larry Holmes insisted all along, the best available competition. Not that the praise did Spinks any more good in the ring than the cheers of inner-city Detroit, where he now roams the streets between fights. He was doomed even when the timekeeper mistakenly rang the bell with twenty-five seconds left in the second round and gave him a chance to whack Holmes, who had obediently dropped his guard and his five-inch reach advantage. "You seen what happened after that, didn't you?" Holmes said Saturday. "I fought right through the bell when it rang for real. I hit Leon good with a right hand." The blow was a preview of coming concussions.

Spinks absorbed them all in a third round that lasted just two minutes and thirty-four seconds. The deluge began with a right to his chin. "Leon fell right into me," Holmes said. "If I'd backed up, he woulda landed on his face." Instead, the champion had to shake himself free with a series of equally vicious punches before Spinks finally hit the deck. He got up out of sheer orneriness, assuring himself of further punishment and touching off a bizarre scene that featured a towel being thrown in the ring and his brother Michael begging the referee to stop the fight. When Michael got his wish, there shouldn't have been anyone left to quibble about Holmes' stature among the heavies.

"You think I got recognition now?" the champion said. "The people didn't have no baseball to watch; they only had me. I'm not on strike, baseball is. I proved to the people I don't have to run out and stand in the rain with my T-shirt on. I don't have to hang around Forty-second Street in New York with the hookers and the pimps. I don't have to do any of that crazy stuff. I'm still a great fighter, and now the people know it."

Still, there is a question of whether the public will be satisfied with Holmes' 38-0 record and twenty-eight knockouts. As long as Gerry Cooney is around, the cry will be for the thirty-one-year-old champion to take him on. "I don't need Cooney," Holmes said. "I'm already a millionaire." But surely he is willing to forget that, or Don King wouldn't be waving a $5 million offer under Cooney's battered nose. The white hope's guidance counselors have countered with a $5.5 million bid of their own, but obviously they are eager to let their man fight World Boxing Association titleholder Mike Weaver while Holmes grows older. "Screw it," Holmes said. "Me and my wife are going on vacation in our new Rolls-Royce. If we see y'all on the road, we'll honk the horn."

So he headed for the door of his hotel, the king with his court, and in the lobby, he found Cooney waiting for him. The white hope had his hands on his hips and a scowl on his face, but Holmes went past him like he wasn't even there. The champion's message was clear: If you're going to fight, do it in a ring for money—not when Howard Cosell's big mouth is in the way.

Cooney: A Gentle Giant Plays Bully
Las Vegas
June 9, 1982

For the moment, they would like you to think about the sparring partner's distended eye. If you can imagine how it ballooned until everyone watching was certain it would explode, then you might be able to forget that Gerry Cooney is an overgrown kid who thrives on pretty girls, Pac-Man, and rock-and-roll. The music fills the ballroom in Caesars Palace that has become his personal gymnasium, and he mouths the words to every song as if he were driving to the movies or the beach. There is so much innocence about him, such a blissful lack of malevolence, that it's hard to believe he threw a punch that unhinged his sparring partner's eye.

Cooney didn't know his own strength when he did it, for he was new to the fight racket and innocent of the sound of faces crumbling. All he saw was the warhorse that his managers had shipped in from Memphis, Tennessee, for target practice and he proceeded to bang away on him until the damage was done. In Cooney's camp today, there is no precise recollection of what bone shattered in the sparring partner's face, just a careful recitation of the dialogue that followed.

"Who assaulted you?" asked the doctor examining the sparring partner.

"Nobody assaulted me," the sparring partner replied. "I'm a boxer."

"But for an injury like this, somebody must have hit you

with a blunt instrument," the doctor insisted.

"The only blunt instrument that hit me," the sparring partner said, "was Gerry Cooney's fist."

The object of the story, of course, is to let heavyweight king Larry Holmes know what awaits him Friday night when he puts himself between Cooney and the World Boxing Council crown he has defended so nobly eleven times. But whether the story has been polished over the years is something you have to wonder about when Cooney refuses to appear at a press conference with Holmes. "I wanted to sit across the table from Cooney," the champion says, "and tell him what I'm going to do to him."

Since the undefeated challenger declined that dubious honor, you have to believe he has a softer side than the one the image-makers are peddling. After all, his trainer has described him as "a real Dr. Jekyll and Missy Hyde," and in that malaprop, you may find a truer picture of Cooney at twenty-five than you will in the mountain of propaganda.

Beneath the sense of menace that he wears like his ever-present newsboy's cap, he is just another dutiful son carrying out his father's wishes when he likely would rather be back in Huntington, New York, hanging out and looking for good times. He writhes under boxings' prescribed strictures of sexual abstinence and he winces at the memory of the damage he has done, yet he continues to clear the road to glory with his left hook because this is the way the late Tony Cooney decreed it should be. The old man was a steelworker who forced the kid to fight, to do roadwork at 4:00 A.M., to suffer for a craft he wasn't sure he loved, and the kid rebelled so violently that the love between them vanished until cancer had Tony Cooney in its relentless grip. "I think one of the saddest things in my life is that I told my father that I loved him only once," the kid says. "That was two days before he died."

Now Gerry Cooney acts as if he must atone for such neglect, and the object of his affection is the sawed-off slave driver who treats him worse than his father ever did. After a lifetime of training mostly mediocrities, sixty-four-year-old Victor Valle sees a champion on the horizon, and even though he occasionally serenades his charge with a song called "Gerry Boy" (to the tune of "Danny Boy"), he does everything else in the key of vehemence. And he gets results because the immense Cooney responds like a lantern-jawed puppy dog to the man he calls "Pops." Obviously, Cooney wants to dethrone Holmes, but you can't help feeling that he also wants something else.

"Will you still be with me when I'm not fighting anymore, Pops?" he asked one day.

"Sure, kid," the startled Valle replied. "Sure, I will."

It was one of those scenes that erases the scowl from Cooney's public face. There is no question that he understands that. If he didn't, he wouldn't have asked New York's boxing writers to lay off the story of his winter of agony. It didn't have anything to do with boxing, anyway.

It had to do with a girl he loves, Nancy Greisel, and the automobile accident she was in just before New Year's Eve. She wound up on the critical list and Cooney flew by helicopter from his training camp to be at her side, made sure his managers were paying her medical bills, did everything a man who puts people in hospitals isn't supposed to do. But he never told anyone except his closest friends how depressed he was and the panel on his speed bag that says "Love Nancy" remained his secret until the *New York Post* turned it into a front-page headline.

With such evidence at hand, it is hard to imagine Cooney turning into a monster. His 25-0 record and twenty-two knockouts, however, tell the tale of a split personality and so does his loquacious comanager, Dennis Rappaport. "Five minutes before a fight, something chilling happens to Gerry's eyes," he says. "It's like ice starting to form."

When another victory has melted the ice, Cooney returns to the gentle ways no one around him these days wants to admit he has. They prefer the image of his letting Jimmy Young drown in his own blood, beating Ken Norton until he was a heartbeat away from a coma, rearranging that poor, forgotten sparring partner's eyesight. Violence, after all, is Cooney's ticket to what Rappaport calls "a billion-dollar future—no exaggeration," and Cooney certainly isn't averse to picking up a little pocket money. But the thought you can't escape is that the real reason he wants to win the heavyweight championship is so the people he loves will have a reason to be proud of him.

A Sweet Victory—and a Bitter Holmes
Las Vegas
June 13, 1982

In the wake of the blood, love did its best to blossom. There were encouraging words from the victorious Larry Holmes' camp, and from Gerry Cooney's too. Promoter Don King stopped crowing that Holmes is still champion long enough to blow a cigar-smoke kiss at Victor Valle, the trainer who dragged Cooney out of harm's way in the thirteenth and final round. Returning the favor as well as they could, the challenger's brain trust saluted Holmes for his heart and his hook. But when it came time for this heavyweight for all time to wax gracious, he couldn't bring himself to do it.

He would start, and again and again the old bitterness would ward off the love bug that was buzzing inside the Caesars Palace Sports Pavilion Saturday. Forgotten in an instant were the pure physical relief of having successfully defended his World Boxing Council title for the twelfth time and the simple joy of knowing he would soon head back to Pennyslvania to be with his wife for the birth of their second child. There have been too many hurts in his career that have had nothing to do with punches in the nose, and before he started celebrating, Larry Holmes wanted the world to know that his capacity for forgiveness is nonexistent.

"I'm glad I can sit here as the heavyweight champion of the world," he told his press-conference audience. "I'm glad I can tell you, 'I told you so.' I'm glad I can tell you to stick it up your butt."

Vengeance was his—vengeance for having watched Cooney show up on the covers of *Time* and *Sports Illustrated*, for having seen this unproven challenger get the national commercials that have always escaped him, for having had to let a kid with the good fortune to be born white walk away with a $10 million paycheck identical to his. "Sure, I'll give Gerry Cooney a rematch," he said, "but I don't want parity next time. I want more money."

Oddly, the only outsiders Holmes wasn't vexed at were the ones who appeared to have designs on keeping him from running his record to 40-0 with thirty knockouts. Two of the fight's three judges, a pair of creative mathematicians named

Duane Ford and Dave Moretti, had him ahead on their scorecards by only two points through the first twelve rounds, which would have been disgraceful enough by itself. But referee Mills Lane had also ordered the judges to take three points away from Cooney for repeated low blows, and if that hadn't happened, Ford and Moretti would have had Cooney leading by a point. The whole thing smelled of what the champion was beating out of the challenger.

"No derogation to Gerry Cooney," Don King said Saturday, "but he continued to hit Larry Holmes in the testicles. If Larry Holmes had hit Gerry Cooney in the testicles that many times, the fight would have been stopped and Larry Holmes would have been disqualified and Gerry Cooney would have been the heavyweight champion—and justifiably so."

Holmes, however, didn't share his fearless leader's sense of outrage. Oh, he wasn't overjoyed by having his protective cup tested so vigorously, particularly in the ninth round. "My mother could feel that one all the way back in Easton," he said. But scoring fights is for people who live in a world of pencils and paper, and Holmes, a seventh-grade dropout, figured that his fists were more than enough of an equalizer for the pointy-heads. "I don't care if they had me losing in twelve rounds," he said. "I won it in the thirteenth."

With all due respect, though, he couldn't have done it without Cooney. Imposing as the twenty-five-year-old challenger was at 6'7" and 225 pounds, he came into the fight with too many unanswered questions about himself. It wasn't just that he had fought only six rounds in the last two years and only eighty-six in his entire career; it was that he had never gone beyond eight rounds or found out if he could really take a punch. And Holmes was determined to lead him into those uncharted waters.

"So many critics had said I couldn't go the distance that I couldn't get it out of my mind," Cooney said. "I held myself back and held myself back."

Worse yet, he stopped too many punches in the process. "That never happened before," he said from behind the dark glasses that hid his bruised and stitched left eye, "and I can guarantee it'll never happen again."

It will never happen again because, once his mother finishes calling him "my little Gerry Cooney" and he gets through chasing all the available leg in Huntington, New York, he will be back in the gym learning the things he should have learned before he suffered his first defeat as a professional. "Sure, that's kind of sad," said Ray Arcel, Holmes' wonderful old assistant trainer, "but you have to make life merry by yourself." So if Cooney really wants to have a grand time, he will do more than reconstruct the girlish right hand that now supplements his bone-crunching left hook; he will take a wide berth around the bitterness that has consumed Holmes.

Even at the advanced athletic age of thirty-two, the champion hasn't overcome his social clumsiness. Sometimes it looks like he has, as when he walked out of the ring Friday night and said, "I'm sorry I'm not what you guys in the press want me to be. I'm not Muhammad Ali. I'm not Joe Louis. I wasn't born to be those people. I was born to be myself, Larry Holmes." It was a touching moment, a moment that could have helped win him the admiration he so richly deserves, and then he destroyed it by telling someone with a question, "Shut up and listen to me!"

Larry Holmes is better than that, but there aren't enough people who believe it. He is funny and generous and a marvelous boxer, but his venom hides it all. Because the anger that serves him so well in the ring cannot be controlled outside it, he seems doomed to be ignored as long as he is punching away at his demons. He won't be appreciated until he has no soapbox to stand on, until there is nothing for the public to consider except the silent lines of glory he will leave in the record book.

And that's kind of sad, too.

Punch Lines
Houston
November 26, 1982

"I get tired second round and stay tired. Actually, I get tired walking up the steps. What keeps me going is purity of spirit, I guess. If I got a man in the ring for half an hour and I can't knock him out, well, I figure that's a personal problem."— Randall Cobb, heavyweight philosopher.

As a talker and a target, he is both a hard man to beat and an easy one to beat on. The resident literary critics at an Irish saloon in Philadelphia discovered this seeming incongruity one evening last year when they gathered around him and the newspaper columnist whose point of view he had come to defend. It was an ugly meeting from the start, but when it reached its low and the critics pulled out bats, our hero couldn't stop himself from going for the funny bone.

"Pete," he said to his writer friend, "I hope that's the softball team."

If there was any laughter, however, it didn't last long, for the writer went down in a heap as a bat split his skull. When he finally came to, he looked up through a haze of blood and saw Randall Cobb flattening one mug after another and shouting, "If he's dead, you're all dead!"

It was just like in the movies, even though Cobb wound up in an emergency room. "I didn't break my arm," he says now. "A crowbar did."

Since Larry Holmes isn't allowed to tote such weaponry into the ring, you wonder what he will do to keep Cobb from separating him from his senses and his World Boxing Council heavyweight title. They scrimmage Friday night in the Astrodome—scrimmage is Cobb's word for every fight, great or small—and while the rules call for fifteen rounds, you have about as much chance of seeing them all as the Texas-born challenger does of being mistaken for Robert Redford.

He is a 6' 3", 234-pound monument to the hazards of his trade, with a face that is primarily scar tissue, a nose bereft of bone, and a smile that resembles an open window. "I never made much money being good-looking," he says, "but there's always somebody who'll pay me to take a punch. And I can take a punch, darlin'. It's just a natural gift, like Bob Hayes was born to run. This piece of granite on my shoulders can absorb a lot of punishment, although contrary to popular belief, I do try to make the suckers miss on occasion."

If he can somehow entice Holmes to do that, if he can crowd the unbeaten champion to dull his meat-cleaver jab, Cobb stands a chance of throwing the bombs that have earned him twenty-one victories and the respect of the two sluggers who beat him. "Don't want no more of that stuff," Michael Dokes croaked after escaping with his neck and a unanimous decision, and Ken Norton was every bit as insistent when he should have been rejoicing in a split-decision win. For twenty-eight-year-old Randall Cobb always extracts his pound of flesh.

He may try to do it in a hurry—no marathon man, he—and he may joke about his disdain for prefight exercise. He may even ask the poor devil he is thumping to go drinking with him after the brawl is over. But he raises hell as long as there is hell to be raised, and Holmes should be advised of that no matter how mortal a lock the oddsmakers say he is.

"I can't stand around and wait for a decision," Cobb says, "because that just ain't gonna happen against a champion. I'm gonna throw a lot of leather at him and it ain't gonna be pretty, but that don't mean I don't like him. Hell, he's the same as me, trying to keep from working for a living. If I didn't like him, I'd take him out in an alley and rip his lungs out."

There was a time, in fact, when alley fights were how Cobb kept body and soul together, so to speak. After he had played tackle for Abilene Christian and before he became a kickboxing king, he was a bouncer in joints where the hooch that didn't get drunk was used to unclog drains.

"You could just keep buying a guy drinks, and when he got real drunk, you could snake him," Cobb says. "There weren't any rules meetings and you were always the one who decided what time the fight started. That was one big advantage. The other one was you never got arrested, because you worked for the bar where the trouble started. Life's a funny dog, ain't she?"

Cobb came to that conclusion somewhere between Bridge City, Texas, and Philadelphia, somewhere between breaking people's knees as a kickboxer and dealing with the vagaries of his new trade in Joe Frazier's gym. He didn't like the big city, especially when the first cab driver he encountered conned him into paying fifteen dollars for a five-dollar ride, but he learned—about urban survival, about boxing, about himself. During the day, he received what he calls "negative reinforcement" whenever he failed to keep his dukes up, and at night, he read the Bible and the I Ching and a lot of other books that nourished the human being hiding behind the punch lines.

His bar fights became rarer after that, if you can overlook the one he tried to laugh off as a softball game, and he became more protective of who he really is. "What's inside me, I can't give that to anyone," he says. "All I can tell you is, I don't have any great message for the world. There isn't anything I'm doing that's that important anyway." Not even fighting Holmes, not even trying to take away his championship.

When their Friday night scrimmage is history, Cobb likely will do the same thing whether he has won or lost. He likely will buy a round for the house and toast all the pretty girls everywhere, raise his glass high and leave everybody wondering what the joke is.

"If nothing bothers you, you'll always be happy," Cobb says. "That may be a simplistic approach, but, remember, they don't pay me to be bright."

As always, the last laugh is his.

A Smile Is Cobb's Umbrella
Houston
November 27, 1982

The eye Randall Cobb likes to wink with started to swell early. The rest of his face went along helplessly.

It is not a pretty face, but there has always been a certain rowdy charm about it, an appeal that speaks of tall drinks and taller blonds, and now everything that fed those impressions was in bruised and bloody disarray. Larry Holmes, the best heavyweight champion nobody ever learned to appreciate, was turning that lovably scarred mug into a Halloween mask with his fists, and Cobb just stood there and took it.

The rogue challenger from Bridge City, Texas, has never been off his feet—not in the ring and not in any barrooms where he has worked as a bouncer—and he refused to betray his reputation in the Astrodome Friday night. "I don't back up to nobody," he said. "Besides, I thought the sumbitch might get tired."

No such luck. The 217-pound Holmes kept blasting away, sidestepping Cobb's awkward punches and punishing him for each mistake with combinations as sharp and vicious as an assassin's stiletto. "The real story," the victim said after absorbing fifteen rounds of this abuse, "is that Holmes is one of the most uncooperative people I've ever worked with." It was the only time all night that Cobb's sense of humor got in the way of the truth.

For he was the real story—this hardscrabble street brawler who lost a unanimous decision to the World Boxing Council's masterful king, who won only one round on the three judges' scorecards, who didn't land more than half a dozen solid punches the entire fight.

Even Holmes seemed to understand the situation after running his record to 41-0 and defending his title successfuly for the thirteenth time. "Was he tougher than Gerry Cooney?" someone shouted during the postfight press conference, and the champion fairly sneered. "Gerry Cooney didn't last fifteen rounds," he said. "Next."

Gerry Cooney didn't last fifteen rounds, and he didn't give a national television audience a lesson in take-a-punch bravery, and he didn't resist the urge to fall in with the Great White Hope bigots. Randall Cobb did. He proved the virtue of his stubborn ways, proved it by refusing to go down as Holmes hammered away at him unmolested through the final six minutes. It was not a pleasant spectacle to watch, particularly if you had taken the time to realize that Cobb possesses the brains and sensitivity that are as rare in his cruel trade as diapers. But if you asked why he persisted, you needed only watch him when he finally got the chance to insult promoter Don King to his face.

Cobb was less than an hour removed from combat, and though he was still fumbling to button his shirt, he didn't fumble when someone asked him about King's financial knife.

"This," he said, turning to the leering figure seated at his right, "is the lying, thieving, mother-lover who cut me to $500,000."

That is $200,000 less than Cobb thought he would take to the bank. Obviously, he came to Houston as unschooled in Sweet Science mathematics as he was in cutting off the ring. King, on the other hand, is a master with numbers, just as you would expect from the erstwhile boss of Cleveland's numbers racket.

He looked at the ticket sales that brought only an estimated nine thousand customers into the Astrodome and decided that the blame was Cobb's. After all, the challenger hadn't arrived in town until Monday, thereby depriving the promoter of any chance to capitalize on his Texas heritage. What King neglected to point out, however, was that he—the promoter—didn't show up until Wednesday.

"Heh-heh-heh," the great man said, and even Cobb couldn't keep from laughing. His sense of the ridiculous had survived a painful lesson.

Or maybe he is just a quick healer. "Hell, yes, I'd fight Holmes again," he said. "Right now. Tonight. That sumbitch might get tired." And Cobb certainly would be better educated.

He may be twenty-eight and he may look like he barely made it through the Bataan Death March, but his shot at the title was just his twenty-third professional fight. He may have lost just twice before Friday night—to Michael Dokes and Ken Norton—but he was better schooled in football, kickboxing, and saloon bouncing. "I gotta think I'm one sumbitch got a chance to improve," he said. "I didn't have no amateur career. I turned professional tonight."

Brave as it was, the admission was also inescapable. You could tell it as soon as Holmes stuck his fierce jab in Cobb's face, then danced away before the 234-pound challenger could unload on him. Cobb smiled the first time the champion drilled him and patted him on the rump after almost every round, but being game isn't the same as being good. You knew it when Cobb headed for the wrong corner after the eleventh and fourteenth rounds, for there is only so much punishment any man can take. There just wasn't enough of it to bring him down.

"I feel that I'm one of the greatest fighters of all time," Holmes said after his $1.6 million payday. "Randy can put it down in the book that he's one of the people to go fifteen rounds with me."

There has been only one other since Holmes became champion almost four years ago. There has been only Trevor Berbick, and he didn't survive the hell Randall Cobb did in the sixth and the eleventh, the fourteenth and the fifteenth. He didn't have his left eye puffed up to the size of a cantaloupe, his right eye cut, his forehead scraped red and raw. Nor did he come out of the ring eager to say "How ya doin'" to the first familiar face he saw and ready to meet the public he had won with his show of heart and hardheadedness.

But there Cobb was, weary and battered and answering questions with the same laughing, lunatic honesty as before. The reporters were scribbling and the TV cameras were grinding away, and from off to the right came a newspaper photographer's deadline plea: "Look this way!"

"What the hell?" Randall Cobb said with an impish smile. "You think I got a good side?"

Bobick Circles to Square One
Indianapolis
February 16, 1979

Judging by the sound of it, the Sweet Science should be made to order for fat men. Alas, it is no such thing, because the science is boxing and participants are advised to have washboard stomachs as well as cast-iron chins. Duane Bobick is a well-known failure on both counts, which is why nobody remembers his forty-eight victories and everybody remembers Ken Norton hanging him up to dry in fifty-six seconds. The suet slopped over the top of Bobick's trunks that dreary night and America marveled at the sight of such a large backfield in motion.

Bobick blushed, but he didn't call a cease-fire at the dinner table. Between courses, he began a comeback by starching two heavyweights of indeterminate origin. Kallie Knoetze of South Africa was supposed to be his third victim a year ago. Unfortunately, Knoetze is a disagreeable sort; he knocked out Bobick in three rounds. It was no time to order dessert.

So now we find Bobick at a critical stage in Comeback Number Two, preparing to fight Big John Tate here Saturday for the right to advance to Marvin Gardens in the World Boxing Association's heavyweight Monopoly game. But we don't find as much of Bobick as we used to.

Nothing jiggles as he stalks his sparring partners, not the belly or the thighs or the jowls. And there are three new notches on the belt that holds up his post-workout blue jeans. "Had to get out my knife and cut 'em myself," he says. The idea is that no haberdasher on the planet could keep up with the pace at which he has become a shadow of his former self. In shrinking from 232 pounds to 209, Bobick has lost weight as fast as doomsayers insist California is sinking into the Pacific. But while Malibu has no hope of reclaiming its sand, Bobick has replaced blubber with steel. "Look at his neck," says David Wolf, the reformed sportswriter who manages him. "Used to be a soft sixteen inches; now it's eighteen inches of muscle. He'll be able to take a punch now." That is no small consideration.

The new Bobick was created on Nautilus weight machines and on jogging paths where he logged as many as forty-five miles a week, which is double the fight game's prescribed maximum. He took stretching lessons from the woman whose husband directed *Rocky* and somehow he survived massages by a Russian weightlifter who doesn't think he is succeeding until he hears screams.

"Can you describe what you went through?" a man asks.

"How does hell sound?" Bobick replies, smiling.

The smile is very important. It tells you that whatever he paid in sweat and tears to get his thirty-three inch waist was worth it. It tells you that he has no doubts about where he is headed and what he is going to do when he gets there. And when was the last time Duane Bobick could say that honestly?

Confusion has been his lot from the beginning. "Even before I went to the Olympics, people were calling me the white hope," he says. "I wasn't sure what it meant at first. I was from a little town in Minnesota with 265 people and I guess I was pretty naive. When I finally did find out, I didn't like it. I wanted people to come watch me because I was a good fighter, not because I was white." The wise guys laughed that there was no chance of that happening. They watched Bobick's awkward, plodding style and called the kid stupid for not being able to change it. The kid couldn't help wondering if he was.

"You start asking yourself why you can't learn anything," he says. "I remember fighting Harold Carter one night in West Virginia. It was my twenty-fifth professional fight, and here this guy who didn't have one-tenth of my ability was doing things I hadn't even learned. It got so bad I just dragged him down, and while he was still on one knee, I hit him. I wasn't trying to hurt him. I was just frustrated."

The feeling was born during Bobick's unhappy tenure with the Denver Boxing Club, and it followed him to Philadelphia like Joe Bftsplk's black cloud. It mattered not that Joe Frazier was his manager because Frazier still nursed dreams of fighting again. It mattered not that the esteemed Eddie Futch was his trainer because Futch's supply of energy had seemingly waned. "Oh, that's all in the past," says Bobick. "I hold no hard feelings." Maybe he should.

Frazier and Futch matched him against Norton when a little patience could have gotten them Muhammad Ali. It was downhill from there. Frazier partied with Norton and neglected so obvious a courtesy as predicting his man Bobick would win. Futch, meanwhile, did little more than dream of revenge on Norton, whom he had once trained. No one discussed strategy with Bobick, no one even walked back to his hotel with him in the rain. "For a guy as sensitive as Duane," says Wolf, his new manager, "those things were devastating."

After Norton and Knoetze beat him—the only losses in his professional career—Frazier and Futch pulled up stakes. "They didn't see Duane as a potential payday anymore," Wolf says. They abandoned Bobick in South Africa at the lowest point in his career. "I was thinking about quitting," he says. "I didn't know what I'd do, but I couldn't be any worse at it than fighting."

The people who stayed by his side told him otherwise. There were Wolf and Murphy Griffith, who trained him in the amateurs, and Chico Segura, Griffith's silent partner in passing on the wisdom of the ages. "I probably should have been with these guys all along," says Bobick, "but I had to go for the big names." It was a lesson learned, the first of many for him.

On his way to the eight straight knockouts he brings to Saturday's engagement, the new ruling troika decreed that he become svelte. Then the word came down to pick up some polish in the square circle. "You'd be amazed what Duane didn't know," Wolf says. Griffith and Segura started from Square One and worked from there, all the while keeping Bobick in an out-of-the-way gym in San Diego where no one could laugh at him.

He was like a kid learning the box step in a dance class—one, two, three, four; one, two, three, four. It was painful and embarrassing at first, but gradually it came. And if he still doesn't remind anybody of Sugar Ray Robinson, at least he looks better than the big lug who fights a bear at a county fair. "I never thought I could do some of these things," he says. He imagines it is because of his streamlined physique, but he is only half right. You see, his mind was never in shape before, either.

The Destroyer and the Dinghy
Indianapolis
February 18, 1979

It was sweet and sad, a beginning and an end. And what can you say except that it was a fight only devotees of ships passing in the night could love or understand.

Big John Tate was the one headed in the right direction. He strode out of the ring with a smile lighting up his broad mug and his fist in the air and cheers nibbling on his ears. In his dressing room, the cheers turned to prophesies of a world heavyweight championship and Big John Tate didn't know what to say. "I'm not too good at giving answers," said this thickset kid who was driving a truck for a living just two years ago. And everybody fell for him a little harder.

Sure, he'll get a title shot, they told each other. He'll win it, too.

Through it all, however, a question gnawed at the back of your mind. You wondered whether Big John Tate will remember what happened Saturday if he really does make the quantum leap from athlete to celebrity. You wondered whether he will remember smoky Market Square Arena and the glare of the TV lights and the pitiful gasping sound Duane Bobick made when he got hit.

Duane Bobick was the ship headed in the wrong direction. Big John Tate turned him around himself.

The job only took two minutes and sixteen seconds of what was supposed to be a ten-round fight. That is eighty seconds longer than Bobick lasted against Ken Norton in his last coast-to-coast embarrassment, but it hardly qualified him for an endurance record. "We're going to have to find some place where they start fights in the second round," said David Wolf, Bobick's manager, trying to smile.

Until they do, they will have to contend with instant assaults like the one Tate launched as soon as he heard the opening bell. "Wasn't nothing to do with strategy or Bobick being a slow starter," he said. "That's just the way I fight." Bobick responded by seemingly sinking into paralysis. Maybe he could have survived if he didn't have a fatal habit of dropping his left hand after he jabs with it. Unfortunately for him, the habit is unbreakable.

The first time Tate saw the opening, he shot an overhand right to Bobick's forehead that gave him every reason for great expectations. "I tried to tell myself not to get too eager and make a mistake," he said. But Bobick beckoned him on unwittingly. So Tate threw another overhand right, and another. And Bobick sagged to one knee.

"I saw the punches coming," he said later. "I just couldn't react to them."

He tried to clamp Tate's right hand to his side, tried to tie him up, tried to do anything to get through this inexplicable hell in one piece. But Tate threw his 229½ pounds in reverse and jerked free. Bobick was left helpless.

Tate battered him from one side of the ring to the other. Pressed against the ropes, Bobick covered his pain-flushed face with his red gloves and weaved this way and that while Tate whaled away. "I had lots of combinations I was going to try," said Tate, "but I really didn't get the chance to use them." The overhand right was working too well. He threw five in a row, broke the monotony with the left hook, then came back with five more rights.

Bobick sagged to the sky-blue canvas and struggled back to his feet immediately, like a stubborn broken yo-yo. He took a standing eight count, but it wasn't long enough for his head to clear. Tate was on him again, and all he could do was backpedal and grimace and pray for the bell.

The referee got to him first. George DePabis wedged his

stout body between the fighters and led Bobick back to his corner, beaten again, maybe beaten forever.

Tate didn't watch. He had sparred something like 600 rounds to get ready for these 136 seconds of glory, and now it was time to enjoy the fruits of his labors. He would not celebrate too hard, mind you, for the work ethic is the light of his life. But he was only too happy to sit there in his dressing room, in front of a blackboard with the word "War!" chalked on it, and listen to his virtues being extolled.

"John Tate will be the best heavyweight in the world if he isn't already," said Bob Arum, the nonstop promoter. Of course, Arum may have been gilding the lily a bit because he has Tate under contract with Top Rank, Inc., and there are big plans afoot. From here, Tate will go on to fight Gerrie Coetzee, while Leon Spinks takes on Kallie Knoetze. "The South Africans," Arum sneered. "My guys are going to clean up on them." And then, provided Muhammad Ali retires this fall, Tate and Spinks will battle for the World Boxing Association's portion of the heavyweight championship. "A dream come true," said Arum.

He had a lot of other things to say as well, but Tate tuned out on them. "Why don't you just say I'm one of the best heavyweights?" he said.

"That's right," said his manager, Ace Miller. "Can't ride 'til you get there, fella."

Maybe someone should have told Bobick that. Or maybe he should have known it already. Whenever he has had a big fight, he has lost it. In the 1972 Olympics. In Madison Square Garden. In South Africa. And now in Indianapolis, of all places. It wasn't supposed to turn out that way, especially not in Indianapolis. He had a new manager and his trainer from the amateurs and a team of geniuses who pared his weight down to 207 pounds and built his confidence as high as it had ever been.

And Tate undid it all.

"He just came storming in at me, throwing punches from everywhere," Bobick said. "I was terrible, wasn't I? I just couldn't get any punches off. Jeez, I don't know what I'll do now. Take a rest, I guess. Yeah, I need a rest."

Bobick reached out and took his wife's hand, and the

two of them exchanged smiles that might as well have been tears.

They were still holding hands when a man from ABC-TV ducked into the dressing room and asked if Bobick would mind coming back to ringside for an interview. Bobick went, for he is nothing if not accommodating. While he was out there trying to separate the jeers from Chris Schenkel's questions, a young middleweight was up in the ring getting knocked out in one minute four seconds of the first round. Bobick didn't even look up. He had seen it all before.

Too Tall's Comic Opera
Las Cruces, New Mexico
November 4, 1979

It was not as if Too Tall Jones had never been on his back, of course. Indeed, the computer hasn't been built that could count the number of times he had to pick himself off the ground when he was rearranging bodies in the Dallas Cowboys' behalf. But this business Saturday was different.

Too Tall Jones was going public as a professional fistfighter and there wasn't anybody around to spare him his humiliation in the sixth and final round. With the eyes of the world upon him, he had to gaze up helplessly at the eminently forgettable Yaqui Meneses, who had just heaved him to the canvas like a sack of potatoes.

"How do you feel?" someone asked later.

"Embarrassed," Too Tall replied.

"You weren't hurt?"

"No, I got hurt later."

But not much later. While Jones was still sprawled in his own corner, his massive head resting on the padded blue turnbuckle, Meneses raced in and whacked him with a stiff left hand. Call it overzealousness. Call it frustration at being denied what would have been the fight's only knockdown. Call it a bad habit Meneses picked up while slugging his way out of Mexico. Whatever, Jones looked like a balloon that had just sprung a leak and the great thinkers urging him to arise knew it.

"Foul! Foul!" screamed his manager, David Wolf. "Disqualify the guy!"

Referee Buddy Basilico paid no attention to Wolf's outraged bleating. Perhaps his deaf ear would be fodder for controversy if Basilico hadn't inadvertently overlooked something else in the chaos. As he was warning the suddenly supercharged Meneses to stay in a neutral corner, an ebony hand snaked over the ring ropes and found its way to Jones. The hand belonged to his cagey old trainer, Murphy Griffith, and what it held was a bottle of smelling salts.

"Where's the disqualification?" howled Meneses' manager, Jimmy Montoya. "That's illegal!"

Over in Jones' corner, they were describing it as tit-for-tat. Besides, it worked.

When the mayhem ended and the final bell rang, the 6' 9" Jones would walk away from the Pan American Center with a split-decision victory. It was not what he wanted, obviously. Ever since he abandoned football for good and began training as a heavyweight boxer three months ago, he planned on inaugurating his campaign with a knockout. Never mind that his opponent had fifteen professional fights and he had none. "I thought I could do it, I really did," he said. "I was too tight, tighter than I ever got for a football game. Next time it'll be different." Next time maybe he won't be an unwilling participant in a carnival of tomfoolery.

The tone for the production was established Friday night when Too Tall's manager and Meneses' manager nearly called off the fight and started one of their own. Apparently Meneses and Montoya had just figured out that Jones was going to do better than the $45,000 that promoter Frank Mirabal had guaranteed him; CBS-TV was going to sweeten the pot with $27,000 more for the opportunity to wedge him between the World Series of Poker and the Battle of the NFL Cheerleaders on "Sports Spectacular." Somehow the $3,000 that Meneses and Montoya were going to take home paled in comparison, so they did what they thought was logical: They said they were pulling out if they didn't get any TV money.

"You're trying to shake us down," said Wolf, the brains behind Jones.

"I am not," said Montoya.

"Your man is a frightened dog," said Wolf.

"I don't have to listen to such insults," said Montoya. "I'm a man."

"I'm glad we have your sexual persuasion figured out," said Wolf.

On and on it went in the lobby of the Las Cruces Howard Johnson's, with Wolf and Montoya toe-to-toe and a crowd gathering to watch the chest-puffing and listen to the sabre-rattling. The gawkers bore the same eerie look of expectancy as those who gather for some poor creature's leap from a twelfth-story window.

Only Mirabal, the stubby wheeler-dealer who lured Too Tall Jones to this bone-dry outpost, provided any comic relief. "Gentlemen!" he kept shouting. "Gentlemen!" But Wolf and Montoya paid no attention even though Mirabal later took credit for convincing the unhappy Mexicans to stick around at no increase in pay. As events would quickly prove, the cold shoulder was exactly what he deserved, for everything he touched turned to green cheese.

The ring for the fight served as Exhibit A. It nearly collapsed when Jones was sparring on it earlier in the week. Naturally Mirabal promised it would be reinforced. But when Wolf stepped on it Saturday morning, it nearly caved in again—and bear in mind that Wolf weighs nowhere near Too Tall's 255 pounds. "So there we are," Wolf said later. "It's 8:00 A.M. and we've got saws and hammers trying to put the thing together."

That was just the beginning. When the ring was measured for the record, it turned out to be fifteen feet by fifteen feet, one foot shorter each way than Wolf's contract specified and also one foot shorter each way than the rules allow. On top of that, the covering for the ring was a wrestling mat, which was soft and guaranteed to slow down the nimble Jones. Decorating the canvas were seeds from a watermelon split by a sword-swinging imitation Samurai warrior while it rested on some brave lad's stomach. Mirabal had promised to forego that spectacular preliminary in the interests of better pugilism, and no doubt Wolf would have pointed that out had it not been for the ropes. The ropes, you see, were too loose to keep two heavyweights in the ring.

"Jesus," said Wolf, as he watched two workmen bolstering the sagging ropes with clothesline. "What's next?"

He wouldn't have believed it if someone had told him. Yaqui Meneses, the owner of ten victories by knockout and a reputation for malevolence, came out and played Little Bo Peep for the first three rounds. "I wanted a brawl," Jones said. But Meneses wouldn't give it to him.

Self-preservation helped dictate the strategy, since Meneses was giving away seven inches and fifty-one pounds. So, however, did pure boxing wisdom. "We wanted to make Jones punch himself out," said Montoya. "We wanted to tease him, to aggravate him, to frustrate him." Someday Too Tall may have enough ring savvy to squelch such plots, but not now.

He proved Saturday just how raw he is as he failed to take advantage of his jab, failed to throw anything resembling a straight right hand, failed to corner the perpetually retreating Meneses. "It was a learning situation," said trainer Murphy Griffith. And now Too Tall knows for sure that heavyweights can be created overnight, but heavyweight champions can't.

"Give us time," Wolf said. "Our credibility will improve."

Credibility? What an interesting word to use considering the circumstances of a fight that became a comic opera. Even when it was over, Montoya was claiming victory for his man because of the smelling salts. "I'm going to protest to the state boxing commission," he sputtered. A valiant thought, but also a futile one. New Mexico doesn't have a boxing commission.

Jumbo's New Front Tier and Frazier's New Deal
Chicago
November 30, 1981

The first time he watched Joe Frazier fight, Jumbo Cummings resided in Tier D1 of Cook County Jail. He was still new at being behind bars then, a relative innocent at the ways of caged men, but he thought the sight of a future heavyweight champion belaboring one Scrap Iron Johnson on television would create a bond in blood lust. If the thrill reached some corners of the tier's recreation room, though, elsewhere a sullen silence fell on hard cases who would think nothing of cutting out a young punk's heart.

There had been mutterings in behalf of the prime-time fluff that was as prevalent in 1967 as it is today, and they were replaced by dark looks suggesting the majority should get its ration of electronic sex and silliness. Then as now, however, Cummings knew nothing of democracy and cared less. He was going to check out Frazier on the tube, and he never doubted for a minute that he would get his way.

"It was easy," he insists. "I was the barn boss."

"How did you get a title like that?" someone asks.

"By being the toughest," Cummings says.

He was sixteen years old, and his jailers were waiting for him to turn seventeen so he could be tried for murder. It was an old story, one heard far too often in Chicago's flinty ghettos, one presumably without a prayer for a happy ending. But if you look in the International Amphitheatre Thursday night, you will see that prayers get answered and that endings don't have to be logical to be happy. Joe Frazier has come down from the TV screen and Floyd "Jumbo" Cummings has the shot of the lifetime he almost wasted.

The two of them will whale away at each other for ten rounds or less while the rest of the world tries to separate the sublime from the ridiculous. Going into the fight, Cummings is ahead on points simply because Frazier is making a comeback that his oldest and best friends think was hatched in hell. At thirty-seven, the ex-champion hasn't fought since June of 1976, when baleful George Foreman cracked his skull as if it were a dime-store dinner plate. Add to that the memories of his three strength-sapping wars with Muhammad Ali and you have the meat of the argument against Smokin' Joe's campaign to stoke the fire once again.

Frazier may be fighting for money, vanity, or perverse amusement, but Cummings and his brain-trust don't have the time to pick and choose. "The only thing Joe Frazier is to us," manager Mickey Carioscia says, "is a stepping-stone to the world championship." While the hyperbole may sound like everything else you have ever heard in the fight racket, Carioscia has to think big, because his tiger is now thirty and trying to make up for the twelve years he spent in the state penitentiary. The idea is to make Cummings think of the prison guards who used to bet against him and the luxury he is missing by living atop a Joliet furniture store. And no matter what Frazier used to represent, Jumbo can think about it only in terms of get-well cards.

"I don't give a damn if people say I'm gonna beat up an old man," Cummings says. "I didn't go looking for him. The old man came looking for me."

The search was part of Minneapolis promoter Bill Cooley's campaign to bring Frazier back from boxing's dead. Being the target of the search couldn't have surprised Cummings more, for he firmly believes the fight racket is full of more hiders than seekers. Big John Tate and Trevor Berbick are the first names he spits out while making his case. Just as you are about to sympathize with him, though, you remember that in March he lost a unanimous decision to Renaldo Snipes.

"Yeah," Mickey Carioscia says, "but there were what you call extenuating circumstances." Cummings' trainer developed a fear of flying just before the Atlantic City fight, his corner had to be filled with relative strangers and he couldn't get a break in the scoring. "You put Jumbo in with Snipes again," Carioscia says, "and he'd knock him out, I promise you."

The boast creases Cummings' unshaven mug with a smile. He likes his new manager's quick-draw style, just as he trusts his new trainer, Jimmy Pearce, and revels in the way his punching speed has picked up since he stopped lifting weights. But somewhere in him there is also an emotional cruise control that keeps giddiness to a minimum. "When you be the way I been," he says, "you know how to deal with ups and downs."

What Cummings is talking about has nothing to do with his 17-1 record or his twelve knockouts. His lessons in life's vagaries began barely two months after he moved to the South Side from Mississippi and landed at the wheel of the getaway car in a grocery-store robbery. Inside, where his five partners were marauding, the grocer grabbed for a gun and got himself killed. The only trip Cummings was going to take after that was the one to Stateville.

He could follow Joe Frazier's career from there, hailing each fight by betting ten cartons of cigarettes—a "brick," in prison parlance—on him and wondering how Muhammad Ali could get away with hitting and holding the way he did in Manila. But Prisoner No. C01324 couldn't always see the fights when they were replayed on television because he was a discipline problem, a prison-yard brawler forever in an isolation cell, and he would stay that way until the joint got its first boxing program six years ago. "Boxing was natural for me 'cause all it is is street fighting with a little polish," Cummings says. "I didn't have to prove myself every time some cat woofed at me." He had found his ticket out of prison.

It got businessmen and correction officers behind him, and undid his seventy-five-year murder rap in 1979. It put him in the position to keep punching until he could look at Frazier on film and see him not as someone to be admired, but as a target. "That left hook of Frazier's, it ain't so tough anymore," Cummings says. "He hit Ali and Foreman right on the nub with it and they looked like they didn't feel nothing." Cummings' right fist tightens reflexively. He has notions of giving Frazier something for nothing.

"Tell you how bad I'm gonna beat him," Cummings says. "The only thing I'm bringing to the fight is my two lawyers, so when I'm up in front of the judge, I don't have to answer anything."

Old habits die hard.

Frazier Polite If Not Politic
Chicago
December 2, 1981

Etiquette means no more to the fight racket than toothbrushes do to junkyard dogs. In a sport where bright moments tend to be provided by pinky rings, there may even be a premium on the ability to lie, cheat, or step on people's feet. At the very least, this crooked tree bears some strange peaches, or else Joe Frazier wouldn't have loved it so when he looked up from the speed bag Tuesday to see the hunk of trouble who wants to make his comeback a trip on the Titantic.

If Jumbo Cummings had been caught trespassing in any other athletic venue, he might have been forced to listen to

Howard Cosell's greatest hits, a punishment guaranteed to make firing squads seem humane. But Frazier treated the ill-timed visit to his workout as a favor rather than shameless spying. For Cummings, his first live target in five years, had given the erstwhile heavyweight champion a chance to show his countless detractors that the old reflexes are still there.

"Somebody lookin' for me?" Smokin' Joe growled after rumbling around the Fuller Park Fieldhouse's two boxing rings and putting on his most fearsome scowl.

Cummings grinned as impishly as it is possible to grin after doing twelve years in prison for murder.

Frazier kept moving closer and scowling harder.

"My daddy always told me a scared man can't win nothin' and a jealous man can't work," he said, "and I ain't either one of them."

"Your daddy?" asked Cummings, surprised at the turn Frazier's line of patter had taken. "He still around?"

"No, he's gone," Frazier said. Then his eyes narrowed and he stared evilly at the unshaven jaw he aims to dent with the left hook that gave him a 32-4 record. "You wasn't talkin' bad about my daddy, was you?"

The question was half prefight hokum, half heartfelt. They say that when Joe Frazier came into this world almost thirty-eight years ago in Beaufort, South Carolina, his share-cropper father looked at him and announced, "This is gonna be my famous son." And nothing Frazier has done since he migrated to Philadelphia and punched his way out of anonymity has betrayed that prediction. He took the charnel smell off boxing with his heart and his honesty, waging full-scale war against everyone in his path and never taking a backward step, not even against Muhammad Ali and George Foreman. His place in history was secure long before Foreman beat him in 1976 and he announced his retirement afterward, dancing with joy and relief until 5:00 in the morning. He was not only famous; he was rich, too, and at the time, that appeared to be enough.

But now we realize that it isn't and wonder if the adjective his father chose for him isn't about to be joined, or even replaced, by another one—foolish. To the people who don't live inside Joe Frazier's thick frame or hang on his every word, there are grave misgivings about his ten-round assault on the magnificently sculpted Cummings in the International Amphitheatre Thursday night. Old friends and admirers want to know why Joe Frazier refuses to admit that rust never sleeps.

Maybe it is, as he hints, the sight of a heavyweight division that wouldn't have amounted to an hors d'oeuvre when he was in his prime. Maybe it is, as he would like to have us believe, the fact that his daughters are now old enough to live with the idea of their father sacrificing his brain cells for money. Or maybe it is simply money.

"I always need money," Frazier says. "I love money. I got to have lots of money so I can party."

There is talk, however, that his partying eats up only a fraction of the cash he brings home. He has a limousine service in Philadelphia that barely breaks even, a gym that runs in the red, an expensive taste for gambling, and the memories from a rock-and-roll singing career that was a six-figure sour note. Never mind that he takes home a weekly paycheck from his restaurant or that his business advisers have put him in shape to make $70,000 a year for the rest of his life. Frazier can always use more, just as he can always use the psychic income of being called Champ, of being told he is special.

"I am one of God's men," he says. "I'm a Capricorn. I am the youngest in the family, the seventh son. That makes me one of God's men. When I was born, 300 people gathered 'round the house that night to see if I'd been born with one arm or not, because my daddy had lost an arm in an accident. Now you look at my son Marvis (undefeated as a professional heavyweight). Has there ever been a fighter put something back into the game the way I have? You tell me I ain't history."

That isn't the issue, though. The issue is whether a sterling piece of history will be tainted Thursday night, sullied the way Muhammad Ali's grand name was against Larry Holmes last year and will be again next week against the undistinguished Trevor Berbick.

Predictably, Frazier likes neither the suggestion of failure nor the connection with Ali. In his own eyes, Smokin' Joe is too pure, too hard-working to be connected with either. "I've wrecked myself into shape for Mr. Jumbo," he says. "I train with my sons, my nephew, guys that knows all my tricks. I fight a championship fight every day in the gym. I've made myself into a wrecking machine." And with his 227 pounds cloaked beneath a tattered robe, Frazier looked the part Tuesday until his legal adviser, Sharon Hatch, dawdled out of sight as the press closed in on him.

"Where were you?" he whispered when she finally appeared at his side.

"Don't worry," Hatch whispered back. "I wasn't leaving."

"Then what I'm doin'?" he asked.

"Talking," she said.

"Talkin' about what?" he asked.

If Joe Frazier didn't know, maybe there is still a chance that the fight will just go away.

A Shame and a Sham
Chicago
December 4, 1981

They brought shame to Chicago Thursday night. They swept the dirt under the seats at the creaking International Amphitheatre, put on a Roman circus punctuated by a woman's anguished scream, and fed a paunchy relic named Joe Frazier a draw he didn't deserve. Jumbo Cummings cried a river when the news hit him harder than the forlorn ex-heavyweight champion had in ten rounds, and a sweating, stinking mob belched up its anger with him. But the point that should be made in the haunted aftermath has nothing to do with justice in a sport that never had any to start with. The point that should be made is that Joe Frazier never should have been out there in the first place.

Though he will never admit it, though he undoubtedly will take his early Christmas present as a sign that his retirement five years ago was born of stupidity, Frazier made a mockery of the greatness that used to be his. Gone were the savagery and boldness that once filled the arenas where he fought Ali and Foreman and anybody else brave enough to step in front of his rolling thunder. In the unkind light of a joint that reeks of blood and cruelty, Frazier looked fat, slow, harmless. He was nothing but a dreary pretender.

Fat jiggled around his middle as he rumbled across the ring to draw a bead on Cummings, and his knee-length purple trunks looked just as ludicrous as they should have on a man who will turn thirty-eight in January. You kept telling yourself that he still might have his fearsome hook, the weapon that once equalized the tons of punishment he absorbed. But you knew the weapon was no more as he swung and missed with it for the first three rounds—swung slowly and missed badly. Even when Frazier finally found his mark later on, Cummings didn't buckle, hardly even flinched. At thirty or thirty-one or however old he may be, the Adonis just two years out of the state penitentiary was still the kid in this one. Joe Frazier, smokin' no more, was the old man.

He cringes at that description, of course. It is an affront to his image and his honor, yet no one gives him the respect he expects—not the friends who counseled him against this comeback, not the writers who have chronicled his greatness, not even Muhammad Ali, who revels in these crazy attempts to defy the clock. Ali called Frazier at noon Thursday, called him at the hasty physical examination that was supposed to cloak the Cummings fight in respectability, and instead of stirring up interest, Ali only stirred up the slaughterhouse laborer with whom he made history.

"We gotta make all the old men proud," Ali crowed long distance from his own comeback headquarters in the Bahamas.

"I hear you," Frazier said. "I'm gonna hold my end of the deal up."

"I'm gonna do my best down here, too," Ali said.

"I don't want to hear none of that I'm-gonna-do-my-best stuff," Frazier said, scowling. "I'm talkin' about you holdin' your end up."

"Yeah, we're old men and we gotta show the world we can do it," Ali said.

"Don't call me old," Frazier said.

Somebody had to, for it was the truth. But the truth never means much in the fight racket, and to the dreamers and schemers who led Joe Frazier to market for the first time since 1976, it meant even less. Bill Cooley, who made his millions in the Minneapolis real-estate market, couldn't bring himself to admit that he was gambling with an incurably proud man's life. Cooley had to play games with ticket sales and do tricks with the overseas television broadcast rights he had or hadn't peddled. And while he diddled around on the periphery, he let the easy marks from the Illinois Athletic Commission flirt with hanging themselves.

They had X-rays and a brain scan that were supposed to be Frazier's, but how did they know? They had been shipped from the fallen champion's personal physician in Philadelphia and, for all anyone knew, they might have been Pete Rose's. But the commissioners blissfully went along with the charade, promising they would check Frazier harder Thursday. Once again, the truth lay bleeding. All Frazier got, in commission doctor Jorge Tovar's words, was "a superficial examination."

It was as if the infamous Long Count from half a century ago wasn't enough, nor September's pathetic Mike Weaver-James "Quick" Tillis waltz, either. It was as if Cooley and the commissioners figured the only way they could put Chicago on the map again as a boxing town was to feed the howling public a tragedy.

That they escaped without one, naturally, will be their defense in the days and weeks to come. You can even imagine them having the gall to suggest matching Frazier and Cummings again, for the fight was a draw, and an undeserved one at that. Only referee Nate Morgan touched on reality as he voted for Jumbo 46-45. Judges Collins Brown and Harold Marovitz defied the obvious and did Frazier a disservice by letting him escape with the even scorecards that should haunt them the rest of their days. Brown and Marovitz must have taken the fifth round, Frazier's only good round of the night, and multiplied it over and over again. They must have used the new math and dressed it up with visions of the way Frazier humbled Ali a decade ago. And in their eagerness to please the shades of the past, they blinded themselves to the good Cummings did.

Oh, he threw some marshmallows himself, threw them with the bulging arms that seem to grow short whenever there is a live target in front of him. But for seven of the ten rounds, Cummings took the fight to Frazier, and in the eighth, the rush almost swept old Joe to oblivion. He was pinned in a neutral corner, his lower lip split and bloody, his arms weakly waving at the punches Cummings rained down on him.

The beating may have lasted no longer than thirty seconds, but it seemed like forever as you watched the soft-bellied figure soaking up the abuse. You knew then just how old and tired Joe Frazier really is. There was no way he could summon the power he used to have in his fists, and it didn't matter that his heart remains as big as ever. Inside that well-padded frame was the dust of his greatness. It was something Joe Frazier shouldn't have been allowed to show us, something that will sully his name for the rest of his days. When people think of Chicago and boxing from now on, they should remember that. They should remember that and blush for a city that has no shame.

6.
Little Big Men

He didn't last long.

They seldom do.

But while he was king of the world's flyweights, Danny "Little Red" Lopez raised enough hell to satisfy a dozen giants. He thundered out of L.A.'s Olympic Auditorium, where anything less than World War III is grounds for civil disobedience, and to the best of my knowledge, he never took a backward step. As a result, there weren't many punches that missed him. In fact, one of the first I saw flying his way sent him spinning on the seat of his pants.

"Trouble," the cigar smoker beside me grunted.

"For Lopez, huh?" I said.

"Uh-uh. The other guy."

In the next round, Little Red, properly indignant, knocked his nemesis colder than a clam.

He's a Man of Stone
Montreal
June 15, 1980

The legend does not serve Roberto Duran well. He has soared to the heavens of boxing, a sport in which simply escaping the gutter is an accomplishment, but the spotlight has done little beside capture his shadow. To people who should know better, Duran has remained a runty Panamanian savage who can drop a horse with one punch and has suffered loss after loss to the English language. And no doubt he would have gone to his athletic dotage neglected and misunderstood were he not where he is now, blinking in the reflected glory of Sugar Ray Leonard.

It shouldn't be like this, of course, this stealing into the public consciousness because a fighter five years his junior, with less than half his experience, deigns to give him a shot at the World Boxing Council's welterweight championship. Life isn't always fair, though, and the fight racket never is. So Duran must squirm indignantly while Leonard, headed back to Montreal, the scene of his Olympic triumphs, plays the lord of the manor.

Most of the time, the Sugar Man handles the role with consumate grace and intelligence, but every now and then the temptation to gloat and preen becomes too much to resist. Witness his act in New York at the press conference announcing the fight that will earn him $10 million and Duran $2 million. He stood tall on the dais and glared down at the opponent everyone in the room expected him to respect grudgingly.

"I want to kill you," Leonard said.

Duran did not need a translation.

Even now, two months later, with the fight just five days away, he bristles at the thought of such insolence, such macho posturing. There is no calming him with Leonard's innocent plea that he was only trying to speak the little assassin's language. Indeed, there is nothing to do but flinch at the thoughts of vengeance those ill-chosen words have aroused.

"If he wants to kill me" Duran says, "he has to stand up and fight."

A cold smile twists Duran's face into a death's head. It is the same smile so many of his victims have seen before he sent them reeling to the canvas, jaws unhinged, senses unraveled.

"How in hell is Leonard going to stand up and fight?"

Now Duran's eyes dance crazily.

"He'll be running once he feels my punch."

It is not for nothing, after all, that Roberto Duran is called Manos de Piedra. He has just what his nickname says he does—Hands of Stone—and if you doubt it, you need only think of the damage he has done while winning sixty-nine of seventy fights and knocking out fifty-five targets. "If the foundation crumbles," says the man in charge of demolition, "the building will come down." Lord, how he loves that sight, loves to break his opponents into small pieces and dance on the rubble.

When the once great Carlos Palomino fell before him, he sneered, "Quit. You don't got it no more." When Ray Lampkin got carted off to the hospital, the victor shouted that next he would get in shape and, yes, "kill him." Heartless cruelty, perhaps, but in the Panama City slum where Roberto Duran grew to manhood, heartless cruelty was an impregnable defense against street-corner extinction.

He was a fighter from the start. Fighting went with carving out the turf where he shined shoes, peddled mangoes, and danced in saloons. He played the drums, too, and maybe he would have been the star of his high school band if he had survived that long in academia. But the third grade was it, and his hair-trigger right hand—what else?—was his undoing. He was thirteen years old.

Two years later, he stepped into the ring as a professional for the first time with a jockey as his manager and a zest for violence as his foremost weapon. The jockey soon vanished, selling Duran's contract to a millionaire sportsman named Carlos Eleta for the magnificent sum of $300. The zest for violence remained, waiting for Duran to put together his two-fisted attack and flee Panama for Madison Square Garden. When he finally arrived there, in December of 1971, the crowd belittled him as a skinny fraud until he knocked Benny Huertas still as death for six minutes. From that night on, people began to understand what Duran's hands were made of.

The stone in them destroyed everyone blocking his way, made him the lightweight champion of the world, turned him into his native land's tax-exempt hero. But in the United States, where the money was, the coast-to-coast infatuation with heavyweights proved too much to overcome. "Small guys can't raise any hell," Muhammad Ali said. It was poppycock until Duran ballooned into the welterweight division and became the butt of cruel jokes and insidious whispers. Since then, his knockout punch has disappeared and, at times, so has his enthusiasm.

"When you're fighting smear cases and you're the best fighter around," says Ray Arcel, the mouthpiece for Duran's braintrust, "it's hard to be interested."

Now that has changed. At twenty-nine, with the end rapidly closing in on him, Duran finds himself faced with a challenge so all-consuming that he doesn't care whether he steps into the ring as a 2-to-1 underdog or whether he takes home only one-fifth as much loot as Leonard. "I no happy for the money," Duran says. "I happy for the fight." Happy because this is his one real chance to wear another crown, to prove his greatness and to win the love he has been denied throughout his career.

On the surface, the need for love would seem totally foreign to Duran, and yet to see him being honored as one of the two Fighters of the Decade was to see the thing that could get him past Leonard. Never once did he fret that the New York boxing writers were abusing propriety by calling him Ali's equal. He had chills running down his spine, and he let it be known. "I speak English because I am learning from my teacher," he said. "I am glad to be here. I thank you very much for this award." For just a moment, those crazy eyes of his were calm and the room was quiet. For just a moment, you could tell what Roberto Duran will have on his side Friday night. Emotion.

At Long Last, Duran Can Rest Easy
Montreal
June 22, 1980

He was in bed now, his phone silenced by growls to the hotel operator and the hallway outside his room patroled by Panama's answer to the Prussian Guard. The well-wishers who were turned away nodded knowingly, their smiles saying that after a night of fighting and partying, even the strongest of men—even this champion—would have to sleep the sleep of the dead.

What none of them realized was that after he threw his last punch and before he set foot on the dance floor, Roberto Duran cried himself a river.

The tears streamed down his cheeks and into his scruffy beard. They came in rivulets that could not be stopped in the dressing room or in the limo carrying him to the celebration. They came and came and came, and it was not just because Duran had unhorsed Sugar Ray Leonard and been crowned king of the World Boxing Council's welterweights. It was also because he had defeated the demons he couldn't see.

"So much trouble, so much trouble," Luis Henriquez said in a hoarse whisper, and shook his head slowly, as if there were weights attached to it.

At Long Last, Duran Can Rest Easy

This was Saturday morning and Luis Henriquez, honorary Panamanian vice consul and friend of Roberto Duran, nevertheless managed to look impervious to suffering. He was leaning against a lushly papered wall in the Bonaventure Hotel, wearing a sport coat made of raw silk and flashing enough gold jewelry to finance an emerging nation. The only thing that didn't jibe with the rest of him was his line of conversation.

"Did you hear what that television announcer say about Roberto?" he asked. "Even after Roberto win, the announcer is saying he look like a villain and that he was a thief and all that bull. Listen, my friend, in the ghetto in Panama, all of us had to steal to eat."

If those days had a virtue, it was that the poor woke up every morning knowing they weren't going to get a break. After two weeks in Montreal, Henriquez wonders if breaks weren't just as hard to come by for an underdog in a championship fight, even if he was going to earn $2 million.

The underpinning for such skepticism is the five trips Duran was forced to take to the hospital and the three electrocardiogram tests to which he was subjected. "What was that all about?" Henriquez said. "They say Roberto has an irregular heartbeat? Fine. Check it out. But why again and again?" A sad smile. "They only make Leonard go once and then it was to another hospital. How do we know he even go?" That was the maddening, almost paranoid question that drove them into a memorable rage.

Duran's boiling juices were the easiest to spot, of course. The first punch he let fly Friday night caught Leonard squarely on the protective cup, and from that point on, good manners were past tense. "My guy's got lumps all over the joint," said Angelo Dundee, the sweetest thinker in Sugar Ray's corner. Duran hit Leonard with head, fists and, it is rumored, knees. And the reason he got away with it is that Freddie Brown was equally teed off about the shabby treatment Duran was getting.

"You ever see Freddie happy about anything?" Dundee asked. He had a point there. The three greatest joys in the seventy-four-year-old Brown's life appear to be molding fighters, chewing on cigars, and griping constantly. Next to eighty-one-year-old Ray Arcel, Duran's other trainer and a picture of pugilistic courtliness, Brown comes on like the wrath of God. "You think that ain't for a purpose?" said Dundee. "Hey, those two guys been around. They're as old as water."

No wonder referee Carlos Padilla didn't dare say anything when Brown accosted him in the ring before the fight. Padilla obviously respects his elders, even if they are shouting and waving fingers under his nose. "I seen the guy work before," Brown said. "He wouldn't let my fighter work inside and it cost him the fight. So this time I was straightening him out ahead of time. You know, tellin' him there'd be a Senate investigation if he didn't let these guys fight."

"Did you get what you wanted?" someone asked.

"No. Hell, no," said Brown. "Every time the ref broke 'em up, he pulled Duran away and held him while that damned Leonard sneaked a couple punches in."

Do not get the impression, however, that Sugar Ray overflowed with fistic inspiration. If anything, he waged the most chuckleheaded war of his career. He is an artist at sticking and moving, at attacking from one angle and then another, and yet he was bound and determined to go toe-to-toe with Duran. "Ray got all macho," Dundee said. "He thought he could beat the little mother at his own game." Obviously he was dreaming.

Oh, the three WBC judges scoring the fight did their utmost to keep Leonard in the hunt. Ignoring how cowardly it is to call a round even while using the ten-point-must system, one judge copped out ten times while the other two followed suit a total of nine times. Yet even that couldn't keep Duran from the unanimous decision that moved him to tears and shoved him to the kind of prominence he never had when he was the lightweight champion.

Suddenly, after fourteen years of knocking around the world's rings, he is a hot commodity among the welters. After giving up the battle to keep his weight down two years ago, he has advanced to boxing's new glamor division—a division that features Pipino Cuevas and Thomas Hearns as well as Leonard—and if the WBC won't pay him what he wants, then the World Boxing Association will. As Don King, the polysyllabic promoter, said Saturday: "Roberto will be happy to take on anyone in order to become a notch in the annals of immortality."

Please understand, though, that there are certin segments of society in which Duran's name already has been bronzed and put in the trophy case. In New York, the little drummer boy is very big at Latin music festivals. And at home in Panama, he is the reason for a holiday that began Friday and will run through Monday. Soon Duran will be there himself, dancing all night, eating what he pleases, and washing it down with his beloved Coca-Cola. Soon he will be there reveling in the fruits of his sacrifices, with no more sacrifices to make for the time being. Just let him sleep a while longer before he goes.

He Cramped His Own Style
Chicago
January 27, 1982

Good times never last long enough and bad ones always last too long. Barbershop philosophers can explain the phenomenon in a minute, but Roberto Duran gives the impression that he doesn't hang around barbershops. He has a head of inky black hair that he combs straight back, hair so wild and shaggy that it must be modeled after his pet lion's mane. The ragged pompadour suggests a man in a hurry, and Duran certainly was that until he got trapped by a moment's indiscretion.

Just a moment, nothing more. Oh, he may have thought about quitting earlier in the fight that rewrote his life. Sugar Ray Leonard was carving the macho right out of him that November night in 1980, hitting him at will and making him swing wildly and laughing with delight. Never in his fierce, crazy life had anyone done that to the urchin revered at home in Panama as Hands of Stone. But when Duran finally did something about it, when he decided that two minutes and forty-four seconds of the eighth round was as long as he could stand to be humiliated, the good times stopped and the bad ones began.

He meekly waved his right fist and uttered the words that haunt him still: "No mas! No more!" They echoed through the funky streets outside the Louisiana Superdome and on into boxing's infamous history. True, Duran has argued ever since that he was done in by stomach cramps, not cowardice. But it doesn't matter. He failed himself and his image when the world was watching, and in that fleeting instant, the good he had done for a far longer time in a far lesser light was rendered inconsequential.

Suddenly, he was the fight racket's answer to Roy Riegels, who ran the wrong way with a Rose Bowl fumble, and Tracy Stallard, who got nailed to the cross of Roger Maris' sixty-first home run, and Ralph Branca, who fed Bobby Thomson the gopher ball that cost the Dodgers a pennant. Duran had done something so memorably bad that its brevity didn't matter. And now it has lived so long and thrived so relentlessly that it seems he never did anything else.

How else can you judge your reaction to his assault on Wilfred Benitez' WBC junior middleweight championship? They will fight in Las Vegas Saturday night—age against youth, savagery against subtlety, scowl against smile, Panama against Puerto Rico—and the chemistry should be all you are thinking about. But it isn't, and Duran knows it, and everyone around him knows it. They can tell at a glance that you are thinking about his fall from grace, if you are thinking about him at all.

"A tremendous tragedy, a great tragedy," says Ray Arcel, his eighty-two-year-old trainer. "I don't condemn him for what he did in New Orleans. But it was a tremendous tragedy."

In the fifteen months since then, there has been no place for the tale of how Duran was born to the slums of Panama City and how he shined shoes, caught fish, and fought off the thugs who tried to prey on him. Once, he was a success story fashioned by his fists, a street child whose incomparable punch made him the pet of Panama's president and its richest man. He flattened a horse with a straight right and almost killed the poor devil who opposed him in his Madison Square Garden debut. He was a pro at fifteen, the world's lightweight king at twenty-one, the world's welterweight champ at Leonard's expense. He was truly Hands of Stone and then, in the rematch he sneeringly granted Sugar Ray, he showed his public what it never suspected he had—a heart of mush.

Even Arcel, who guarded him paternally before that

debacle and has returned to do so now, wept bitter tears in the long hours afterward. "Duran quit," the old man said, and the quaver in his voice fueled resentment. It was as if Duran had betrayed the people who thrilled at his rage, painted him as the embodiment of violence and bet their ranches on him. Now they were going to get him. They were going to make him pay for not being what they had imagined him to be. And most of them haven't let up yet.

The reaction is human enough—which of us has not dreamed of revenge of one kind or another?—but it fails to take into account that maybe Duran is human, too. He doesn't always show it, of course. Indeed, you can find him in Las Vegas sneering at reporters who ask him about the night he quit and why he thinks Leonard should give him another shot at the welterweight title. The studied surliness is vintage Duran, yet it may also mask the desperation that has come to mark his life.

At thirty-one, eight years Benitez' senior, his powers are slipping away faster than he discovered them. Though he snarls at the suggestion, surely he must know it is true. It has been happening since his insatiable appetite pushed him into the welters, a weight class where his knockout punch lost its authority and his reputation began to lose its lustre. Leonard drove the point home but, lest you forget, so did Zeferino Gonzalez before that and Nino Gonzalez and Luigi Minchillo afterward. Now the lethal Benitez awaits him with a dose of punishment, but no one begs Duran to turn back before it is too late, no one offers him the kindness that soothed Muhammad Ali and Joe Louis and so many other fallen champions.

In one sense, that may be only fair, for Duran never offered anyone mercy. Violence was his key to boxing's kingdom and so it shall also be his destruction. The violence he suffers, however, comes not just from the men he fights but from the public he betrayed on a night that should be nothing more than a line in the record book. For a moment, he forgot he was Roberto Duran and waved the white flag of surrender. He waved it until he realized his mistake, but by then there was no escape. His moment of shame would last him a lifetime.

The Warm-up Heats Up
Las Vegas
September 13, 1981

They don't need any of this. They really don't. All they want is to put Tommy Hearns on high and Sugar Ray Leonard on ice, but nobody out here in the devil's desert workshop seems to comprehend the purity of their purpose. The bright lights keep blinking, the dice keep rolling, and the hookers keep marching from one side of Las Vegas Boulevard to the other to peddle their questionable wares. Temptation curls a come-hither finger at every turn, and when the friends of Tommy Hearns think they are about to succumb, they hide behind the absurd. They pretend they are back home in Detroit.

It seems a defense designed by a masochist until you bow to the fact that on the east side of recession-ravaged Motown, in the middle of poverty's Desolation Row, there stands a dream temple called the Kronk Gymnasium. From its basement boxing factory comes a spirit that defies the street punks smoking reefer out front and the junkies nodding off in the hotel across the way. It doesn't matter that you can dent your skull on low-hanging water pipes or that the ring sits on the floor. Tommy Hearns and the multitude in his wake—each in a gold-and-red Kronk T-shirt, each seemingly the owner of a 15-0 record—understand that now. The indignities of the past were just a warmup, a tank-town preliminary if you will. Vegas is the big test and Leonard is the holy war.

They've got to be tough.

They've got to be loud.

"Ladies and gentlemen," says Shelly Saltman, the Hearns mouthpiece whose next quiet day will be his first one, "history will be made at this workout. When Thomas Hearns walks through the door over there, we're going to play for the first time a record that you'll be hearing a lot of in the months to come, a record that will go on sale next Wednesday. The title of it is 'We Are the Champions,' the group singing it— I'm sure you've all heard of them—is the Dramatics, and the lead singer is a young fellow from Detroit by the name of . . . Thomas Hearns."

Too bad he couldn't carry a tune if it was in his suitcase. But then there are a lot of things he can't do. Can't skip rope, can't make the speed bag do tricks, can't recite the last page of *The Great Gatsby*. Tommy Hearns just knocks people out.

There have been thirty of them in his thirty-two professional fights, thirty left stiff as mackerels as he marched undefeated to the World Boxing Association's welterweight championship and the chance to snatch Leonard's World Boxing Council title. The damage has been done with a right hand forged in the Kronk, and surely forged is as accurate a word as there could be in this case. For in the Kronk, the temperature always bubbles in the nineties, just the way it is in the Caesars Palace Sports Pavilion, the cement quonset hut where Hearns is stoking his furnace now.

"Hot enough for you?" someone asks Emanuel Steward, the hardnose who has driven Hearns and himself to the top.

"It's never too hot," Steward replies without a smile.

Maybe he would change his mind if he got a load of Angelo Dundee, who doubles as goodwill ambassador and master tactician of the Leonard camp. Dundee has a wife soaking up sun by the pool, the latest in tennis clothes on his body, and a joke he hopes is fresh. "You hear about Reagan and Begin?" he asks. Nobody has. Everything is just the way Dundee and Leonard and everybody else on their side of the fence like it. Everything is cool.

The closed workout, a good-luck charm that helped clear the way to the humiliation of Roberto Duran, is over. The tape that patched a hole in the canvas protecting Leonard from prying eyes has been removed. The collection of movies in Sugar Ray's suite has been readied for another night of taking his mind off the fifteen rounds or less that await him Wednesday night. "We watched Bruce Lee, the kung-fu man, in *Street Fighter* the other day," Leonard says, "but I don't think I'm going to borrow any ideas from him. And I'm definitely not going to fight in the street. You don't get paid for that."

He has everything Tommy Hearns doesn't. He can turn on the television and see himself peddling Seven-Up. He can answer the phone and listen to none other than Muhammad Ali tell him that this is "a fight for the ages, a rumble that's gonna rearrange the planets." He can laugh at the memory of Shelly Saltman trying to put him on one train and Hearns on another, start each fighter on a different coast, and have them spar their way across the country until they collided at mid-continent. And all Tommy Hearns and his friends can do is work all day, work a little longer.

The scheming is up to Emanuel Steward, and he obviously is up to it. Just last Thursday, he fired off a telegram to the WBA proposing that the welterweight brawl might just as well be for Leonard's junior middleweight championship, too. "You can talk about a separate fight," Steward says, "but I think Ray's gonna get messed up so bad in this one that people won't want to see him in the ring again."

Steward smiles at last, smiles so evilly that there couldn't be a more perfect villain for the cartoon fight he has just scripted.

Beside him, Hearns drums his fingers nervously.

The noise is deafening, or maybe that is just your imagination adding to the havoc cobra-thin Tommy has wrought in training. He has broken jaws, carved up faces, and done more damage than napalm in a dry forest. "These aren't bums he's sparring with, either," Steward says. "They don't drink all night, then come out knowing they're gonna get their asses kicked. These guys are contenders." But Hearns chops them into ground beef, cuts them up and waits for Sugar Ray to enter his slaughterhouse. "It's my turn to do commercials," he says. "I hope they're not as hard to do as the Johnny Carson show." It would sound like a joke if Hearns laughed. He doesn't.

"I don't understand that," says Mike Trainer, the Washington, D.C., lawyer whose brains are a perfect complement for Leonard's fists. "I don't understand any of the things they're doing over there. All that running around and screaming. Beating up sparring partners the way they do. Really, what kind of person is Tommy Hearns?"

Angelo Dundee provides an answer of sorts by—what else?—cracking wise. He is filming a television interview, and the lady sportscaster wants the cameraman to take a shot of her over Dundee's shoulder. He is supposed to keep talking for appearance's sake, not for the sake of anything that will make it onto the tape. So he stares at this sweet young thing and says: "I'll tell you what Tommy Hearns is. He's a guy who likes boys better than girls. That's the truth, really it is."

The word will get back to Hearns soon enough, and the

anger inside him will rise a little higher, the punches he throws will burrow a little deeper. Don't tell him Dundee was joking. Tommy Hearns doesn't believe in jokes. Not now anyway.

No Grit Rings So True as Vito's
Las Vegas
November 30, 1979

It is a fighter's face, with the nose steamrollered and the eyes turned sad and ugly by scar tissue. Vito Antuofermo wears it proudly through casino crowds of friends who tell him he used to be a handsome kid and strangers who flinch at the residue of 300 hasty stitches.

There is an equation involved, one that seems simple to Vito Antuofermo: If he weren't willing to suffer, there would be no crowds and he wouldn't be the middleweight champion of the world. But the outsiders are repelled by such harsh logic, and when he turns to the fight crowd for spiritual sustenance, he hears only cruel laughter.

In dank gyms and stuffy arenas, wise guys belittle him as the second coming of Chuck Wepner, the Bayonne Bleeder, the human punching bag who once got cut by the first sharp in the National Anthem. And what can Vito Antuofermo say in return? Can he tell them he has never taken more than eight stitches in one sitting? Can he lecture them on what the scars symbolize? He tries, but it does no good.

"At least my wife loves me," he says forlornly.

She sits at home in Brooklyn with the month-old son who will never know what his father really looked like or, maybe, never even know his father as a champion. The oddsmakers, you see, have cast Vito Antuofermo as a 4-to-1 underdog to lose his title to Marvin Hagler at Caesars Palace Friday night, and Marvin Hagler has already started punching.

"Isn't it tough training out here with all the beautiful women wandering around?" someone asks him.

"Hey, man, I haven't had sex for two months," Marvin Hagler replies. "But every time I see a lady I like, I just put Vito's face on her body and the desire goes away."

It is such an inviting target, this face with the brows that jut out over the eyes like balconies. The big hitters and the big talkers bang away at it ceaselessly, and only rarely does it dawn on them that another part of Vito Antuofermo's anatomy means much more to him in the ring—his heart.

Without it, he would not be the one champion on the planet who is recognized by both the World Boxing Association and the World Boxing Council. Nor would he have peered through a veil of blood last June to knock the crown off Hugo Corro's head. Nor would he have risked his old job loading soft-drink delivery trucks all those times he sneaked away to fight four-rounders for $75. But he did, and still he must listen to the rhapsodies about what Marvin Hagler had to endure before he got a title shot.

"I don't understand," Vito Antuofermo says. "So what if Hagler had to wait? I didn't get no fight for the championship until I'd fought forty-eight times. And I fought a lotta guys that had been champions—Corro, Emile Griffith, Denny Moyer, that guy Dagge in Germany. The only guy Hagler fought that was recognized all over the world was Benny Briscoe, and I beat Briscoe before he did. Now you tell me what's the big deal about Hagler."

The sentiment is understandable, for Vito Antuofermo takes a back seat to no one when it comes to rising above his roots. Born twenty-six years ago in Bari, Italy, the center of grape country, he emigrated to Brooklyn at fifteen with his mother and father, brothers and sisters, aunts and uncles. "My father wanted to make it better for us," he says. All the brood got for openers, however, was a two-room hovel.

There would be no school for Vito Antuofermo. He spent his days on a construction job and his nights trying to figure out what was happening. "I couldn't speak no English," he says. "Everything was pretty much by hand." Or fist.

He fought a lot—for squatters' rights on street corners, for girls, for the hell of it. And finally he fought too much. The cops slapped the cuffs on him and tossed him in the rear of a squad car. "Tough guy, huh?" one of the cops said as they pulled away. Vito Antuofermo didn't answer. The cop kept talking until he realized why the kid was so quiet. "Then he started in on me in this broken kind of Italian," Vito

Antuofermo says. "That's how I found out about the Police Athletic League gym."

The story belongs to another time in this country, a time when immigrant kids got off the boat and punched their way out of poverty. Yet it is hard to believe that even the old-timers could have added such nice touches to their tales. For one minute Vito Antuofermo was getting his first professional fight as a substitute for a preliminary boy who didn't show up, and the next he was looking for the cop who steered him straight.

"It's kinda hard, you know?" he says. "I never even learned the cop's name."

A decade later, Vito Antuofermo wouldn't make the same mistake. He is a different person, and not just because he has a 45-3-1 record and a championship. He has a working relationship with the English language and enough poise to do public relations for the outfit he used to load trucks for. Why, when Marvin Hagler presented him with a Vito the Mosquito flyswatter the other day, he responded with a pair of boxing shoes whose soles bore a special message: "Have a Coke and a Smile. And Good Night."

While the challenger struggled in vain for a retort, Vito Antuofermo laughed and laughed and laughed. It was only the scars over his eyes that made him look like he was crying.

Champion of the Wait Class
Chicago
September 30, 1981

They sang "God Bless America" the night Marvelous Marvin Hagler won the championship that boxing's power brokers had kept away from him for so long. It was in the wee small hours of the morning, in an out-of-the-way London hotel, and the people around him—his manager and trainers and sparring partners—thought they had run out of ways to celebrate the fury with which their tiger had ripped the middleweight title off homeboy Alan Minter's head. Then there was a stroke of inspiration born in the memory of the fight's angry ending and the bottles full of beer that had rained down on them as retribution for the blood Minter spilled.

It had been the War of 1812 all over again, and somehow "God Bless America" seemed meet and right in the aftermath. So they belted it out the way they still do every time Hagler wins another big one. They had their anthem of triumph, a source of communal pride beyond hokiness, and the only thing they might do to improve it now is to add a verse blessing Marvelous Marvin himself because, Lord, he has suffered for his art.

The pain, as anyone can tell by examining his 56-2-2 record, has been more mental than physical. He is black, left-handed, and unwilling to sell his soul to either Bob Arum or Don King, and for all of that, he has paid. In the unhappy days before he ruled both the World Boxing Association and World Boxing Council, Hagler saw champions dodge him, got stuck with a controversial draw the first time he got his hands on Vito Antuofermo and, finally, had to travel across the Atlantic knowing the only way he could beat Minter in England was to destroy him.

"People thought they was cutting the heart out of me," Hagler says, "but all they was really doing was making me meaner. Ain't no sense in telling you I changed since I been champion, either. Anybody tries to hurt me I'll hurt 'em back worse."

There is something about the way Marvelous Marvin's eyes turn cold and flinty during his discourse that should make believers of everyone within listening distance. Yet Paddy Flood, one of boxing's few remaining merry pranksters, insists that the guy should go one-on-one with a lie detector before further attempts at sounding as tough as he looks. "What kinda gobbage is he trying to feed us?" Flood asks in his best Brooklyneese. "Who is this bum anyway?" For those asking the same about the gentleman speaking, it should be noted that he manages and trains Mustafa Hamsho, otherwise known as the Syrian Buzzsaw, and Hamsho will go after Hagler's crown at the Horizon Saturday night, and there you have the reason for the difference in opinion.

"I'm getting Marvelous Marvin crazy," Flood confides. "I keep telling him that he's a dirty fighter, that he uses that shaved head of his to cut people up. He gets all teed off, and then I really go after him. I tell him I got Al Braverman coming in, and Al Braverman's been teaching Mustafa how to fight dirty for two months. Like Al Braverman is a Mafia hit man or something."

"But has he really been teaching Mustafa to fight dirty?" someone asks.

"Sure," Flood replies cheerfully.

The answer makes Hagler wish he were marching off to war against Flood, not Hamsho. "What I got against Hamsho?" Marvelous Marvin wants to know. "He can't hardly talk English. Paddy Flood's the one doing the talking. But he ain't the one gonna be getting in the ring, so I guess it's Hamsho's head I gotta beat in." Seldom have the principles of success in the Sweet Science been simplified so beautifully.

Then again, maybe there never has been a fighter who, at twenty-nine, appreciated his success as much as Hagler does. "I had all those bad times," he says, "and now I know why I stuck with it." He has basked in the love of Brockton, Massachusetts, his adopted hometown and the birthplace of Rocky Marciano. He has heard a Boston rock 'n' roll band sing an ode called "Marvelous Marvin" to him. He has gazed for hours at the sterling silver globe that British boxing officials gave him for dethroning Minter and surviving the riot afterward. But the biggest prize of all awaits him Saturday night: For working fifteen rounds or less, he will be paid $1 million, which is not only $250,000 more than WBA heavyweight champion Mike Weaver will make on the same card, but more than any middleweight ever made anywhere.

"I like the money, I like it a lot," says Hagler, who is as eager as anyone to retire young, "but it ain't gonna change me." As if to prove it, he turned down the chance to do the color commentary on the cable telecast of the showdown between two other undersized millionaires, Sugar Ray Leonard and Tommy Hearns. Marvelous Marvin had begun training for Hamsho by then and he wasn't about to break away for a meaningless fling at celebrity. "I'm a fighter," he says. "Nothing else."

Such restrained rhetoric hardly befits an age of nonstop self-promotion, but that is not to suggest that Hagler is without ego or goals. He has both, in proportions as big as the punch that has stacked up forty-three knockouts for him. "I want to bring the respect back to the middleweight division," he says. "I don't want to be no cheese champion like they had lately. I want to be great like Sugar Ray Robinson and Jack LaMotta." Granted, he may have to wait for Leonard and Hearns to grow into his weight class before he has a shot at the magnitude he dreams of, but patience is a virtue he is long on.

Hagler perfected it in the endless years before his friends and countrymen sang "God Bless America" in that London hotel room twelve months ago. There were plenty of opportunities for him to pack it in—the rotten decision he lost to Bobby "Boogaloo" Watts in 1976, for instance, or even the bloody draw with Antuofermo—and now they don't matter. He has survived to win the undisputed championship, to throttle Antuofermo in their rematch, to become a millionaire middleweight.

He has endured in man's cruelest sport and now he waits like a Venus's-flytrap for Hamsho, for Leonard, for Hearns, for any fighter bold enough to want a piece of him.

He waits, and there is nobody better at it.

A Touch of Class
Miami
November 12, 1982

Class always tells. It speaks volumes about where a man has been and where he is going, and maybe it can also point others in new directions. At least that is what you wind up thinking when you see Aaron Pryor, the World Boxing Association's junior welterweight king, putting a white cap on his gold tooth and refusing to insult the wrong people. He has taken a lesson in class, and that tells a lot about Alexis Arguello, the best challenger an untamed champion ever had.

In a sport long on both sweat-stained T-shirts and ersatz finery, Arguello is a custom-tailored, double-breasted blue blazer. He looks like a Nicaraguan Omar Sharif, handles himself like a diplomat, and sounds like he ought to be selling Monet originals to Palm Beach dowagers. "To throw a punch through the air, to make it land where you want it to," he says, "that is an art, a beautiful art." Predictably, when Pryor first heard that, he mistook Arguello's appreciation of beauty for a weakness of the spine.

There was no energy expended considering the three world titles Arguello has won in other divisions or the seventy-six victories and sixty-two knockouts he has rung up in eighty fights. There was no time for contemplating the history Arguello would make by winning a fourth championship or the arguments that already call him our greatest active boxer. There was just the macho cry that meant so much on the streets of Cincinnati where Pryor grew up poor and tough: "I want that sissy! I want him right away!" Yet now that Pryor has him, now that they are counting down to their fifteen-round showdown in the Orange Bowl Friday night, you can see how things have changed since Arguello stepped up beside the champion and wrapped an arm around his shoulder as if to tell him they are brothers in an ugly business.

"We are not just boxers," Arguello says. "We are human beings, too, and I respect all human beings. Respect is a beautiful thing, although the writers may not think so when they ask me questions. I cannot predict that I will beat Aaron Pryor. Maybe I won't. I will try; that is all that I can do. I wish Aaron Pryor good luck and I wish myself good luck, too."

And Pryor says, "I agree with Alexis." The refrain is there whether they are discussing their pleasure at the size of the purse—$1.6 million for the champion, $1.5 million for the challenger—or the wisdom of Sugar Ray Leonard's theatrical retirement. Deep down, Pryor may believe that, at twenty-seven, he is too young for the thirty-year-old Arguello and that his buzz saw style will overwhelm the perpetually slow-starting challenger. But Pryor is too classy for such brash pronouncements now, and perhaps too wary as well.

"Alexis is a different type of fighter—just look at the way he's dressed," says the champion, himself a devotee of ski caps and jogging suits. "Alexis is conservative, he don't mess up, and he fights the same way. If you make mistakes, he'll compensate you for them. Yeah, you guys like him so much because he's nice, got so much style. But I'll tell you something: When he gets you in trouble, he forgets how nice he is.

He takes you home."

The choice of words is intriguing, for Arguello can't go home again. Though his picture hangs next to Jesus Christ's throughout his native Nicaragua, though his battle with Pryor will be televised there despite a countrywide ban on boxing, he is persona non grata with the ruling Sandinista regime. Maybe it is because he once rode in a motorcade with the now-overthrown dictator, Anastasio Somoza, or maybe it is because he let himself become an honorary lieutenant in Somoza's bloodthirsty national guard. In both cases, the politically naive Arguello stepped out of character and defied the advice of his mentor, Dr. Eduardo Roman. But it wasn't until the Sandinistas took power in the civil war of 1979 that he realized the smoke he smelled was from the bridge he had burned behind him.

The Sandinistas seized his home and his car, his chicken-raising business and the $500,000 he had in the bank. They drove him into exile in a Miami suburb, penniless and petrified, and it didn't seem to matter that his teenage brother, Eduardo, died fighting for their cause. When Arguello squared off against Bazooka Limon, he carried a Nicaraguan flag into the ring to mourn his brother's passing and the chaos in his beloved country, and the Sandinistas refused to believe that his grief was personal, not political. "If I try to return home," he says, "I will be killed."

So he dwells in a land where he is free to be who he wants to be, free to rebuild his fortune, free to try to become the first fighter ever to win four titles. "If you want something, you must go get it," he says, and that is as close as he comes to talking about the killer instinct that already has made him the WBA's featherweight champion and the World Boxing Council's lightweight and junior lightweight champion. Only five other fighters have worn three crowns at once, an accomplishment that would stamp Arguello as special if he weren't already special in another, more important way.

You could sense it when he embraced Ray "Boom Boom" Mancini after thrashing him last year, embraced that tough little mutt and told him to take good care of the father to whom he had fruitlessly dedicated the fight. And the feeling remains whether Arguello is calling promoter Bob Arum

"Mr. Bob" in all sincerity or refusing to make his admirers pay to watch him work out. But never does the essence of the man shine brighter than when he dismisses the trauma of winning and losing.

It is all around him and Pryor, of course. It is part and parcel of any fight for any championship, yet Arguello refuses to cave in to the hype and the hysteria. Someone else can gape at the money these two little big men are pulling down. Someone else can babble happily about how this will be the fight of the year. "I must remember one thing," Arguello says. "I am still the same person no matter what happens. I am still a human being." In that case, he can never lose.

For Pryor, the Party's Not Over
Miami
November 14, 1982

His voice was a whisper that kept getting carried away by the tropical breeze caressing the courtyard. What he had to say was shouted down again and again by the ache in his ribs and the pain in his swollen fists. He should have been resting, but the postcard sunshine had lured him out of his hotel room, out to where the men with questions lay in wait, and when he tried to smile at them, they could see a fleck of blood in the white of his left eye. Aaron Pryor was the winner.

He had gone to the hospital to see the loser Saturday morning and discovered that Alexis Arguello was already home with his broken nose and his stitched-up eye and whatever tears he had left to cry. For thirteen rounds in the Orange Bowl Friday night, Arguello had waged a classic war for Pryor's junior welterweight championship, only to be brought up short in the fourteenth by one concussive right-hand lead. Then Pryor had pinned him against the ropes and battered him with a lack of mercy that was, at least in part, a tribute to Arguello's stature. "I never fought a man like that before," Pryor said in his morning-after whisper, and the courtyard grew very still.

For what had transpired barely twelve hours earlier had been the greatest fight since Muhammad Ali and Joe Frazier dueled in Manila—the greatest for sustained fury and brilliant cruelty and somber postscripts. It was a terrible thing to behold, yet you couldn't take your eyes off the punishment Pryor the dervish and Arguello the craftsman inflicted on each other in this campaign to prove that size doesn't matter in the ring. The challenger was seeking his fourth title, seeking a goal no one has ever attained, and the champion was struggling for the esteem that only a crown can bring him, and their violence hypnotized you.

They were so perfectly matched, so elegantly brutal that one of the officials scoring the fight ruled five rounds even while the other two said the same of four. In another time, another ring, the officials would have been chastised as cowards for such a performance with pen and paper, but this time they were reflecting exactly what they were witnessing—a battle so well-balanced that it would not end until twenty-seven-year-old Aaron Pryor dipped down into the reserve of dignity no one knew he had.

"I was glad to have the opportunity to let a lot of people know that I fight from my heart," said the undefeated king of the World Boxing Association's 140-pounders. "There's people who don't understand me and some of the things I do, but when I fight, I fight for my pride."

Surely Pryor had tried to make his point before Friday night. Surely he had done his best to prove that he is more than his pock-marked track record would have you believe. But always there was Arguello, and with his courtly manner, his double-breasted blazers, his tales of being exiled from his beloved Nicaragua, he represented what Pryor was never supposed to be outside the ring or inside it. Lord, how that must have grated at the champion and the countless minions surrounding him. Yet Pryor played along as best he could, showing up on time for press conferences and asking for moments of silence for dead fighters, and even after he had walked out of the ring victorious, he held his tongue. One of his court jesters, alas, could not.

"Why you always writing that Aaron had two wives?" Booker Griffin whined to the reporters he found in the hotel lobby Saturday morning. "Why don't you ever tell the people Arguello had three?"

"Because none of Arguello's wives ever shot him," came the reply.

For Pryor, the Party's Not Over

It didn't matter that Theresa Pryor hugged and kissed her husband when the photographers focused on her after the fight, or that she vowed she would never try to hit him in the face even if she does own a black belt in karate. The bullet that scraped Aaron Pryor's midsection two years ago left him scarred in more ways than one.

From that day forward, you expected only the worst from Pryor, and he never seemed to let you down. If he wasn't trying to break a contract with his manager, he was losing a paternity suit back home in Cincinnati. If he wasn't flitting from one promoter to another—he may have been the first great fighter Don King gladly watched join forces with Bob Arum—he was partying when he should have been training. Erratic was the best word to describe him, and the only time it didn't seem to apply was when Sugar Ray Leonard walked into the room or simply got mentioned in a conversation. "Aaron has always been paranoid about Leonard," said Pryor's estranged manager, Buddy LaRosa. "He was jealous of Leonard, just crazy jealous." It was consistency of the most exasperating sort.

Now, however, it may have evaporated after a week that Leonard began by retiring from the ring and ended by watching Pryor rise up and smite Arguello. The Sugar Man was there as a cable-television sportscaster, an electronic totem geared to building ratings, while Pryor strutted toward glory in new-found freedom. "Sugar Ray gone," the champion's trainer, Panama Lewis, observed as if he were speaking of the dead. "Aaron the man now."

He has been released from the shackles of his emotions. He can tell the boxing world that he wants to fight Boom Boom Mancini next and the boxing world will pay attention. He can say he is heading for Las Vegas to boogie, then stay in Miami to check on a fallen foe, and no one will growl about his indecisiveness. And it is all because of the message he hammered onto Arguello's head and shoulders.

"Maybe it was a great fight," Pryor said. "Myself, I'm still trying to figure out what went on in there." His voice was softer than ever now as fatigue and pain battled to consume him. He had thrown too many punches, and caught too many as well, and that was all he knew. Soon enough, the gladhanders would be hoisting him to their shoulders, echoing his trainer's praise and carrying him to the gaudy retreats where his seductive old demons dwell. The party would start shortly, and the very thought of it left you wondering if Aaron Pryor wouldn't be safer marching off to another war.

Postscript

It was farewell for Roberto Duran after he lost to Wilfred Benitez, or so we were told. As for Vito Antuofermo, nobody has heard from him since his moan signaled the last stitch in his face. Though they are better off for being gone, they probably would give anything to trade places with Tommy Hearns and Marvin Hagler. Hearns must rebound from his loss to Sugar Ray Leonard and Hagler must count the days until his competition catches up with him. For little men, big loads.

7.
Beautiful Losers

If you saw On the Waterfront, *I'm sure you remember the scene. Marlon Brando is the ex-fighter who got snookered into taking a dive and now he is sitting in the back seat of a cab with Rod Steiger, the brother who deceived him. "I coulda been somebody," Brando says mournfully. "I coulda been a contender." The thought echoes through the Sweet Science like a funeral dirge, yet I am not sure it does justice to many of the men who utter it. I have seen enough courage, resilience, and integrity in dank gyms and forgotten arenas to believe that you don't have to be a champion to be somebody.*

Murderer Loses His Right to Punch Free
Marion, Ohio
March 7, 1977

Prison is bad enough when you have been on the skids from day one. It is even worse when you have had something and lost it.

Tap City Harris, Inmate No. 136132 at the Marion Correctional Institution, thinks about that a lot in the gray light of Cell 16, Cell Block 5. Four and a half years ago, he was a professional boxer with a 25-0 record and designs on a championship. Now he is an admitted murderer desperately looking for a way to salvage his life.

The best way he knows is boxing, and Sunday he got the best chance he has had to do anything about it since the prison doors slammed shut behind him. He was fighting before 1,399 fellow inmates in the MCI gym as an added attraction in the latest installment of Don King's U.S. Boxing Championships.

The fight would mean nothing to Tap City Harris and it would mean everything to him. Even if he won, he would not get another big-time bout, for the tournament must move on while he stays put. But if he won—and won big—people from the outside would know who he was. They would know his plight. And they might be willing to help write his parole.

It was a wonderful dream until Tap City Harris clambered through the ring ropes and discovered he was in the middle of a nightmare.

His opponent was Johnny Heard of Chicago, a nobody with just three wins who didn't turn pro until he was thirty-three. Heard should have been a pushover, but he didn't topple easily. He fought from an odd crouched stance that made him seem more like a dwarf than an overweight middleweight.

The effect on Harris was devastating. He was awkward and tentative. A study in confusion. He didn't throw his first decent punch, a crisp left, until the third round. And even though he went on to land enough telling blows to make Heard surrender after the fourth, Harris had been forgettable when he wanted to be memorable.

In his dressing room, he tried at first to cover his failure with braggadacio that is clichéd no matter what side of the bars you are on. "I would have got him in the next round," he said. "I would have knocked him out." But the lie failed to convince even the man who was telling it.

"I'm sorry I didn't look better," Harris said mournfully. "I wanted all you reporters to come in here and rave, 'Boy, you a tough stud.'"

But the reporters said nothing of the kind. Finally the twenty-five-year-old Harris started interviewing them. He asked the ones who had seen him in his last main event, back in 1972, how far his skills had eroded.

"Well," one reporter said hesitantly, "you weren't putting your combinations together the way you used to."

"You looked rusty," another reporter said.

Tap City Harris slowly put down his can of soda. "You don't think I'm through, do you?" he said.

It was a poignant ending for what Don King called "a convivial gathering." No one had more reason to be convivial than King. He was back in the same slammer where he did four years as a convict. But he was back as the P.T. Barnum of boxing.

He watched the fights with Joe Louis on one side of him and Warden E.P. Perrini on the other.

He puffed a foot-long cigar and flashed a diamond ring the size of a baby's fist. Still, he could not forget what it was like to be No. 125734.

He met inmates who were at MCI when he arrived on October 15, 1967, and were there when he left on September 29, 1971, and are still there. "Hey, Jackson," he said to one, "I thought you'd gone home."

When the mayor of Marion gave him the key to the city the other day King said, "I didn't get no keys the last time I was here."

And when he pulled up outside MCI's twin barbed-wire fences Sunday in a blue, chauffeur-driven limousine, he recalled his first ride to prison. "They had a bunch of us in an old truck," he said, "and we were all chained like animals."

He was doing one to twenty for manslaughter. Ronald "Tap City" Harris, who grew up in the same Cleveland ghetto as King, has it tougher. He is doing ten to life for second-degree murder. "My mother was attacked, beaten up, and robbed by some maniac," he said, "and I ran into him by chance."

When Harris did, he pumped five bullets into him. The only thing Harris could do afterward was plead guilty.

"I have a debt to pay society," Harris said. "I've been paying it for the past four-and-a-half years. Now I think I deserve a second chance. I hope society thinks I deserve a second chance. That's one of the reasons I was fighting. There was important people out there watching, people who can help me."

"Who?" someone asked.

"Wasn't the governor out there?" Harris said. "Yeah. Him mainly."

When Harris entered the ring for the day's last fight, however, another important person was out there—Michael Dokes, now a promising young heavyweight but once a kid Harris used to provide with candy money. Dokes tried to make Harris believe that his nickname stands for someone going for broke, not for someone who is broke. "This is for freedom," Dokes yelled. "Fight for it, baby."

But when Dokes and Don King and all the outsiders who came with them were gone Sunday night, Tap City Harris was still in Cell 16, Cell Block 5, wondering if he will ever be free.

Some Dreams Never Go Down for the Count
Chicago
October 26, 1977

The bad back had gone out on him four days before, but Big Jim Beattie showed up at the Aragon Ballroom anyway. He is thirty-four years old and the ache in his sacroiliac was far worse than the first time he felt it, a decade ago. And still he had flown down from St. Paul believing he would be ready to fight in the semi-main event. You would think Big Jim Beattie would know better by now.

There was no mistaking him as he strode through the decaying lobby Tuesday night, for even in this age of mammoth heavyweights, nobody can match his dimensions of six feet nine inches and 240 pounds. When the curious and the concerned asked him about his display of—what was it, courage or foolhardiness?—he shrugged it off as a debt to Ernie Terrell, the pug turned promoter, after pestering him for action for nine months. "We go back a long ways," Beattie said. "We were on the same card in Madison Square Garden three times. Of course, Ernie always had bigger billing." And that was supposed to explain everything. You would think Big Jim Beattie would know better by now.

With him was his nine-year-old son Jeff, all red hair and eyes as big as silver dollars. The two of them munched popcorn and watched the fights from seats next to the eagle eyes from the State Athletic Commission. Beattie had to rise just once, when Terrell introduced him to the roistering crowd. "Here he is," boomed Terrell, "the Great White Hope." Beattie was standing tall and handsome in a corner of the ring when he heard the words by which he will forever be identified. They made him flinch. You would think Big Jim Beattie would know better by now.

Only seven years ago, he quit boxing because he hated what it was doing to him. He celebrated his decision by getting a role in the film version of the Broadway hit *The Great White Hope*. He played the title character. "I was acting a part I lived," he says.

It was not a life James J. Beattie sought. True, he had spent the summer of his sixteenth year fighting all comers for a traveling carnival, and true, he had won fifty of fifty-five amateur fights, thirty-eight by knockout. But all this Minnesota farm boy wanted to obtain with his fists was a college education. He thought he had a boxing scholarship to the University of Wisconsin until one of the school's fighters was killed in the ring and boxing was de-emphasized. Then the man who had steered him to Wisconsin had another idea: Why didn't he turn professional? "No matter what sort of doubts I had," says Beattie, "I knew I was too good a fighter not to."

His supposed benefactor steered him toward a New York-based consortium headed by Gene Schoor, the author-restaurateur. They had been looking for a white heavyweight, taking out ads in *The New York Times* and promising up to $150,000 a year, but they had no luck until the dubious Beattie fell into their laps. "It didn't take long for them to win me over," he says. "I was a poor farm boy and they came at me with fists full of $100 bills. I'd never even seen a $100 bill before."

Beattie received only $50 more than that a week for his efforts, and in the beginning, his efforts were just what the Schoor gang had dreamed of. He knocked out each of his first three opponents in one round. Then he ran into an artless brute named John Barrazza and was beaten bloody before he collapsed in the fifth round. When the hospital finally released him six days later, his troubles really began.

"Schoor and his buddies had me pegged as a smart ass," says Beattie. "I never knew who was calling the shots on my career, but I kept asking questions. I guess they got tired of me after I lost for the first time, because when they got the chance, they set me up. I got assassinated. I walked into a buzz saw."

The buzz saw's name was Jim Woody, and after he was through, the New York State Athletic Commission revoked the carved-up Beattie's license. Scared, confused, Beattie, just twenty-three, went home to Minnesota and tried to fight again. He lasted almost four years before he walked into consecutive knockout punches thrown by Buster Mathis and

Tommy Fields. "I thought I'd be better off living off my reputation in boxing," he says of his 1969 decision to retire. "After all, I was Big Jim Beattie."

He got in the movies, he owned real estate, and he had pieces of drug stores, fast-food restaurants, life insurance companies, and an outfit that manufactured emergency-squad equipment. Everything was fine. Until his business partner died. Until the economy got tight and the banks started calling in their loans. Until he tried to ease the pain with pills and booze. "I became my drug stores' best customer," he says.

It took Beattie ten months to dry out. In the process, he ballooned to 300 pounds. His New Year's resolution for 1974 was to pare the bountiful flab. The first forty pounds were easy, the final twenty an impossibility save for one method: He had to get back in the ring. Thus was begun the comeback that found Big Jim Beattie in the Aragon Ballroom Tuesday night, sporting seven straight victories and cursing his aching back for costing him what he was sure would have been his eighth.

To listen to him, it was hard to believe that this was the executive director of Nexus, Inc., a community treatment center for chronic young lawbreakers. Nor did he sound a bit like the community-theater thespian who will play Lenny in *Of Mice and Men* and who missed his first flight to Chicago because he was filming a TV commercial. Instead, for a few hours, he was simply one more fighter with a dream.

"It has nothing to do with being the Great White Hope," Beattie said. "Maybe once that gave me an identity, made me somebody. But now it's just a part I played in a movie. Now I've learned to love boxing because it excites me the way nothing else can, and there aren't many things that give you a real tingle. I'll tell you what else. I think I can be the heavyweight champion of the world. It's only in the last couple years that I've matured physically and mentally, and I really think I can be champ. I'm not kidding myself. I don't do that."

You would think Big Jim Beattie would know better by now.

Fight Game Has Lira on the Ropes
*Chicago
July 1, 1979*

The leg was full of buckshot, put there by a teenaged gangster hiding in the dark of an alley. The doctors said amputate and Johnny Lira's mother and father agreed. But when they came around to get the kid's name on the dotted line, Johnny Lira told them to go spit in their hats. Once the coast had cleared, he got a friend to sneak into the hospital with a pair of crutches and a fifth of vodka—and off Johnny Lira went for a month on the lam. He poured some of the vodka on the leg to kill the pain. The rest he drank.

Ten years later, the story still lives on the street corners and front porches of the hard-scrabble Italian stronghold where Johnny Lira became a man before his time. Now, at twenty-six, he struts through the West Side on the leg he made the doctors save, and everybody knows him, says hello to him, gives him respect. It starts with the elders and carries all the way down to the angels with dirty faces playing softball in front of the Union League Boys Club.

"Hey, who's the toughest guy in the neighborhood?" he shouts.

"You are, Johnny," the angels sing.

Too bad the neighborhood stops at Grand and Ashland. Too bad for Johnny Lira. Because in the territory beyond, there are men who care not how tough he is; their fountain pens make them tougher. And though Johnny Lira is fighting the idea, fighting it with everything in his barbed-wire body, he is losing this one on points. If that weren't the case, he would still be the U.S. lightweight boxing champion.

He lost the title on a curious technicality: He and his manager, Mike Sarge, didn't get along. The schism between them was so wide that Sarge, who deals out of Las Vegas, never even bothered to tell the defeated Johnny Lira what was happening. Instead, he sent a telegram bearing the bad tidings to *The Ring* magazine, which sponsors the championship. The telegram was a one-sentence knockout:

"Due to Johnny Lira's negative attitude to perform in regard to defending U.S. title, I as manager hereby relinquish title. Mike Sarge for Johnny Lira."

The news was broken by the ring announcer at a Vegas fight show two weeks ago. "Isn't that a helluva thing?" says Johnny Tocco, the wizened trainer who has become Johnny Lira's chief ally. "You don't blast something like that without all the parties knowing what's happening. And they never told me and Johnny." Maybe Sarge and his associates were too busy toting up the money Johnny Lira should have made for the fights they claim he passed up between January and April. "It comes to $93,000," Sarge says.

Now Johnny Lira is no scholar and he realizes it. "I got kicked out of every grade school in Chicago for fighting," he says. But last winter he turned down only one fight, a $6,500 shot in Madison Square Garden, and that was because the flu had him on the ropes. Even if he stands on his head, he can't make $6,500 look like the bankroll Sarge is talking about.

"He never told me about none of those other fights—you got to believe me," Johnny Lira says. "Here I am starving and they're saying I didn't want to make $93,000. I can't afford a car; I got to drive a ten-speed bike. The only money I've made since April is $4,500 I got for fighting here in Chicago. I used to make $270 every two weeks for coaching boxing at the Boys Club, but now because I'm a pro, I can't get paid no more. Man, I'm scratching and these dirty bastards are trying to squeeze me out of the box. You'd think they'd have bigger problems than one little kid."

But since Sarge is throwing around a figure that Johnny Lira hasn't made in all nineteen of his fights combined, what better occasion to counter with the wildest sporting proposition imaginable?

"For $93,000, I'd fight the heavyweight champion and light-heavyweight champion and the middleweight champion," Johnny Lira says. "I'd fight all three of them in the same ring at the same time. Tell some promoter that; you could get a helluva crowd. Give me a knife and I'll fight a lion. Don't worry, I'd beat him; I'd bite his nose off. I'm a tough kid. For $93,000, I'd fight anything, not just anybody. I'd fight the devil. With these guys, I guess that's what I'm doing."

It seems a safe assumption that Johnny Lira's need for exorcism coincided roughly with the upset victory last August, when he put Andrew Ganigan of Honolulu in the hospital and stole his lightweight crown. On the plane back to Las Vegas, Sarge suggested bringing in another trainer, an old crony from Philadelphia, to join Tocco in molding Johnny Lira. The idea was vetoed by both Tocco and the fighter, but Sarge had scarcely begun to scheme. His next move was to sign Johnny Lira to a three-year contract, ending in August of 1981. And once the contract was signed, Sarge tried to saddle his property with a three-fight package with Don King, the ultimate pinky-ring promoter. To his everlasting credit, Johnny Lira said one fight was enough.

"All I ever did was treat the boy good," Sarge says. Indeed, he never took the one-third share of the purses that the contract entitled him to. Moreover, he recently turned over his duties as manager to Rico Peone, who has known Johnny Lira since they went to karate school together. But Johnny Lira remains unimpressed. "Rico told me once not to trust no one, not even him," he says. "That's what I'm doing."

His logic is unimpeachable. He has sat through too many meetings where he was the only person in the room without a lawyer at his elbow. He has heard too many of the characters who say they aren't interested in money change their tunes when someone suggests selling his contract. "Let 'em take whatever they want," he says. "I'll fight for free." But even that doesn't satisfy all parties concerned.

There are still whispers that he won't climb in the ring again if he doesn't have the right connections. There are still accusing looks from the hard hearts who think his imagination is working overtime. "I'm willing to take a lie test," he says. "Let's see Sarge take a lie test." The challenge sounds good, real good, to Johnny Lira, and a smile spreads under his misshapen nose. For a moment, the toughest guy in the neighborhood can forget that he is one more piece of meat for the fight racket to chew up.

How to Pass the Bar Exam
Chicago
March 10, 1982

Cynics may find it amusing to learn that there is a criminal lawyer afoot in Chicago who has launched a second career as a fight promoter. The news suggests that the city's knaves and varlets are in a slump that has driven the poor devil to take a recruiting trip into the sport most likely to yield him some new clients.

With all due respect to the legacies of such fistic felons as Sonny Liston and Jake LaMotta, however, Jack Rimland will jump from the Cook County Criminal Courthouse to the seedy, old Aragon Ballroom Thursday night because of a kid boxing kept out of prison.

"I'm not going to try to paint Johnny Lira as a saint," counselor Rimland says. "He's been arrested for almost every charge there is, from burglary right on up to murder. But when you look at him now, when you see what wonderful things he's done with his life as a fighter, you know what an exceptional person Johnny is. He went through the revolving door of our justice system, but unlike so many others, he came out of it."

Lira and Rimland were shoulder to shoulder in Judge Marvin Aspen's courtroom when the door spun in the right direction. It was 1972 and Lira was staring at ten years for filling his pockets with diamonds that weren't his. Under the circumstances, he wasn't doing much daydreaming about the amateur boxing career he had put in high gear so quickly, but then Aspen brought it up. "The judge told me if I won my next fight, he'd have a surprise for me," Lira says. So the kid from the West Side streets raced off to win the Illinois middleweight championship, and when he returned, Aspen sentenced him to two years on a work-release program. There was no hard time. There was only the understanding that, once and for all, Johnny Lira had to prove that honor meant something to him.

"I ain't disappointed the judge yet," he says. "My life ain't over, but I've kept my word this far. I always had respect for the people who had respect for me. All the bad things I done, maybe that's the only good quality I had. I know there's lots of other guys out there waitin' for me to screw up, to go back to bein' a burglar or a thief. They wanna go, 'Ha, ha, that kid Lira's still a bum.' But I couldn't do that to the judge. He's a federal judge now. I couldn't humiliate him."

No wonder Lira has become the darling of the John Howard Association, the prison-reform group whose membership he describes as "them rich liberals." After winning twenty-eight of his thirty-one professional fights, losing only to champions of various venues, and evolving as a character who is fueled by equal helpings of showmanship and business sense, he is what the reformers see as the shape of things to come.

They preach the evils of extended incarceration and the virtues of work-release, and in the twenty-nine-year-old Lira, they have the broken-nosed hero who could serve as their poster boy.

Or so the representatives of the Howard Association intimated when they began talking with Jack Rimland about his suddenly marketable client a year ago. They wanted to back Lira in his grand adventure and, of course, feed off him, too. "The only legitimate thing I know is boxing," Lira says, "and me and Jack had plenty of ideas about that." They had seen Chicago become one of the fight racket's ghost towns and they had suffered through promotions they thought were an insult, and now they were getting the encouragement to test their wings.

Perhaps that is as simple an explanation as exists about how Rimland came to be the brains behind the card at the Aragon. As his client flew higher and higher as a lightweight, the attorney became more and more enraptured with boxing, so much so that eventually he could mastermind the six-fight card that should have the John Howard crowd all atwitter.

For openers, Jumbo Cummings, a veteran of both a murder conviction and solitary confinement at the Illinois State Prison, will use a three-round exhibition to display the muscle that drove Joe Frazier back to retirement. And for a grand finale, Lira will bang away at former Canadian lightweight champion Al Ford for ten rounds or less as he attempts to regain his national ranking. What that will add up to is as much a sociological highlight as it is another night at the fights. The proof is there whether you are reading the fighters' rap sheets or listening to Rimland talk about Lira before he found salvation in a left hook.

"When I first met Johnny, he was in County Jail awaiting trial on a charge of murder," Rimland says. "There'd been a street-gang shooting and he'd been identified as one of the participants. His mother got in touch with me and I went out to see him. Right away I liked him. There was some kind of magnetism about the kid. He was very much under control, which you don't always see when a white kid lands in jail. But with Johnny, you got the feeling he could handle any situations that arose. How old was he? Oh, seventeen."

Twelve years later, with the murder rap erased by insufficient evidence, he appears no different as his attorney carefully navigates his maiden voyage as a fight promoter. Jagged shoals are everywhere, disguised as matchmakers and managers, and having been snagged on them a time or two himself, Lira is supposed to be standing watch. "I gotta make sure Jack don't get it stuck up his dupa," he says. Little did he know who was going to do the sticking, though.

"The John Howard people said they were going to get support for us," Rimland says. "They made it sound like they were going to find some backers for us and some people to help us get some publicity, and then they didn't do a thing. The way it's turned out, I'm putting up the money and all they put up was the promises."

Maybe someone should remind them that if Johnny Lira wasn't any better than that at keeping his word, he'd be behind bars.

It's a Waiting Game for Blevins
Chicago
September 19, 1979

The voice on the phone said the fight was off, and Little Jimmy Blevins tried to act like it didn't matter. He would go back to the grinding monotony of roadwork up the lakeshore and crosstown el-train rides to the noise and stink of the Woodlawn Boys Club. Sooner or later, he told himself, there will be a lightweight somewhere who doesn't care what Little Jimmy Blevins has been doing to the hard cases who thought of him as mere meat for the grinder.

"I can wait," he insisted. "I'm only twenty-four."

The truth had to scramble back to its feet to beat a ten-count.

Tinkering with age is nothing new in the fight racket, of course. Cain may even have thrown away his birth certificate

It's a Waiting Game for Blevin

before he slew Abel. To his eternal credit, Little Jimmy Blevins is neither as nasty nor as devious as Adam and Eve's firstborn son. "You want the real truth, or what you want?" he said at last. "The real truth is that I'm twenty-eight, but there's some people out there that would ridicule me for that. They'd ridicule me and they'd freeze me out until I was too old to fight these guys that's duckin' and dodgin' me." So he turns back the clock for the outside world, turns it back to a time when it is meet and right for a child of the streets to discover that violence can pay.

The record book shows that Little Jimmy Blevins has been a professional fighter for two years, but all that does is prove that lines of type have nothing to do with the way of the flesh. In truth he began fighting as soon as his father checked out of the Navy in Pensacola, Florida, in 1960 and brought nine squawling youngsters to the South Side of Chicago. Love can get spread pretty thin in a brood that big, and Little Jimmy Blevins wanted more than could be had at home. He was a perfect candidate for gangsterhood.

"That's just the way it works for a lot of black kids," he says. "There's nothing happening at home for you, so you go out on the streets and get with a gang. Everywhere you go after that, you got guys that stick with you."

He was fourteen when the Valiant Lords came to call, boasting of their ties with the arrogant, all-powerful Black P. Stone Rangers and swaggering beneath the black tams that were supposed to identify them as certified bad dudes. Little Jimmy Blevins enlisted on the spot. There was no basic training, though, nor were there any lessons in battle tactics. He could have used both, for one night he was drinking cheap wine with his new comrades and the next he was blazing away at the Mighty East Side Disciples with a snub-nosed .38 revolver.

"You should have seen the polices when they got there," he says. "They was lined up like they was gonna start a parade."

Nothing scared Little Jimmy Blevins in those days. Life was a blur of small crime and large threats, rumbles and reefer. He ran and ran and ran, and four years later, when he finally decided he should get out and travel in another direction, it was almost too late. "People get to know you one way," he says, "and they think you can't never change."

The Disciples were foremost among the doubters, which explains why six of them launched plans for mayhem the minute they stumbled across Little Jimmy Blevins on the corner of Thirty-ninth and Calumet. He was jiving with some buddies before heading upstairs to a pool room where he planned on winning the week's grocery money. And then he heard the pounding of footsteps, the thunder of curses. Two of the Disciples had guns, two others were waving golf clubs, of all things. Little Jimmy Blevins, who wasn't completely reformed yet, stuck a hand inside his jacket and pulled a .22 caliber pistol from a shoulder holster. "Like a real live gangster," he says. The move may have saved him from becoming a very dead statistic.

He fired twice and the Disciples turned to retreat. "I was glad they did, you know what I mean?" he says. Relieved or not, he kept on firing, hitting one of the enemy in the arm and another in the rump. It was a great triumph until the cops showed up to arrest him for attempted murder. The charge was later reduced to aggravated battery, another triumph in itself, but not one so great that it could keep him out of Pontiac State Prison for two years.

Little Jimmy Blevins wasn't quite nineteen when the steel doors clanged shut behind him. It is hard to believe that now when he recounts the story of the life he has made into a success. There is one chapter about his wife and four-month-old daughter, and another about the work he has done helping rehabilitate other ex-convicts. "I can go across the water and get along with anybody," he says, and who is to doubt him?

But the question of the moment concerns the boxing career that began in 1977 when he walked into the Woodlawn Boys Club on Sixty-third Street out of nothing more than curiosity. He fought in the amateurs just long enough to find out how his fists should be wrapped, then went pro in the Aragon Ballroom by walloping a stumblebum who outweighed him by ten pounds. "I didn't care," Little Jimmy Blevins says. "It was a start." It was also $100.

He earned $1,500 his last time out, winning a split decision over a tough mutt named Rick Falstaff in Orlando, Florida. Little Jimmy Blevins has been big stuff in Orlando since he beat homeboy Larry Stanton to a pulp there. Detroit, Kansas City, and Milwaukee also know who he is, even though he is unranked and has only been around long enough to pile up an 11-2-1 record. But Chicago? "People are surprised when I tell them I'm a prizefighter," he says. "They think I'm in some kind of office work." He is left to wonder if that is because he snubbed the local establishment by putting his future in the hands of Jerry Mullen and Tony Arvia, the people he wanted. And now the doubts have been compounded by that call from Detroit, the one that said tough old Ralph Racine wanted no part of him.

"Tell every lightweight in the world that I want 'em," Little Jimmy Blevins says. "Nobody got to give me no set-ups or nothing. Just bring 'em in. I got to have my big fight."

Somebody should tell him that he already had it. And won.

A Nose for Boxing
Chicago
March 3, 1980

Ron Stander would like to shrug off the Picasso-esque structure of his nose as one of the hazards of fistiana. No doubt his sentiments are tinged with guilt, for he used to take as much delight as anybody in asking Chuck Wepner, the old Bayonne Bleeder, what that was under his eye. The answer, of course, was that it was Wepner's schnozz. But now the joke doesn't seem so funny, perhaps because it is on Stander himself.

Every morning he awakes to find that his twisted nostrils have let him down again. "I got to breathe through my mouth," he says, "so there's all this stuff caked around my lips." It is a heavyweight's way of admitting that he drools in his sleep, drools like a baby.

Only an operation will spare him this daily indignity, and Stander can't afford one right now. It has been eight years since he fought for Joe Frazier's championship, and even then he earned only $50,000 for seventeen stitches' worth of punishment. Now, with his best behind him, he peddles body and soul for three grand and hopes it will be enough to keep himself fed and the ex-wife and the kids happy. Nose specialists are out of the question, replaced for who knows how much longer by simple ingenuity.

"If I wanta breathe through both nostrils," says Stander, "I got to do this."

He twists his nose sharply to the right and somehow manages to stifle a scream.

The time is wrong for looking vulnerable, you see. On Monday night, in the International Amphitheatre, he will fight ten rounds or less against a promising young stud named James "Quick" Tillis. Such an occasion calls for Stander's meanest face, the one with the missing teeth, the one crosshatched with scars. But even when he has it on, his vulnerability still shows.

Perhaps the tipoff is the gently spreading belly that Stander's T-shirt doesn't quite hide. He weighs in on the far side of 230 pounds, which is a considerble load to carry on a 5'11" frame but far from his most embarrassing public posture. "One time I was fightin' this bum up in Providence, Rhode Island," he says, "and when the scale hit 250, I jumped off. Hell, I knew it wasn't gonna stop there."

He laughs and his one-man audience laughs with him, and the shame of it is that it can't always be like this for Ron Stander. But the fight racket isn't made that way, so you find Stander managing himself after discovering that three other men couldn't do the job for him.

Alone in a South Side hotel room, he waits for a promoter from Omaha, his hometown, to fly in to be in his corner Monday night. He talks about eating dinner by himself, taking spiritual sustenance from a brief meeting with two pretty girls and the word that he almost got to meet Walter Payton. It is as close to a monk's existence as Stander ever will live, and yet only one thing about it really bothers him: At age thirty-three, after forty-three wins, fourteen losses, and two draws, he is the trial horse who is being brought in to lose to Tillis.

"Hey," he says, "I know the score."

It seems he has been on the losing end of it ever since he was yanked from oblivion after eighteen professional fights and thrown to Frazier. Granted, Stander was a celebrity, but a curious one. The image makers took advantage of his Iowa roots and called him the Council Bluffs Butcher, even though he had never done anything to a piece of meat except eat it. "Everybody's gotta be something," he says with a shrug.

That is not to suggest, however, that there was a consensus on what his identity should be. After noticing his seemingly unquenchable thirst, some critics suggested that he might better be described as a drunk. "Ah, I wasn't that bad," he says. "Don't get me wrong now. I like my beer; I can drink a case in one sitting. But I wasn't doing it before Frazier." Sober or otherwise, Stander couldn't satisfy his wife, who uttered perhaps the most unflattering commentary. "Yeah," he says, "she thought she was being cute comparing me to a Volkswagen in the Indianapolis 500."

She left his life afterwards almost as fast as fame did. One day he was the toast of the Omaha Civic Auditorium, the next day he was a face in the crowd. The passing years have done nothing to change his status. In Omaha, the resident sports celebrities are Bob Gibson, whose pitching brilliance bankrolled a restaurant, and Bob Boozer, who uses a telephone company public relations job to reminisce about the National Basketball Association. "Me?" says Stander. "All I've got is a suitcase."

And so, appropriately enough, he travels. New York, Los Angeles, Fort Lauderdale, Tucson—he hits them all. "There's always somebody who wants to hang out," he says. Or somebody who needs a bodyguard or a bouncer. Yes, he does that, too. He has watched over the Rolling Stones and Fleetwood Mac, Buck Owens and Robert Goulet, not to mention P.J. Clarke's, the fashionable Manhattan gin mill. It's an honest buck, and an easy one, and surely he will have to consider that when he spits out his mouthpiece for the last time.

"Why don't ya gimme another year fightin'?" he says.

It is as if he can't forget coldcocking Earnie Shavers and Terry Daniels, and can't remember being humiliated by Boone Kirkman, Horacio Robinson, and other assorted tomato cans. For three grand, any promoter in the county can have Ron Stander, who has been everywhere and fought everyone. For smaller change, he will be a sparring partner, he will try to give a kid the lessons he never got. There will be bruises, scars, aches, and pains, but it doesn't matter, not as long as the pay is on time.

"Those nose jobs," says Stander, "they don't give 'em away."

Capuano Took the Blows and Did It His Way
Chicago
February 23, 1981

The door was open when Luke Capuano got to his hotel room. He looked inside and saw three friends who hadn't been there four hours before, saw them standing guard as if they were trying to keep everything just the way he had left it. The bed was still unmade, the TV in the corner was still on, and the breeze was still stirring the curtains ever so slightly. But when he walked in, Capuano could sense something drastically different.

It was he.

Luke Capuano had been to war and lost.

For ten rounds downstairs in the Conrad Hilton's Grand Ballroom, he had suffered while a suede-sport-coat crowd digested the Sunday brunch that was part of the bacchanal. The fans had loved him, too. They had loved the way he went after Mike Rossman even when the blood was streaming into his left eye and the best he could draw a bead on was a sickly red blur. "Lukie! Lukie!" they chanted, pounding their tables and stamping their feet. But all those voices, flooded with all that emotion, couldn't drown out the unanimous decision against him.

And they couldn't ride the elevator to the twenty-ninth floor with him, either. It was just the beaten light heavyweight, his handlers, and his thoughts.

"Shoots another rematch in the ass, don't it?" he said.

In his hometown, he was 0-and-2 against Rossman now, 0-and-2 against an ex-champion who must have hocked his greatness for another leg tattoo. "Yeah, I know what they say about the guy," Capuano said, "but he's still a tough mother." Capuano pulled his black ring robe tighter around him. "Jesus, my head hurts. Hey, order me some beers, will ya?"

He had never needed Heineken's pain-killer quite so badly. In twenty-three previous fights, twenty of them victories, he had been bruised and nicked, but he had never encountered anything like the gaping wound he was trying to cover with a flesh-colored Band-Aid. "You shoulda heard how bad Lukie was hurtin' in the corner," said his trainer, Primo LaCassa. Maybe there were some people who did, for the pain was the result of a resounding first-round collision. In the midst of a flurry of punches, Capuano and Rossman banged their heads together, and from that moment on, the fight was painted red.

The jagged gash over Lukie's left eye must have been a sight on national television. At ringside, it was almost too much for the two twentieth-century foxes who took turns telling the crowd what round was coming up. They flinched and looked away, keeping their wide eyes fixed on the ringpost, the ceiling, the doorway—anything except the stunned Capuano.

The pain didn't hit him at first. "When I saw the blood on my shoulder, I thought it might be Rossman's," he said. No such luck. The blood was his, and with it came the fear that referee Stanley Berg might get a queasy streak and stop the fight. Maybe Berg would have if Capuano hadn't had wise, old Syd Martin on his side to dip into a medicine bag that contained every healing potion the law allows.

"How'd you stop the bleeding, anyway?" Capuano asked up in the hotel room.

"That's my business," Martin said with a smile.

It was also his business to concoct a fight plan that would give Capuano revenge against Rossman and make him more than the World Boxing Association's tenth-ranked light heavy. But when the blood started to flow, it carried away all the wisdom that Martin had brought with him from New York. "I went right back to the old Lukie," Capuano said. "I started brawling. I guess that's what you do when you're hurt: you go back to what you know best." Damned if he almost didn't get away with it.

He had Rossman pinned in a neutral corner in the fifth round, the two of them just banging away at each other's heads and rib cages, and suddenly he could feel the hard guy out of Philadelphia turning soft. It must have been the right cross that did it, so Capuano threw another one. Now there was a cut beneath Rossman's left eye, and he was trying desperately to hang onto Lukie's arms. Capuano shook himself free and kept whaling away with the same hands that will be holding a newborn baby any day now.

"I called your wife," said Ralph Sanmarco, a friend for a lifetime.

"She watch the fight?" Lukie asked.

"Yeah. She almost had the kid in the fifth round."

Capuano smiled as much as the pain would let him, then motioned for another beer. The guys on the West Side will be talking about that round until they get over the loss. They will be saying that if Lukie had had another thirty seconds, he would have walked out of the Hilton a winner. And all the while, he will know that it was he who let Rossman get away, not the clock. "I shoulda hit him a left hook right in the gut." But he didn't, and now he had to sit there an stew in the juices of defeat.

He had to remember how lifeless he was in the final rounds and how Rossman wouldn't let him get off a decent punch. Capuano's only hope was the beer, and it was warm. Worse yet, every time he took a drink, the pain shot through his head and left him wondering about the fifteen stitches that awaited him. "Jesus," he kept saying. In the past, he had never felt like this after a fight. Maybe he wasn't ready to go dancing, but at least the wages of war hadn't caught up with him until the morning after. What Capuano was getting now, though, was a look into a future he didn't want.

"Tomorrow is gonna be a mother," he said.

Sparring Partner
Chicago
May 29, 1981

Like sweat and pain, anonymity comes with the job. It really doesn't matter that his face is hidden by leather headgear, that his high cheekbones are masked with Vaseline. Nobody would notice him anyway. They want to see the champ, and Larry Holmes is always there, filling the gym with the jive he earned a right to by unhorsing Muhammad Ali. Sometimes the champ tries too hard to be funny, maybe even betrays his own insecurity, but what can LeRoy Diggs do, no matter how much he likes the guy? He's just the champ's sparring partner.

To get the fight crowd's attention, he'd have to knock Holmes on his dime, and you can tell right off that Holmes doesn't think there's much chance of that happening. "We got us a bet going with Larry, me, and the other guys he spars with," Diggs says. "Any one of us put him on his butt and he'll pay $10,000." The offer—or is it a dare?—brings a smile to territory where one seldom appears. "I'm tryin'," says the heavyweight no one knows. "I'm tryin' like hell."

It's easy to forget that when the lights from the TV cameras are in your eyes, and Holmes compounds your memory lapse every time he climbs aboard his soapbox. You listen to him tick off the dire things he will do to Leon Spinks when he defends his World Boxing Council title two weeks from now in Detroit, and you don't even realize that LeRoy Diggs has slipped your mind. Maybe that's the hardest thing for him to accept. He stands 6'3" and weighs 220 pounds, yet to the public, he is like morning dew—scarcely noticed, never missed.

"That ain't right, but what you gonna do?" Diggs says. "You understand what's your job, so you just get on with it. They tell you to come to camp in shape and you do it. Larry, it don't matter that much for him. He can get in shape as he go along. There's three of us spars with him and we got to get him mean, got to get him being two different people. Goddamn right he can get that way. You make him miss in the ring and he want to kill you. Don't matter how nice he is when we're sittin' around nights playin' cards. His ass gonna be up for a whippin' when he's fightin' for real, not mine."

Because Diggs understands that and reacts accordingly, he gets the kind of gigs that the Sweet Science's has-beens and never-weres can only dream about—eight weeks in good hotels, with three square meals and a $1,000 paycheck every Friday. Sure, there are Holmes' fists to worry about, but he's used to them by now. It's getting so he's even used to the questions about why a strapping lad like him, just twenty-seven and brimming with aggression, isn't out there chasing a championship of his own.

"I don't love boxing no more," Diggs says. "I used to, but the love is gone now. Everything I do with boxing these days is for the money. Yeah, go ahead and tell me I could do better fightin' ten-rounders in Atlantic City. I'll tell you you're wrong, man."

He'll do it with the story of his life in the ring.

It began in 1974. He was pumping gas back home in Cherry Hill, New Jersey, and a long, cool Cadillac pulled up bearing Joey Giardello, a former middleweight champ looking for easy money. Giardello thought Diggs might be it, even though the kid was barely out of high school and had never thrown a punch in a ring. "Joey told me to call him at this gym in Philadelphia, so I did," Diggs says. "Two months later, I had my first pro fight. Stopped a guy named Joe May in the second. It's in the record book." What the book doesn't show is that Diggs drove from Philly to Waterbury, Connecticut, and back the same night for $75 that became $35 after he had shared the wealth with everybody in his corner.

Maybe he wouldn't dwell on that so heavily if the succeeding chapters in his story had been happier. But there were problems that surfaced when Giardello's personality went sour and soared out of sight two years ago when he had to fight Randy Stephens in Monte Carlo on three days' notice. Diggs had a makeshift entourage that couldn't speak English and a promise that he would be rewarded for substituting for Alfredo Evangelista. But even after he walked off with a decision, it meant nothing.

For a while, he thought it would be better to be a small-town cop. The feeling lasted until the first time he pulled over a carload of drunks at four in the morning. "Your heart be beatin'," he says. "You know they're bombed out of their gourds. Mother love, it's all you can do keep yourself from turnin' around and runnin'."

When Diggs took off his uniform for keeps, though, he heard no cries of "Coward!" First, Earnie Shavers wanted to hone his fists on him. Then it was Leon Spinks lying in ambush for Ali. "The crazy mother," Diggs says. "He let that money he made after Muhammad swell his head up." Larry Holmes isn't like that. Even when he's flattening Diggs' nose, it's hard to work up any hate against him. There is never a sense of lord and master about the workouts, never a feeling that a sparring partner must grovel to be appreciated.

"He gives you your respect," Diggs says. "It's like he be thinkin' the same thing I am when I watch the Superstars and all that trash on television. How those people get there anyway? It was the people underneath that helped them. It was those guys carryin' the Gatorade to the football players and the caddy for that what's his name. Yeah, Jack Nicklaus. See, Larry know that. You just listen to him."

There is just one problem: The words from his mouth that get recorded for posterity are the ones full of bombast, not thanks. It has been that way in the past and it will be that way again in Detroit. The gawkers and the gladhanders will swoon at Holmes' pronouncements and fill his ears with praise. When the ring glows under the lights and the bell for the first round sounds, nobody will realize that LeRoy Diggs had anything to do with it.

The Buzz Saw
Chicago
October 1, 1981

Geopolitical niceties escape Paddy Flood, which is one of the problems with having grown up around wise guys whose destiny was life in prison if they were lucky and the electric chair if they weren't. When Paddy took his first look at Mustafa Hamsho, a middleweight with decidedly violent tendencies, he pegged the kid as the toughest sell since somebody tried peddling thermal underwear in the Mojave Desert.

"You're a foggin' Arab," Paddy blurted in the genteel manner that has made him the toast of Manhattan.

"No, Paddy, I am no Arab," Hamsho replied patiently. "I am Syrian."

"Fog you, I can see the price of gasoline," Paddy said. "You're a foggin' Arab."

With that in mind, the resourceful manager tried to pass the kid off as an Italian or a Greek. He called him Rocky Estafire and Mike Estafire; then he called him in for a heart-to-heart chat. After twenty professional fights and absolutely no publicity, it was time to reverse the field for Hamsho.

"I said, 'Mustafa, lemme see that hat you're always wearin',"' Flood says. "I call if a kaffir now, like I'm some foggin' Middle East politician, but back then it was just a hat.

I said, 'Mustafa, would you like to wear your hat in the ring?' He don't know the difference, so what the hell. We go walkin' into the Jersey Arena like a couple big shots, boom-boom, and they introduce him as Mustafa Hamsho, the Fighting Arab, and all of a sudden, a bottle comes flyin' through the air. Fog that. I said, 'Gimme the hat, Mustafa. I'm puttin' it back on the sideski.'"

There it has stayed while Hamsho, now billed as the Syrian Buzz Saw, has cut his way through the middleweight division to a 32-1-1 record and the promise of a Saturday night bloodbath with undisputed champion Marvin Hagler. It will be the first title fight in the short history of the Horizon and, presumably, not much of an advertisement for future brawls if cleaning bills are any consideration.

Anyone who has watched Hagler in person or on television should remember the impromptu surgery he performed on the faces of Alan Minter and Vito Antuofermo. While he moves in the ring like a dance master, Marvelous Marvin punches as though his gloves were razor blades. The result is his reputation for being a beast, a reputation that puts most fight men back on their heels, but only infuriates Paddy Flood.

"A beast?" he sputters. "Whaddaya foggin' think my guy is? Style? He got no style. He's like a crab; he comes at you from every-foggin'-place. Hagler wants to fight dirty, let him. Mustafa will split his head open. The kid's a foggin' animal."

"Thank you, Paddy," Hamsho says.

The kid is a sweetheart that way. Get him out of the places where Darwinian theory rules and you will learn that he worships Flood, loves his family, and thinks every New York cop he has ever met is a candidate for sainthood.

When cops get shot, Hamsho is the first civilian to give blood. When cops need someone to spread the word in Brooklyn's tense Arab community, Hamsho steams in from his Bayonne, New Jersey, home. "If we don't call him," says Richie O'Neill, a honcho from the New York Policeman's Benevolent Association, "he gets all bent out of shape." So the cops not only call him, they follow him to all his fights, even the ones in Chicago. There will be a couple of busloads of them at the Horizon Saturday night—narcs and guys who walk beats and every other kind of cop imaginable—and that isn't bad for a fighter who hopped off a boat from Syria just nine years ago.

He had gone undefeated on the streets of his hometown, Latakia, and as soon as his cousin, a Brooklyn grocer named Sammy Mustafa, started talking to him, Hamsho didn't see why his lot should be any different in American rings. His confidence got him past a loss in his first professional fight, and his guts did the rest until Flood landed him 6½ years ago.

"Heart?" Flood asks. "I never seen such heart. Lemme tell ya, this is a smart kid, a decent kid, a brave kid. He never paid nobody to win. What the fog, I had to beg to get him on television."

In his national debut, the erstwhile dockworker was supposed to be a sacrificial lamb. He was fighting Wilford Scypion, who had made his name by pinning Willie Classen against the ropes in Madison Square Garden and beating him to death. It was the ugliest of memories, and Flood's best friends in a cruel business told him that Hamsho was too nice to walk into the same trap. "That's when they found out how foggin' tough Mustafa is," Flood says. He battered Scypion senseless and sent him flying through the ropes, an obstacle no more.

"I give Hagler the same thing, you watch," Hamsho says. "I see him fight before and he don't show me nothing. If he want to beat me, he better bring baseball bat. It mean to me my life, this fight. He'll have to kill me."

It is standard pre-fight hyperbole, the stuff of which the racket is made, yet Flood flinches when he hears it. "What the fog you sayin' that for, Mustafa?" he asks. "Stop it with this 'kill' stuff, huh? You're givin' me the creeps." The sentiment doesn't go with the wise-guy pose Flood lives behind; it suggests that he might really be a softy, that he might really think of his fighter as more than a piece of meat. "Foggin' cuckoo," Flood mutters. God forbid that his image should be ruined now.

8.

Champions Forever

Despite the considerable baggage of his ego, Muhammad Ali used to flinch when someone hailed him as Champ on the dim, dark mornings after he had been dethroned. "Don't call me that," he would say softly. But to tell someone that in this country is to seek the cancellation of a national impulse, for ex-champions are like ex-presidents; they are revered as if the past lives on and the present doesn't exist.

Mr. President.

Champ.

I didn't understand how the titles stuck until I followed Joe Louis through the airport in Columbus, Ohio. It had been more than a quarter of a century since he ruled the world's heavyweights, yet almost everyone Louis walked past recognized him. And if they were too surprised to speak, they turned their heads and stared, and the looks in their eyes explained how a champion can be forever.

Fifty Years and No Decision
Chicago
September 21, 1977

They say the boxing ring is still somewhere at Soldier Field, probably hidden away in one of those musty old corners that looks like it belongs in *Les Miserables*.

Jack Dempsey once knocked Gene Tunney stiff in that ring, but instead of getting his heavyweight championship back, Dempsey heard only the discomfiting tones of what came to be known at the Long Count. In another age, he might have wryly attributed it to the New Math. But this happened fifty years ago. To be exact, it happened fifty years ago Thursday.

There will be no moments of silence, no drums banged slowly, for golden anniversaries in sports don't pack much punch. Most of the people who saw events half a century ago are gone, or their memories are. And even if that weren't so, their stories might not be straight, for athletic history can be as much fable as fact.

Think of what you know about Al Gionfrido's catch in the '47 Series or Citation slopping past his stablemate, Coaltown, in the '48 Derby or the Bears leaving the Washington Redskins in the rubble of a 73-0 demolition. You know the names, and that's about it.

Dempsey and Tunney have had decades longer than any of those characters for their images to be blurred. If anything can help bring these two brilliant, vastly different fistfighters back into focus, it is a history lesson.

It begins in Philadelphia, on a rainy September night in 1926, when Dempsey slogged into an outdoor ring to battle Tunney for the first time and discovered he had nothing with which to hit him. Dempsey should have known he was in trouble before the fight. He had been sick to his stomach for more than two hours, and in the dressing room, he had broken out in a rash. But he was a brawler in the best saloon tradition and he kept telling himself all he needed was one lucky punch.

Tunney, possessed of the same classic reserve as a symphony cellist, never gave him the room to throw it. He pounded away for ten rounds before Dempsey's heavyweight crown toppled from his head. Tunney scooped it up and was gone.

Dempsey was left with nothing to do but search for a reason for the pummeling. Food poisoning received most of the blame. But the dethroned champ would have been more honest if he had said he suffered from frazzled nerves.

His former manager, Doc Kearns, hit him with seven court summonses while he was training, and his newest wife, Estelle Taylor, kept nagging at him to leave the fight game so she could concentrate on her career as a movie actress. Dempsey couldn't help wondering if she was right. After all, he had been champion since he whipped Jess Willard in 1919. Now he was thirty-one, and every time the crowd yelled for him to keep fighting, his body yelled louder for him to call a cease-fire.

He was ready to call one after the Tunney debacle. Then Tex Rickard, who was from the same school of snake-oil salesmanship as Doc Kearns, confronted him with a chance for a rematch with Tunney. When Dempsey said no, Rickard responded the way Hollywood says conniving fight managers are supposed to.

"Maybe you're right, kid," he said. "Maybe Tunney's too tough for you. No one likes to get licked by the same guy twice."

"Wait a second, Tex," sputtered Dempsey.

What happened next was almost predictable. Dempsey knocked out Jack Sharkey in Yankee Stadium and was deemed ready to meet Tunney again.

The fight was made for Soldier Field because the promoters there could get $40 top for seats while the best New York could demand was $27.50. With the 145,000 people who were eventually jammed into Chicago's concrete mastodon, boxing had its first $2 million gate.

Dempsey was the madding throng's favorite. He had mauled his way out of the Colorado mining town of Manassa with a no-holds-barred style, and that was how people thought fighters should operate. Tunney, on the other hand, was suspect even though he had been a Marine Corps lieutenant. He quoted Shakespeare and spouted high-falutin' words. The normal reaction was to question his manhood or the believability of his image. As one critic said, Tunney owned several books and may even have read one of them.

Maybe the general dislike of Tunney accounted for the odds favoring him dropping from 9-to-5 to even by fight time. Or maybe it was because bettors saw newspaper advertisements saying Dempsey drank Chippewa Natural Spring Water— "the world's purest spring water" —at his training camp.

If Al Capone had had his way, it would have been foolish not to bet on Dempsey. The heavyweight champion of mobsters offered to fix the fight, but Dempsey turned him down in a letter. Even so, Capone's henchmen still scared the bow tie off one referee, who quickly decided he would rather see Dave Barry officiating.

The fighters scarcely noticed the change when they entered the ring at a little past 10:00 P.M. on September 22, 1927. Barry explained that they would have to go to a neutral corner on any knockdown. He explained it once. He explained it twice. Then he told them to come out fighting.

Tunney won four of the first five rounds, opening a mean cut over Dempsey's left eye. In the sixth round, Dempsey finally retaliated with left hooks, straight rights, and the rabbit punches that Tunney complained about all night. In the seventh, Tunney really got something to complain about.

Dempsey dropped three bombs on his jaw—right, left, right. "Tunney bounced backward against the rope and, helpless, his legs collapsed under him, slid like a drunken man to the floor," John W. Keys wrote in the *Chicago Daily News*. "There was a foolish expression in his eyes and a dazed look on his face. . . . He clutched feebly and frantically at one of the ropes."

Dempsey didn't realize it, but he was in worse shape. Instead of immediately going to a neutral corner, he paced in a circle in the center of the ring. Barry, who had started the count on Tunney, stopped and waited for Dempsey to mend his ways. When Barry resumed the count, Tunney struggled to his feet at nine. He had been prone for fourteen seconds.

For the rest of the round, Tunney ran. It may not have been what his fellow marines wanted, but it worked. Dempsey had no more energy, and after the tenth round, Tunney walked away the winner and still champion. Dempsey just walked away. It was his last fight in anything but a sideshow.

"Gettin' What I Deserve"
Chicago
September 14, 1977

He left the streets of New York as an aspiring burglar and returned as middleweight champion of the world. He threw punches at the biggest names of his era, and he threw a fight, too. Outside the ring, he piddled away $2 million, broke rocks on a chain gang, and celebrated his fiftieth birthday as a strip-joint bouncer. Somehow he also found the energy to go through four wives.

In the enduring saga of Jake LaMotta, only one thing is missing: a dull moment.

"Gettin' What I Deserve"

Hollywood and Broadway, which have enough dull moments as it is, are both getting ready to do LaMotta up big, provided they can make sense of the crazy-quilt pattern of his life. To help unravel it, Robert DeNiro, the Academy Award-winner who will portray LaMotta on the screen, has begun studying at the master's feet. He watches the stout, fifty-five-year-old LaMotta fill up a room with his swagger and listens to the pugilistic patois resonate through a nose that has been broken six times. Forever incredulous, he is like an entomologist examining an unidentified mosquito, but LaMotta doesn't seem to mind.

"Marlon Brando himself told me this guy DeNiro is the greatest actor in the world," says LaMotta, who drops names faster than he does consonants. "I was talkin' to a neighbor of mine a couple blocks down the street—Richard Harris, the actor—and he told me the same thing. I never thought it'd be like this, me gettin' what I deserve."

This must be the season for making a fuss over the hard guy they used to call the Bronx Bull. He is going to be in Chicago Friday to be inducted into the newborn Italian-American Boxing Hall of Fame, and to revive some old memories as well. The most vivid of them should focus on his last fight here, the one in which Sugar Ray Robinson plucked the crown from his head after a thirteenth-round technical knockout.

"That was the St. Valentine's Day Massacre of 1951," LaMotta says. "I think I'll tell the Hall of Fame people a joke I always use. I'll tell them if the referee hadn't stopped the fight, I would have won it, because Robinson had t'rown so many punches he was ready to collapse of exhaustion. I always get a big laugh out of that."

The story LaMotta probably will neglect to tell is the one about what happened the night before the fight. With the weigh-in twelve hours away and LaMotta 4½ pounds over the required 160, his trainer smuggled him into a steam bath at 10:00 P.M. and didn't let him out until 1:00 A.M., when he had sweated off his excess pasta—and his punch.

"Ah, hell," says LaMotta. "I been on a diet all my life."

He indulged his appetite as a man because he had gone to bed hungry too many nights as a boy. He was the son of a struggling immigrant fruit peddler on New York's lower East

Side. "It was the kind of place where you steal to survive," he says. "You break into places and you rob clothes, you rob food, you rob whatever they got in the cash register." And if you're lucky, you don't get caught. LaMotta, at sixteen, was not lucky.

Or maybe he was. The police picked him up carrying a set of burglar's tools under his arm and shipped him to the reform school where another kid from the neighborhood, Rocky Graziano, was already studying better manners. LaMotta not only improved his comportment, he learned how to jab and hook. When he was back on the street, he learned he had a marketable skill, one that would get his family off relief and keep him out of the slammer.

"What would I have been if I wasn't a boxer?" he says. "A t'ief."

Incorruptibility, however, has never been synonymous with the name of Jake LaMotta. He became an untrustable in 1947 when he remained upright for only four rounds before collapsing in front of harmless Billy Fox. And thirteen years later, he told the Kefauver committee on boxing corruption what everybody had suspected: He took a dive.

The indignation his admission aroused was righteous, and also loud. It drowned out his explanation that going in the tank was the only way he could get a shot at the title, and it erased, at least temporarily, the legend he had carved for himself. "I always fought the guys nobody else wanted to fight," he says. There was Sugar Ray Robinson six times, and Fritzie Zivic four times in ten months. There was the night he knocked out Marcel Cerdan to win his beloved championship, and the night he saved it by knocking out Laurent Dauthille with thirteen seconds left in the fight.

There was all that and so much more, but few people wanted to hear about it. They were more interested in the seedy side of LaMotta's life. It began when he ended his boxing career in 1954, took the $2 million he had earned to Miami Beach, and began frittering it away as a nightclub owner.

That was bad enough. Things got a lot worse when a certain lady of the night started hanging around LaMotta's joint. She turned out to be fifteen years old. "Hey, fighters ain't too much on intelligence," LaMotta says, "but I ain't so dumb I'd get hooked up with a broad like that." A judge and jury said he was. He did six months in a Florida jail, part of it on a chain gang, part of it in a hole in the ground that was the size of a closet. A small closet. "It was as close to hell as I ever been," says LaMotta.

Recuperation was slow, both personally and financially. LaMotta acted in good movies like *The Hustler* and bad movies like *Cauliflower Cupids.* He did commercials. And he kept the peace, so to speak, in a Manhattan fleshpot where he refused to ogle the merchandise. "You see one topless broad," says this four-time husband, "you seen them all."

The pieces of his private life came together in an odd way for a man whose fortune had been won through violence. "I decided I wasn't mad at nobody," he says. "It's like when you hurt for a long time and then all of a sudden you get lucky and you forget the pain. Well, I forgot my pain."

LaMotta forgot it because of the movie that is going to be made about his life and because of the actor who is going to portray him. If there is anything wrong now, it is that Robert DeNiro won't be with him at the Holiday Inn-Rosemont Friday night when he takes his place in the Italian-American Boxing Hall of Fame. In that moment, Jake LaMotta will reign as the two things people in the fight game appreciate most—a champion and a survivor.

LaMotta Learns to Control the Rage Within
Chicago
December 19, 1980

She keeps dabbing at her left eye with a hanky as soft as an angel's breath—dabbing, then smiling and pretending nothing is wrong. Maybe this is the way all beautiful women growing old protect themselves. When nature can't be depended on anymore, they master the art of illusion and produce what Jake LaMotta sees before him now. She is no fading flower. She is, rather, the same long-legged honey blonde he met beside a Bronx swimming pool thirty-seven years ago.

"That's the Vikki that's in the picture," LaMotta says.

The hanky comes away from her eye quickly.

"He loves to say my name," she purrs.

Once they were man and wife. Now they are friends and business partners, reunited by *Raging Bull*, the movie of LaMotta's star-crossed life. They may even be more, but time apparently has taught them the virtue of discretion. When they checked into the Continental Plaza, their request was simple: same floor, separate rooms. "All I'm gonna tell ya," LaMotta says, "is that I don't go for that brother and sister stuff."

Under the scarred brows that were part of the price he paid for the world's middleweight championship, his dark eyes twinkle roguishly. It is what you expect, but it is not the complete picture of Jake LaMotta crowding sixty.

There is no more of the fire, the savagery, the craziness that could have made this untamed street kid a murderer if he hadn't discovered the joy of mayhem in the ring. In a deftly-tailored gray suit, with his chair adjusted so you can speak into his good ear, he seems totally incapable of destroying his championship belt or, worse yet, punching his beloved Vikki.

"Feelin' any better?" he asks her.

"I'm gonna go see the doctor in just a little while," she replies.

She turns to a visitor.

"Isn't Jake cute?" she asks.

Vikki LaMotta used different adjectives for him that grim day when his jealousy boiled over and he accused her of rampant infidelity, garroted his brother on a hunch, and blackened her eye. It was the same one that is bothering her now, and the funny thing is, her latest injury can be blamed on Robert DeNiro, the actor who plays Jake in the movie. Vikki was holding DeNiro's picture the other day, and when somebody tried to grab it, she pulled back and poked herself in the eye. Just like that, history had repeated itself.

If Jake LaMotta flinches at the thought, you need only see *Raging Bull* to understand why. He has sat through it twice, and twice may be all he can bear. "I come out a bad guy in the picture," he says. "It's the way I was, it's the truth, but that don't make it no easier on me. The first time I watched it, I didn't know what happened; I didn't know whether to like it or dislike it. There was something wrong, and I couldn't figure out what it was until the next day: I was reliving my life."

It was a life in which the good times were almost extraneous. Sure, LaMotta waged a glorious holy war with Sugar Ray Robinson for the better part of a decade. Sure, he poleaxed Marcel Cerdan to win the championship in 1949. Sure, he refused to concede that Laurent Dauthille had him beat and knocked the stubborn Frenchman stiff with just thirteen seconds standing between him and ignominy. But the bulk of LaMotta's legacy is as sad as a cauliflower ear and as ugly as a nose split down the middle.

The ruination of Jake LaMotta began with the fight he threw to Billy Fox in '47. The mob may have been leaning on him and he may have had to play along to get a shot at the title, but he went in the tank all the same, and when he did, he stamped himself as a bum forever. No wonder people were saying it figured years later when LaMotta got run in for letting a teenaged hooker operate out of his Miami strip joint.

He wound up on a chain gang, did time in the rat hole dedicated to incorrigibles, and never heard a word of sympathy. Maybe it would have been different if the word had gotten out that he pried the diamonds out of his championship belt to pay for a defense attorney, but Hollywood wasn't going to make *Raging Bull* for another twenty years.

"When I done that to my belt," he says, "I was symbolically—is that the word?—destroying the thing that made me the way I was. See, I was like one of those dogs that go to war. They're trained to be vicious, they're rewarded for it. But when the war's over and they're back with their civilian masters, they can't understand why they're punished when they attack people. That's the way I was, and I had to figure it out myself. I couldn't afford no psychiatrist. I had to adjust by myself. There's the word. I had to adjust."

Not until now, however, did LaMotta have the chance to prove that he has succeeded. With *Raging Bull* hitting theaters across the country, he gets paid to leave New York and hold court in fancy hotel rooms in the cities where he used to fight. He does Marlon Brando's back-of-the-taxi speech from *On the Waterfront*, and when the telephone rings, he leaps from his chair and shouts, "What round is it?" And always there is Vikki, the second of his four wives, the mother of two of his six children. She is up from Miami, back into his life, and for just a while, Jake is young again.

"You know why she didn't play herself in the movie, don'tcha?" he asks. "I didn't want her kissin' Robert DeNiro."

"You mean you didn't want me to kiss Bobby's booboo?" she teases.

"That's the truth, Vikki."

He loves to say her name.

Nowhere to Run
Chicago
April 1, 1979

It was a glorious place, the Del Prado Hotel was. If you listen closely, you can still hear the echoes of the young lovers and swaggering big leaguers who used to make its lobby so fresh, so vibrant. But to open your eyes in there is to see the other side of midnight. The furniture is cheap and frayed, and the old folks arrayed on it live with a fear dramatized by a sign taped to the front desk: SORRY, NO MONEY ON PREMISES—PLEASE PAY RENT BY CHECK OR MONEY ORDER. Yes, that is what has become of Hyde Park's leading hostelry, and the change is a hurting thing for everybody except the lost soul dozing in the corner, the one the fight crowd used to call Honey Boy.

He lives in a world that skirts reality, a world filled with panhandling buddies and visions of old movies, a world where no one can hurt him. Late at night, when he is alone in the lobby, alone with his jumbled thoughts, he will rise from the couch where he sleeps and slowly walk toward the full-length mirror. He will raise his fists and bend at the knees and, suddenly, he will be Johnny Bratton, welterweight champion, once again. Never mind that his hair is more gray than black or that he is an easy fifty pounds over his fighting prime. You can't take the past away from him.

He bobs and weaves, jabs, recalculates the old combinations—all in slow motion. How sad and yet how perfect for the setting. It is as if you aren't allowed in the front door of the woebegone Del Prado unless you, too, represent faded elegance.

Johnny Bratton showed up one evening last winter, in the middle of his one-way trip to nowhere. A chill ran through the lobby, for its elderly white denizens did not know how to deal with a black drifter who was caked with street grime and whose long silences were punctuated by bursts of unexpected laughter. There was no predicting that he would soon be running errands for new friends, receiving invitations to breakfast, or whistling at Patricia Bock, the hotel's salty manager, and getting away with it. Indeed, Patricia Bock had to be grabbed by the arm and shaken before she would stop looking down her nose at this uninvited guest.

"Don't you know who that is?" asked the man who runs the variety shop.

"No," she said.

"That's Johnny Bratton."

"So?"

"Do you remember Joe Louis?"

"Oh, he was my idol."

"Well, that man there was as famous as Joe Louis."

The point would have been exaggerated anywhere other than the South Side. But on the turf where Johnny Bratton discovered that he could be somebody, however briefly, it was the stone truth. So he found a roof to cover his head during the blizzard of '79 and, no matter how ragged he was, the Del Prado boasted its first celebrity since American League teams declared the neighborhood unsafe for their precious athletes. "The hotel doesn't look like the Astor anymore," Patricia Bock says now, "so why should anyone care?"

Johnny Bratton wasn't supposed to have to rely on charity, though. In the late forties and the early fifties, when he was fighting in Chicago Stadium and on TV, when it was all you could do to escape reading about him getting ready for a fight or winding down from one, he thought he had gone over the wall from hard times. He was a taxi driver's son, a Du Sable High School dropout, but he wore zoot suits and gold cuff links and cruised the city in a Cadillac bearing the name "Honey Boy" and a Jaguar bearing the name "Johnny B." And the marvel of it was, the soft life didn't make him a pushover in the ring.

"I could do it all," he says, "but I had to do it under my conditions. You understand? My conditions."

He had a style that would have become a man trying to sneak into the house past his sleeping wife. It was capable of turning crowds venomous even when he was beating Charlie Fusari for the old National Boxing Association's welterweight title in 1951. Still, there was something about Johnny Bratton that endured longer than the memory of his caution. Perhaps it can best be described as courage.

He came to the fore when boxing moved at a relentless pace. A victory meant the loser got another fight, and if the loser won that one, there had to be a rubber match. Just look at Johnny Bratton's record. He fought the brutal Ike Williams three times. He battled Holly Mims twice within twenty-one days, with a lesser bout sandwiched in between. And nobody who witnessed his last chance to regain the championship, when Kid Gavilan carved him up for fifteen rounds, ever will forget his absolute refusal to retreat or surrender. Afterwards, he lay on his dressing room table unable to speak.

The problems Johnny Bratton had always were supposed to be physical—an impacted tooth that led to a fractured jaw or tiny hands that crumbled like potato chips. But what got him in the end was his mind.

He was not punchy.

He was mad.

"It started getting worse after my last fight," he says. "I got beat by Del Flanagan. The referee patted me on my back and told me I was through. I was twenty-six or twenty-seven. A couple years later, I went to the state hospital at Manteno. I had a private room. Do you think they were giving private rooms to psychopaths in 1954? I wasn't no psychopath. I even had my picture in the paper. Do you remember that? They had a picture of me looking out the window. I was in my room."

There were other rooms in other hospitals and, finally, Johnny Bratton was allowed to step back onto the streets seventeen years ago. He has walked them ever since, refusing to settle at a halfway house or with an older brother. There is always a letter from Hitler or a covered wagon surrounded by Indians to distract him, to let him know he must keep moving. "You don't understand, do you?" he says, and looks for a bus that will carry him to safety. If he is lucky, it will pass a movie theater and he can hop off and take refuge there.

Movies give him something to cling to, something he can't seem to find anywhere else.

"That fella next to you kinda looks like Paul Muni, don't he?" Johnny Bratton says. "I seen Paul Muni in a lot of pictures. Him and Errol Flynn. I don't think Errol Flynn ever made a bad picture. But he got in trouble, right? Him and all his women. Me, what I think you got to do is live a good reputation, like James Cagney. Yessir, the Yankee Doodle Dandy hisself."

On Rush Street, that mecca of clip joints and cut-rate love, they say they have never seen anyone who knew as much about movies as Johnny Bratton. Sooner or later, he makes it up there every day to win his daily bread—and drink—with his vast knowledge. And if that fails, there is always out-and-out panhandling. "He can put the arm on you pretty good," says one old fight guy. "I figure it's good for a sawbuck if he sees me." To be sure, Johnny Bratton is always looking, always moving. He pauses only to gaze at his reflection in the windows of a disco.

What he sees is a slightly stooped figure cloaked in a dirty overcoat; rising up out of the coat's collar is a face on which scar tissue and a goatee fight for prominence. What he sees is what the conventioneers and the swinging singles don't always want to see. The pattern is never altered: a handout here, a turndown there, and don't scare any well-dressed women. He can get by that way, Johnny Bratton can. He won't get rich, but another day will be done and he will have bus fare back to Hyde Park, back to the Del Prado.

The septuagenarians who live there worry about him on those nights when he doesn't show up, and he seems to sense it, even enjoy it. But just as he is getting comfortable, perhaps for the first time in a long time, some hotshot outfit is pumping $4.5 million into the Del Prado to gussy it up again. When the old furniture goes, Johnny Bratton will have to go, too. You can say time is running out on him if you like, but of course that really started long, long ago.

In a Class All His Own
Chicago
September 9, 1979

When Archie Moore came around, the fight racket never seemed like the sewer it was. He had the sagacious Doc Kearns for a manager and Redd Foxx for a court jester, and best of all, he had himself. Lord, has the ring ever known a more masterful counter-puncher, a more delightful storyteller, a more elegant gentleman? And yet he was misunderstood and unappreciated for two decades, the classic example being the numb silence in the Montreal Forum before he battled Yvon Durelle.

Moore was the light-heavyweight champion of the world then, and in an effort to be appropriately regal, he appeared at the weigh-in wearing a homburg and a midnight-blue shawl-collared tuxedo and carrying a silver-headed cane. The cigar chewers would rather have seen the emperor with no clothes.

"I'm only trying to give boxing a touch of class," Moore sputtered exasperatedly. "Why, Durelle, there, is dressed like a farmer."

The cigar chewers grumbled that it was the old con again.

He had that kind of a reputation, Archie Moore did. It mattered not that he would fight anybody, anytime, anywhere, or that he was on his way to an unsurpassed 141 knockouts.

He was seen more often as a mystic fraud, proclaiming the wonders of pigeon soup and sucking the juice from his steaks, then throwing the meat away. Yvon Durelle, on the other hand, was a thumb-in-the-eye brawler, and when he knocked Moore down three times in the first round, justice was supposedly being served. "I hated to spoil the party," Moore says now, twenty-one years after the fact, "but that seems to be my nature." He weathered the savage first, you see, and in the eleventh he finally put out the lights for this brute who was young enough to be his son. Suddenly, it was all right to love him.

They showed a movie of the Durelle fight at a restaurant in Oak Park the other night, and Moore sat through it for perhaps the four hundredth time. "It was my pleasure," he said afterwards. For one thing, he could take a look into his hallowed past. For another, his hallowed past could become reality to James "Quick" Tillis, the apprentice local heavyweight he has been training for the last two weeks. When the movie was over, Tillis could see at last that there must be something to "Escapeology," "Breathology," and the rest of Moore's venerable gambits.

"I can't talk about 'em," the kid said. "They're trade secrets."

"Excellent, excellent," Moore said when apprised of Tillis' zipped lip. "If he continues to listen and to believe, I can have him fighting for the championship in eighteen months."

That would seem to be the least a young fellow could expect from the self-proclaimed "world's greatest boxing instructor." But as part of the bargain, Tillis should also receive continued helpings of the charm Moore tosses around like confetti. During his short stay in Chicago, the man they used to call the Mongoose has already identified at least half a dozen relative strangers as his assistant trainer. He has dropped tickets to the fights into every outstretched hand he has found and never once admitted that he didn't recognize someone claiming to be a childhood friend from St. Louis. The admirers came to press the flesh, to be in the presence of greatness, to listen to the yarns the fight game doesn't produce anymore.

It has never been a secret that Archibald Lee Moore is an original in the same sense as Muhammad Ali, Sugar Ray Robinson, and precious few others. He fought from 1936 until 1963, and when he finally retired, he refused to say whether he was forty-nine or fifty-two. His mother always insisted that he was born on December 13, 1913, while he argued that the year was 1916. "Certainly, she was there," he said, "but so was I. I have given this a lot of thought and have decided that I must have been three when I was born."

The only thing that created as much continual consternation in his career was his weight. Out of the hullabaloo came his Australian aborigine diet and a wardrobe that contained clothes for when he was a heavyweight, a light heavyweight, and lighter than air. Alas, the final category was seldom used. "I am not a glutton," Moore said in his own defense, "but I am an explorer of food."

Such eccentricities tended to cloud the magic he could perform on an elevated, 20-by-20 hunk of canvas. He did his tricks against the best fighters in two, maybe three eras—Jimmy Bivins, Joey Maxim, Harold Johnson. And to this day, he remains convinced that he had Rocky Marciano beaten when he was thirty-nine, or forty-two.

"In Yankee Stadium, before 60,000 people, the referee forgot that there was no mandatory eight count after I knocked Marciano down in the second round," Moore said. "He yanked Marciano by the hands and yanked him out of his stupor." In the ninth, Marciano bid good night to the Mongoose for keeps and the Mongoose began wondering what the referee, Harry Kessler, had against him. "This man, a metallurgist, a philanthropist, had been giving me a hard time since the old days in St. Louis," Moore said. It is an old refrain, of course, but pride is pride.

Moore always guarded it, even when he was doing nothing more exhausting than sparring with George Plimpton, the daredevil writer. After an easy, abbreviated first round, Plimpton made the mistake of strutting over to Moore's corner and asking him if he was all right. "There was a whole bevy of Park Avenue beauties there and they all started tittering," Moore said. "The next round I led with a nose-breaking left jab. George started bleeding all over and there wasn't anymore tittering."

There is a moral there about keeping strangers off your turf. Someday Moore's protégé, James "Quick" Tillis, may understand it, but for the moment, he must be satisfied with learning his craft. His latest lesson took place at the Chicago Circle Campus gymnasium Friday night, when he needed only two rounds to unhinge Jimmy Phillips, who both looked and fought like Gene Shalit, the NBC movie critic. Tillis stood in the ring afterwards, unsure of how to react to such easy success. "Bow, bow," Moore shouted from the corner. The kid did and the old man smiled. Class will always tell.

A Preacher and His Cadillac
Miami
November 13, 1982

In the gospel according to Hammering Henry Armstrong, the acts that save a man are acts of providence. Hammering Henry has delivered his sermon since the Lord woke him from a bourbon slumber by shoving him out of a bed and onto the floor and intoning, "Preach, preach." So he became a Baptist minister, and when he looked over his shoulder at a past sparkling with three of boxing's championship crowns, he realized that providence must have visited him early, swirling in on the wind and bearing a message about a Cadillac car.

Hammering Henry was laying down his tools back home in St. Louis that fateful day in 1929 when the dust began whipping around him and a newspaper fluttered at his feet. He was seventeen then, a pint-size laborer for the Missouri and Pacific Railroad with no greater expectations in life than his next good time. But one look at the page that the wind opened before him provided the goal he had always been without.

"Must have been the sports page," Hammering Henry says, "because the headline said, 'Kid Chocolate Beats Al Singer for Featherweight Championship; Wins $75,000 for a Half-Hour's Work and Goes Back to Cuba in a Cadillac.'

"Man, I stared at that and stared at that, and all the time the foreman was hollering for me to come get my money. It was payday and he wouldn't pay off until everybody was there. He was hollering, 'Come on, come on,' and when I finally went over there, I told them, 'Well, fellas, I'm not going to be with you no more. This is the last time you see me. I'm going to be a fighter.' And they said, 'You're crazy. You can't fight. You're just a little guy.' And I told them, 'If my idol Kid Chocolate can be a champion at 126 pounds, I can do it, too. And when I come back, I'm going to come back in a Cadillac of my own.'"

He would do it just as sure as he was born Henry Jackson seventy years ago; just as sure as he started boxing as Melody Jackson "because I like to sing a little"; just as sure as he borrowed his trainer's last name so he could try the amateurs again before setting professional history on its cauliflower ear as Hammering Henry Armstrong.

In less than twelve months splashed across 1937 and 1938, Armstrong earned a right to his seat of honor at the Aaron Pryor-Alexis Arguello junior welterweight championship fight Friday night. He lured Petey Sarron back from a European hideaway and knocked him off the featherweight throne. Next was the welterweight championship that Barney Ross treasured so dearly. Armstrong had to put on twenty-two pounds to win that one, and the added weight didn't make him slower, just tougher. "I gave Barney Ross a pretty bad beating," he says. "He never fought again."

It sounds cruel, but Armstrong could take as good as he gave. If he couldn't have, he wouldn't have gone on to capture Lou Ambers' lightweight title. "I had some cuts in my mouth from training camp," Armstrong says, "and Ambers found them." They bled so badly that the referee wanted to stop the fight in the twelfth round, only to be talked out of it by Armstrong's promise that he would stop the crimson flow. And stop it Hammering Henry did by swallowing his own blood until the final bell sounded and he had his historic third championship.

Only five other fighters have collected as many crowns, and only one of them, the artful Arguello, ever dared go for a fourth. He did it against Pryor with Armstrong watching and smiling at the knowledge that no matter what happened, Arguello couldn't face as much treachery as he did when he shot for the moon in 1940 against Ceferino Garcia, the king of the middleweights.

"I'd heard underground that the gamblers bet a lot of money on the fight," Armstrong says, and the night of the fight, they showed up in his dressing room with a pitch that proved it. First, they offered him $75,000 to take a dive in the fourth. "Get out of here," he said. Then it was $100,000 for a dive in the fifth. "Get out of here," he said again. So the gamblers went and found a referee who would call the fight a draw even though Hammering Henry pummeled Garcia for eight of their ten championship rounds. "What can you do?" Armstrong asks now.

His question is borne on the weary tone of a man who

knows the taste of defeat too well. For he fell as fast as he rose to the top, and his manager gambled away the riches he had won with his fists, and he still has trouble believing that Arguello and Pryor will split $3.1 million when the most he ever made for a fight was $85,000. The only thing that fate never stole from Hammering Henry Armstrong, it seems, was the Cadillac of his dreams.

When he called himself Melody Jackson, he went to Pittsburgh to punch up enough money for his car, only to return with one win, one loss, and the same rusty hulk he had left in. "It was like a covered wagon," he says, "and everybody started jiving me about it. I listened to them long as I could, and then me and my manager hoboed out to Los Angeles. It took us eleven days."

He was Hammering Henry Armstrong by the time they arrived, and he had enough energy left to throw so many punches that the L.A. press called him "Perpetual Motion." He had style to go with his heart, and the beautiful people from Hollywood went for him in a big way. Al Jolson and George Raft, the actors, bought his contract, got him fights with their clout and put him in enough chips to buy his Cadillac.

It was waiting at the train station in St. Louis the next time he went home. But none of his old crowd put the two of them together until his chauffeur opened the door for him. "It's mine and it's paid for," he said. And this time no one laughed at Hammering Henry Armstrong.

No One Could Hold a Candle to Joe Louis
Chicago
April 13, 1981

He probably never realized how dank and dimly lit the basement hallway was. On his way to the ring, everything in Chicago Stadium must have been a furious blur—his handlers surrounding him protectively while he stared at the floor and contemplated the violence that was about to come pouring out of him. And as he returned to the dressing room, tasting the fruits of victory again, he made people wonder if he even noticed that his magic filled the hallway with the candlepower it lacked. Maybe that was why it seemed drearier than ever Sunday. Joe Louis was dead.

The news arrived as you waited outside the Boston Celtics' dressing room, poised to wade into another victory celebration and swath another hero in rococo prose. It is a strange business, this deciding who's to bless and who's to blame, who's a story and who's history, but with Joe Louis, there was never a question.

He was a champion for all time, a man who was remembered as the sleek, sleepy-eyed Brown Bomber even when he was up to his thick neck in unpaid taxes and the demons in his mind were telling him that the walls had ears.

The last of his sixty-six years on earth trapped him in a wheelchair, left him leaning on a nurse who could dab the sweat off his brow, but the people who saw him being rolled up to ringside for the fights in Las Vegas never varied in their reaction. "Hi, Champ," they would say, just the way the awed and the innocent did when he was the greatest heavyweight who ever laced on a pair of eight-ounce gloves. The thick middle didn't matter; neither did the cowboy hat that hid his bald head. Until his heart gave out, Joe Louis managed to retain the magnetism that was best illustrated when he ventured onto the Soviet side of the Berlin Wall in 1967, long after his last fight, and watched his guide aim a camera at him.

"No pictures, no pictures!" shouted a Soviet lieutenant, rushing over in a haughty rage.

Then he recognized the object of his imperiousness.

In a minute, all the lieutenant's soldiers were taking Joe Louis' picture.

There couldn't have been a more natural response, for Joseph Louis Barrow, Jr., was bigger than boundary lines, bigger than color lines, bigger than any barrier that ever confronted him. The unlettered son of an Alabama sharecropper, the unpolished product of Detroit's most heartless ghetto, he became a champion that America's white power structure wasn't ready for. Only Jack Johnson before him had been black, and Johnson had been written off as a self-destructive aberration. But Joe Louis was different. "He came forth," the Reverend Jesse Jackson once said, "and the cotton curtain came down."

No One Could Hold a Candle to Joe Louis

Nothing and nobody could withstand the power in his fists. He beat Buddy Baer and Tommy Fall, Jersey Joe Walcott and Two-Ton Tony Galento—beat them so badly that Galento was moved to pugilistic hyperbole. "He musta used an ice pick," growled fat Tony. And the beauty of Joe Louis was that he didn't deny it, didn't try to hide behind artificial modesty. Just remember what he said as he prepared to stalk the clever, courageous Billy Conn: "He can run, but he can't hide." The man wasted neither words nor punches. But his gift didn't flower until after he had lost to Hitler's pet heavyweight, Max Schmeling, and heard the cry of Aryan supremacy.

They met a second time after Joe Louis had won his championship, and in Archery, Georgia, the black hired hands at Earl Carter's farm gathered round the boss' radio to listen. The fight ended in one round with Schmeling stretched on Madison Square Garden's hallowed canvas and Joe Louis vindicated. Swiftly, quietly, the hired hands went back to their shacks. "All the curious, accepted proprieties of a racially segregated society had been preserved," Earl Carter's son Jimmy wrote years later as he pursued the presidency. They were preserved, that is, until the hired hands were alone, and then there came a shout of joy that Jimmy Carter heard all night long.

At last, Black America had a hero whom white people couldn't ignore. Joe Louis was a great athlete and more. He never ducked a challenge, provided psychological relief from the Depression, answered the nation's call to duty during World War II. And all the while he was showing his brothers and sisters by skin that it was possible to rise above the hate and squalor that was supposed to be theirs for eternity.

It was for other pioneers to integrate schools and get blacks on the voting rolls—to move to the front of the bus, if you will. What Joe Louis announced was that the future would not be monochromatic. When it finally arrived, though, he had become a tragic figure. His millions had been squandered, he struggled with drugs and the Internal Revenue Service, and he fought to keep his sanity. The best job he could find was as a greeter at Caesars Palace, and though the gawkers still called him "Champ," they did their best to pretend he didn't matter anymore.

Maybe all of us did until his big heart began short-circuiting three years ago and it became obvious that Joe Louis was not forever. Suddenly, there were high-rollers in Vegas willing to fly him to the world's foremost heart specialists. Frank Sinatra snapped his fingers and every bright light in Hollywood turned out for a banquet in the Champ's honor. It was as if everybody realized we were about to lose an irreplaceable natural resource.

The inevitable finally happened Sunday, just as you knew it would the night you saw Joe Louis on the dais next to Sinatra, shivering in a wheelchair, waiting for someone to pull a blanket tight around him. He was helpless, and yet he wasn't. As a fighter and a human being, he had been something that even death won't erase. He was too big for it, just as he was too big for life. What better way, then, to remember him? The candle is out, but the light still shines.